Fire and other images

Fire and other images

PARITOSH SEN

Published by
Tulika Books
35A/1 Shahpur Jat, New Delhi 110 049

ISBN 81-85229-82-1

Typeset at
Tulika Print Communication Services
35A/1 Shahpur Jat, New Delhi 110 049

Printed at
Pauls Press
E44/11 Okhla Phase II, New Delhi 110 020

Contents

To

SATYAJIT RAY, RADHAPRASAD GUPTA,
SHANTI P. CHOWDHURY, NIKHIL SARKAR (SREE PANTHA)
who encouraged me to write

Preface

The essays and stories in this book, originally written in Bengali, have been selected from three of my books – *Zindabahar*, *Abu Simbal*, *Picasso o Anyanyo Tirthe*, and *Amsundari o Anjanyo Rachana*. Writing came to me by sheer chance when I was about sixty years old. A request from a Bengali little magazine titled *Kabipatra* to write my childhood memories kindled in me a hitherto unperceived urge to express myself in the form of *belles lettres*. The initial efforts, I felt, suffered from literary pretension. This failure prompted me to rethink and make a fresh beginning. It then occurred to me that I was gifted with a pair of painter's eyes. Why not let my eyes do all the talking? Since my art school days, I have always been good in portraiture. I decided to draw pen-portraits of people, places and objects that have remained stored in the inner recesses of my mind. As I started writing about them, they came gushing forth, like fossilized images suddenly coming to life.

The first story I wrote was 'A Tree in my Village'. To begin with, I made a pen and ink sketch of the tree. I then contemplated it for two or three days, trying to figure out how to transform it into words that would convey its visual richness. Altogether, it was an exciting experience. After completing it I passed the story on to Satyajit Ray, Radhaprasad Gupta and Shanti P. Chowdhury for their comments. I had great respect for their literary taste. To my surprise, all three of them expressed their unqualified praise and asked me to keep going. Ray even suggested that I devote more time to writing than painting. In fact, I did not touch paint and brush from then on until my first book, *Zindabahar*, was ready for publication.

One after the other, the stories and essays (translated into English) in this book came to be published in such well-known Bengali little magazines as *Ekshan* (jointly edited by Nirmalya Acharya and Saumitra Chattopadhyay, Ray's favourite actor) and *Krittibas* (edited by the famous poet and novelist Sunil Gangopadhyay), and, of course, in the popular Bengali weekly *Desh*. A few were also published in the now defunct weekly *Amrita*. A facsimile deluxe edition with numerous illustrations of 'A Tree in My Village' was published in the form of a portfolio by the National Institute of Design, Ahmedabad. It became a collectors' item and soon went out of print.

The present volume is the result of many friends' urging that I should reach out to a wider readership by publishing a selection of my writings in English. This would not have been possible but for the magnanimous offer made by Ms Enakshi Chatterjee to do the tedious job of translating the prose pieces from Bengali into English. Except for 'A Tree in My Village' which I translated, and 'The Devotee' which was translated by Ms Ela Datta, the rest have been translated by Ms Chatterjee. I will remain ever grateful to her for the time and care she has so ungrudgingly given to the task. My gratitude is also due to Professor Kunal Chakrabarti of Jawaharlal Nehru University, New Delhi, for his help in the selection of the stories. He also suggested the title of the book. It is my honour and privilege that Professor Romila Thapar has written a foreword to this book, despite her many engagements. Last but not the least, I am grateful to Ms Indu Chandrasekhar of Tulika Books for having agreed to publish the book in its present form and for having taken the trouble to oversee its production.

December 2003
Kolkata

PARITOSH SEN

Foreword

I first saw Paritosh Sen's paintings in the home of my friends Santi and Pula Chowdhury and it was also in their home that I later met Paritosh and his wife Jayashree. There were many conversations about the paintings, about Paritosh's writings, much acclaimed, which unfortunately I could not read because they were in Bengali, and most of all about Paritosh's perceptions as a creative person, not only in contemporary India but in the world of today. These ranged from the immediate environment and the present, to the many manifestations of the worlds that he has known. I therefore read these essays anticipating a further discovery of his perceptions, an anticipation well fulfilled.

In these vignettes of his past, Paritosh Sen, in looking back, evokes a world that we have lost. Landscapes have been reworked, cityscapes have taken new forms; the assumptions on which human relationships are based have undergone a mutation. His memories of childhood in Dhaka inevitably carry an evocative quality. What they evoke is a memory of what has been and gone; nevertheless, the act of evocation creates a presence. This is what is not lost and the evocation is a powerful presence. This remains with him in the continuity of his experiences in life that are alive in his paintings and his prose writings. The latter are familiar to a Bengali audience, and it is as it should be that some of these pieces have now been rendered into English for a wider audience.

His family was large enough for him, as a child, to lose himself in his own vision of the world: a vision that has remained with him and becomes real in moments of solitude. His relationship with his father, so much the quintessential *bhadralok* 'gentleman', is at times distant, but despite this is deeply imprinted in him. The fire at his father's cremation rivets his attention to the forms and colours that explode in his mind's eye – a vision that now kindles his remembrance of reading about Duryodhana burning the house of the Pandavas, the vision of the universe that Krishna reveals to Arjuna, and passages from Dante's *Divine Comedy*. In describing the death of his mother he juxtaposes with poignant empathy the anguish of a mother mongoose separated from her captured babies: a juxtaposition that heightens the mother–child relation but also hints at other dimensions of such a relation.

He responds repeatedly to the landscape, trees, plants, birds and people that encompass him. The magnificently large Arjuna tree – the tree in the village – has been profusely illustrated in another publication. He compares the tree to a high-rise building with a hierarchy among the birds that nestle separately in its various branches – a hierarchy that seems to control the varied relationships between the birds in the tree and with the snakes and iguanas in the roots of the tree. The tree becomes its own universe. Suddenly the system is disturbed by an invasion of monkeys. The birds fight back, almost ruthlessly, to regain their branch-hold. There is something almost Hitchcockian in the scene.

On a lighter note one shares his enthusiasm for gourmet meals ranging over a spectrum of cuisine. His ability to laugh at himself is the most appealing part of those narratives where the unspoken, underlying hilarity arises from unexpected encounters, sometimes with women in unusual situations, or with strangers making seemingly incomprehensible demands.

Paritosh the artist comes through forcefully in his recalling his meetings with Brancusi and Picasso. The image of Brancusi in his studio is a splendid glimpse of a sculptor at work. Picasso, he writes, had the most lasting influence on him. One is made aware of the initial awe and then the gradual fading of the awe, to be replaced by a recognition of the immense human qualities, however whimsical, that go into the best creativity and the way in which Picasso epitomized some of these. The artist in Paritosh also surfaces in his stunning description of travelling across the waters at Abu Simbel at dawn, which becomes almost a moment of epiphany.

The creativity inspired by a recollection of a past world and of the attempt to comprehend the present, is preserved in both his paintings and writings. This connectivity is germane to his understanding of himself as a part of the universe and it provides many dimensions to his perceptions. Some enter his consciousness fleetingly and summon links to varied cultures of the world of Asia and Europe. Others are more deliberately called forth. They provide some clues to his reading, his observations and his thoughts, all that go into the making of his articulation as an artist.

One of the most impressive among these is his conviction that creativity can only exist in a condition of freedom. Paritosh believes firmly that if this freedom is shackled by ideologies that are intended to obstruct free expression, such ideologies become an assault on creativity. Assaults of this kind have been made in recent times, in India, and have to be resisted. Both his painting and his writing are statements that endorse freedom as necessary to creativity and as central to the human experience.

ROMILA THAPAR

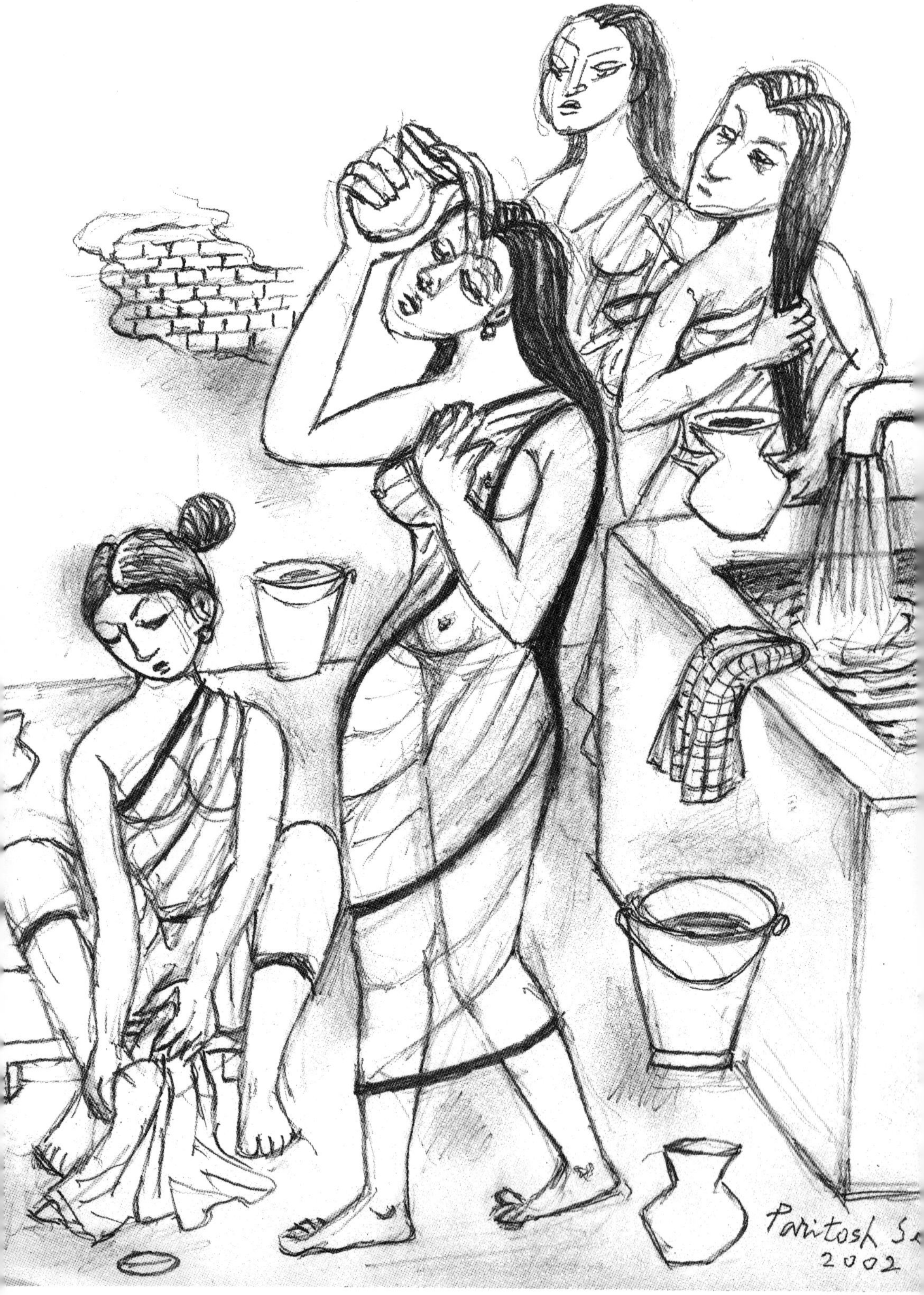
Paritosh S
2002

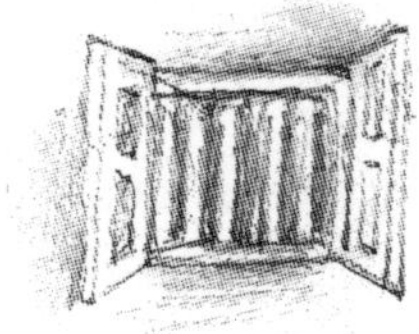

Looking back

It was a huge, old-fashioned mansion divided into two sections, with nothing special to distinguish it from the neighbouring houses. There were a large number of rooms, but they were small. The household was constantly on the move, on the staircase, in the verandah, in the courtyard, by the water tap – wherever you went, you were in danger of running into people. I would get lost in this crowd. Many seemed to forget the fact that I even existed. With daybreak the entire house rose to an extraordinary stir of activity. The chorus of sounds would wake me up. There was no way you could loll in bed, you had to get up. At the sound of the early crows the cleaning procedure got underway – doing the beds, dusting, sweeping, mopping the floor. I came out on to the verandah. Downstairs, near the tap, piles of dirty utensils were stacked – dozens of plates, bowls, glasses, frying pans, cooking vessels, ladles, *dekchis* and hundreds of odd objects. Gopal was doing the mountain of dishes. Among the left-overs a big fish-bone caught my attention. The spinal bone of a *rohu*. It looked like an ivory comb to me, still drowsy with sleep. I walked down the steps slowly, taking them one after the other.

The area adjoining the tap was a busy place. The women of the family were bathing there, some were washing clothes. There was no question of them being bashful in front of a small boy like me. The soft morning light danced over their bare breasts. As I proceeded towards the kitchen I found *Baro Boudi*, my eldest sister-in-law, winnowing the rice. She was doing this with such perfect rhythm that the sound combined with the beat took on the quality of a kind of dance music.

Somebody was powdering spices on the grinding stone, her back turned to me. I saw my mother slicing potatoes, paper-thin, like slices of betel-nut. But she was intent at work, her eyes cast down – she had no time for me. The family constantly demanded her undivided attention. By the time I woke up she had already left her bed. And when I went to bed at night, she was nowhere to be seen. The large family on the one hand, and her husband on the other, were more than she could manage on her own.

The ground floor of the house did not get enough sunlight; it was damp and dark. A musty smell hovered around this floor, in winter as well as in summer. Added to this were the kitchen smoke and the mixed smell of fried spices. At times it was difficult to even breathe. In the rainy season strange patches appeared on the walls, like vague outlines of sketches – unknown faces, unreal animals or fluffy, cotton-like autumn clouds. Sometimes I saw a galloping prince brandishing a sword and disappearing in a whiff of dust. And beyond him the vague outline of a fort on a distant mountain-top, beckoning. I could clearly hear the sound of charging horses. Every year before or after Diwali the masons would come with their thick brushes to put a coat of lime-wash over these pictures. Then once again, in the monsoon months of Ashar and Sravan, an invisible artist would draw a fresh set of pictures. I spent many an idle afternoon visualizing the strange figures in them. A world of fairies reached out to me from this mysterious, half-hidden land. My thoughts fluttered skyward like a pigeon. My heart swelled with pride and excitement. I drew the outlines in burnt charcoal, afraid that I may not find them the next day. The idle afternoons were all mine and I had a wonderful time letting my imagination roam.

I was eight or nine. We were a large family of brothers, sisters, step-brothers and step-sisters. In addition, relatives came by during weddings and festivals. At such times our house began to resemble those modern structures that are rented out for marriage celebrations. At least sixty meals were served each day. I would come downstairs during meal hours to find shining brass plates balancing atop glasses everywhere, not just in the dark dining room. They looked like golden lotus leaves on the dark green waters of a pond. I was attracted by this sight and would hover around till we were called to take our seats. As one batch finished eating, the dishes were promptly washed and laid out again for a fresh batch, almost like at the riverside hotels near the ferry ghat.

Akrur was just back from the market. As usual, all the women rushed to see what he had brought. His sack was full of vegetables – a big *lau* looking like a dumb-bell, a *pui* creeper rolled up like a snake, a couple of *mochas* and lots of other things. The cream-coloured *mocha* flowers set against the dark copper of the *mocha* were as beautiful as *champak* flowers in a woman's hair. A slice of *chalkumro* beside a bunch of *kochu sak* resembled the eleventh-day moon. And that piece of the banana trunk – anybody would mistake it for the tusk of an elephant. The girls were impatient. Where is the fish? Akrur, a mischievous twinkle in his eyes, took his time. He brought out the spices and other things first. Finally, a pair of *ilish* emerged from his bag – *ilish* from the Dhaleswari river. My sisters and nieces fought over the right to dress the silver beauties. Funnily enough, these young maidens were not to be seen anywhere when it was smaller fish like *sarputi*, *falu*, *tangra* or *mourala* that were brought.

It was nine in the morning. A horse-drawn carriage waited outside our house. Father was getting ready for his regular rounds of patients. He came out sticking *attar*-soaked cotton behind his ear and addressed me and my elder brother as we squatted on the ground, poring over books. 'Get ready, quick. You are coming with me', he said, and proceeded to the outer room. Once or twice a month he had these rare outbursts of affection. In no time we were ready, dressed in fresh shirts, shorts, shoes and socks. My heart danced with delight and anticipation. Though I had plenty of playmates at home, the prospect of an escape from these dingy damp surroundings and the narrow confines of school was exciting. I was restless with curiosity and kept fidgeting in the carriage, moving from one window to the other.

In the noisy street teeming with horse-drawn carriages and people, somebody did a *salaam* to Father. The sounds of the bazaar fascinated me. The kite shops displayed at least a thousand different designs. There were shops selling handloom cloth – *lungis* and saris. What a riot of colour! It was as though some master painter had let himself go in gay abandon, dipping his brushes in buckets of colour. Then came the mouth-watering smells of fries, *parathas* and *bakarkhani* from the roadside stalls. Mixed with these was the *zafrani* aroma of Mughlai food. Unconsciously, my jaws began to move, munching invisible delicacies.

The toy shops sported multi-coloured balls and balloons and cheap Japanese toys. Grapes and pomegranates from Kabul were on display in the fruit stalls. Refined *attar* bottles stood in an array in the perfume shop. Porters rushed in from the ferry ghat carrying baskets of mangoes on their heads. The jewelry shops were doing brisk business in gold and silver.

And over there, a little away from the gate of the Nawab Palace, my eyes were fascinated by the sight of clothes' shops which dealt exclusively in *jatra* and theatre costumes. They had just about anything you might need. There were velvet dresses for kings and *badshahs*, magnificent with richly embroidered patterns in gold and silver threads. One particular *jubba* stood out. It was black and gorgeous, fit to have belonged to Shahjahan. Rows of bows and arrows, shields and swords, head-dresses of all kinds, crowns, turbans, greeted the eye. Was that beard and head-gear meant for Sage Viswamitra? Or perhaps it belonged to Narada. A huge pair of moustaches – Bhim's or Kumbhakarna's? Next to these were long Kali-like tresses – those must be for Surpanakha. . . . Brown matted hair, a tiger skin and a trident – must be the costume for Shiva when he performed the *tandava* dance. The shelf below was where women's clothes, including artificial breasts, were kept. The ten faces of Ravana set my heart aflutter. How terrible he looked! The masks of Puloma, Taroka and Bakasur were equally terrifying. I shut my eyes, afraid that they might visit me in my dreams. All the shops were crowded with buyers.

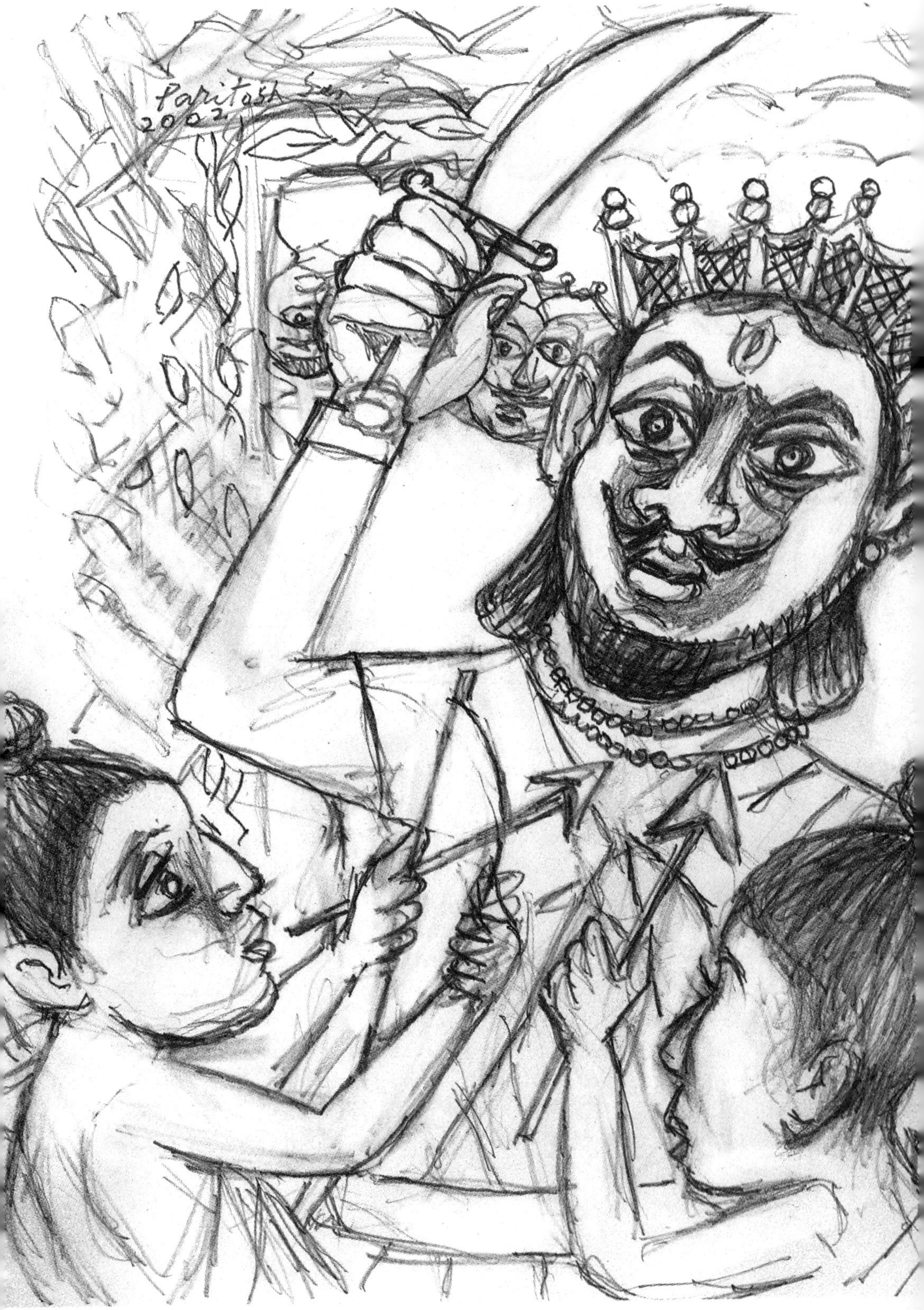
Paritosh Sen
2002

We moved ahead and went past the famous sweet shop of Kalachand Saha. Then came the Kali temple, the church and the mosque. They moved in succession like bioscope images. As the scenes gradually receded I began to feel that we had come a long way from home.

After a few visits to patients, Father asked the coachman to head in the direction of the Nawab Palace. In a short while we passed through the huge gates to enter spacious grounds. The palace stood in one corner of a green field, a structure of burnt brick colour, with a lot of *minars* and domes. The waters of the Buriganga river glistened at a distance, on which sail-boats laden with jute, lime and sand plied, creating ripples as they sailed up the river. Against the backdrop of a transparent blue sky, the scene became a beautifully drawn sketch, like a painting of the Kishangar *gharana*.

Hordes of servants, armed sentries, stables for horses, a Ford car with a folding hood and swarms of people greeted the eye. We were taken to the inner quarters and led upstairs. The rooms had ornamented pillars and porches. Fine *chik* curtains with silk borders hung over the doors through which the movement of people took on an air of mystery. A maid curtsied and lifted a curtain. At once a magnificent scene came into view. One that absolutely matched my idea of nawabi grandeur.

Stained glass windows and doors with heart-shaped coloured pieces of glass. Sunlight streaming in through them in soft rainbow hues. A chandelier lit by the soft sunlight sparkling like multicoloured stars. Our feet sank into the velvet-soft, patterned carpet. The milk-white walls were decorated with gold and silver motifs. The gilded four-poster seemed to be resting on four flower vases. A pink mosquito net graced the top of the bed like a canopy, fine as muslin. To the left, on a black marble-top table, stood an intricately worked silver hubble-bubble. On an adjoining table were a *paan* container, silver tumbler, *attar-daan* and a decanter with a spout made of copper and brass. The beautiful ornamentation was an example of the finest craftsmanship. A few white rose petals floated in a white marble bowl: a charming sight of white on white. A huge spittoon was placed under the bed, and next to it a pair of embroidered slippers. My eyes travelled to the far corner of the room. Kites made of fine Chinese paper lay there in a heap amidst colourful kite-flying paraphernalia. How my fingers itched to touch them! Who in Dhaka did not know of the Nawab Saheb's passion for flying kites?

The Nawab lay half inclined on the bed, supported by a huge velvet cushion. He looked for all the world as a nawab should – pink pomegranate complexion, blue eyes, light hair. He sniffed an *attar*-soaked silk handkerchief from time to time. The exquisite fragrance of *attar* pervaded the room. An expensive Kashmiri shawl covered his body. Was he running a fever? Without changing his position he lifted his right hand in a respectful *adaab* to my father.

Father felt his pulse – first the right wrist, then the left – his eyes closed in great concentration. My eyes moved between the Nawab and the pile of kites. At this point a young girl entered the room from the inner rooms, parting the *chik* curtain. She had the light movement of a colourful butterfly. She was dressed in a silk *salwar-kameez* with her head covered, and was carrying *sharbat* in glass tumblers placed on a tray. She walked up, did an *adaab* first to the Nawab Saheb, then to us, and spoke in chaste Urdu, '*Falsey ka sharbat*. Please oblige us by accepting this.' The Nawab Saheb, his eyebrows puckered in displeasure, admonished her, 'Serve it in silver tumblers.' 'As your honour pleases', replied the girl and withdrew. She was back again soon, with the aromatic beverage poured in silver containers.

There were many stories about the etiquette of the Nawab's family that made the rounds in the city. The great-grandfather of the present Nawab was very particular about manners. His servants were given special training in observing courtesies. To the elite of Dhaka that was the last word in courtly behaviour. This is how one story went. The old Nawab was once having his meal in royal style when his flowing white beard accidentally caught a few grains of rice from the sumptuous plates of Baghdadi *biryani* and Isfahani *malai korma*. Then it caught a few more. By and by his beard began to look like a spotted beehive. The Nawab was not aware of this. One of the servants, obviously a new recruit, in his desire to please the master, blurted out, '*Saab, aapke dari me chawal latak raha hai*.' The Nawab exploded. What impertinence! Streams of abuse were unleashed. '*Bevakoof, battameez, junglee*! If such words are heard again you will have your face broken in.' The poor servant was terrified. He thought he was going to lose his job. But no. The Nawab Saheb interrupted his eating to give the culprit a lesson in etiquette so that he would not repeat this in front of guests. He instructed him that in such a situation he should clothe his words in metaphors and figures of speech and say, '*Huzoor, shakhe me gul aur hai do bulbul*' (there are two bulbuls on the branch). The servant had to repeat this a hundred times, holding his ears and doing sit-ups.

Naturally, the women of the Nawab's household did not think it necessary to observe purdah in front of the aged *kaviraj*. In comparison to the colourless ladies of middle-class Bengali families, these women looked quite unreal. Their portraits still glow in my mind like Botticelli's Venus. Exquisite beauties, they seemed to belong to a fairyland. How could women of flesh and blood be so lovely? Were they human beings or flowers? Perhaps a garden of flowers would be a better description. Perhaps Mirza Ghalib had such beauties in mind when he wrote about how he wished to relish the beauty of the garden and pluck the flowers at the same time. Such slim and tender bodies! Cheeks like freshly plucked, sun-soaked apples from the garden of paradise. Figures that seemed like they were fashioned from the lightning flashes of a strong

Nor'wester, with ups and downs like the wild waves of the seven seas and complexions as white as the foam of the ocean. *Surma*-lined light eyes that sparkled like the blue stars of the night sky. Skin that was smooth and taut like a stringed instrument, ready to vibrate at the slightest touch. Other images come to mind. Like a tightly packed firework cracker fashioned by a master craftsman, at the touch of a lighted match they would sail skyward, shedding silver stars all the way down till they reached the clouds. And as they came down many a young heart would be struck by their light and heat.

A basket full of goodies were packed by these ethereal beings for me and my brother. Kabul grapes in a bed of cotton as if they were precious jewels, dry fruits and raisin, and almond-studded *gajar ka halwa*. Sometimes, we were given specially designed kites with bobbins bursting with treated thread. These appealed to us more than the exotic fruits.

We left the dream-world of the Nawab's residence. Our carriage turned right towards the *kotwali* and we entered the narrow lane to the left of the police station. Strange noises greeted our ears – cutting sounds, grinding sounds – all sorts of smells too. What a unique world! Perhaps nowhere else can one find such peculiar contrasts. The buildings were tall but narrow, hardly five feet in width and going up to six floors. Their weird shapes made me think that they had been pressed together by a mighty blow from a monster. They were supported by arches, had latticed windows as tiny as pigeon holes, and were surrounded by Islamic ornamentation. The doors were just wide enough for a very thin man to slip in. The insides were so dingy and dark that it seemed as though sunlight and air were forbidden from entering. How did people survive in these black holes? Despite this the architectural variety was quite stunning. The inhabitants of these strange houses were even stranger. The rooms and the front balconies were teeming with bare-bodied people, all of them busy at work. They held semi-circular iron gadgets in their hands. A glance at the gadget sent shivers down my spine . . . the lower part, sharp as a sword, glistened in the reflected light of the street lamps. I have seen a contraption exactly like this one. It was designed by Leonardo da Vinci and equally spine-chilling, though machine-driven. At the back of a horse-driven chariot were fitted semi-circular blades of steel in parallel circles, almost like a horizontal table fan. Another spiked circle was attached to this fan. As the horses picked up speed the wheels began to go round at a terrific speed, shredding everything that came in the way.

The workers were holding a solid greenish object between their feet, which they cut with the help of the terrible contraption. Their hands went up and down in such perfect rhythm that I could not take my eyes off them. I asked Father what these people were so busy at. He briefly said that they were making bangles from conch shells. I had no idea that the pure white body of

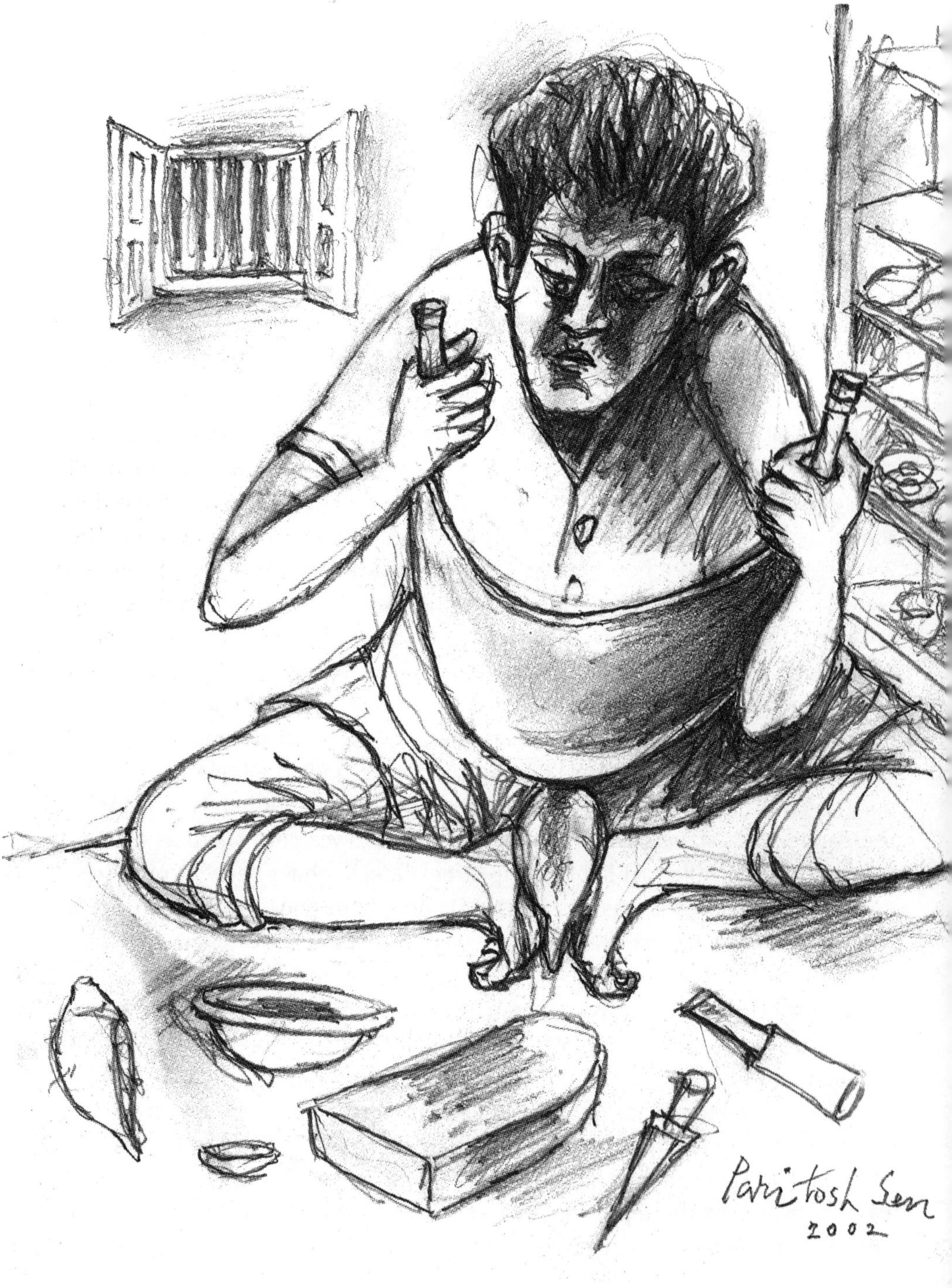
Paritosh Sen
2002

the conch was hidden under the layer of dirty green. As the mystery cleared I began to wonder at this strange transformation. Some of the craftsmen, wearing spectacles, were doing intricate ornamentation on the bangles, very much as with gold bangles. The scene created such a strong impression on me that in later life I made several sketches of it.

Another wonder awaited me the next morning at home. Overnight, a harmonium and a music teacher had materialized from nowhere. I went over to the south veranda to find out what was going on. A soiled exercise book was spread over the instrument. An attempt was underway to teach my sister, *Chordi*, the lines of a popular song, '*Shefali tomar anchalakhani bechao sarada prate*'. *Chordi* was trying her best to master the tune. The music teacher, with *paan*-stuffed mouth and armed with a *paan* box, was trying to pose like a typical *ustad*. He cleared his throat, blocked one ear and kept repeating the first line. The fingers of his other hand played over the harmonium. He wore the slightly annoyed expression of a teacher. He did manage to teach my *didi* a few songs within a month. Not that *Chordi* could sing in tune, but funnily enough, she passed with honours in the marriage test. The harmonium and the teacher disappeared after that. So much for the cultivation of music in our family. Our engagement with the fine arts was no better. A few soot-stained and dusty pictures of gods and goddesses adorned the walls of our sitting room. We also had a few ugly dolls painted in horrible colours in spite of the fact that folk art in this part of Bengal was quite lively. I will come to that later.

It was afternoon now. Lunch was over. The otherwise noisy, crowded household was sunk in a stupor, at least for some time. Silence descended, as if it is a land of ghosts. Unable to take a nap and driven by an uncontrollable desire to read a story book, I roamed the house. But nothing, not even a copy of the *Ramayana* or the *Mahabharata*, was available. The family's collection of books was limited to some tattered medical books and notes which belonged to my father, the almanac and the Lakshmi *panchali*. That was all. Life was a long stretch of monotony, with occasional weddings and festivals to cheer us up. The day-to-day life of the Sen family was drab and dull. It made me restless; I longed to break out of it.

One afternoon, unable to bear it any longer, I sneaked out of the house and set out for the market area known as Babur Bazaar, not more than a few hundred yards away. I reached the rows of food-stalls selling Muslim fare. Appetizing aromas of ghee, spices, onions, garlic and *heeng* wafted in the air. *Kababs* of different varieties, mutton cutlets and roast, *rumali roti*, *phulka*, rice and other delicacies were being cooked in huge pots. The gravy of the mutton curry looked as though it was made entirely of red pepper. The last platter contained sizeable pieces of breast cuts, smeared in rich orange gravy. A charcoal stove giving out low heat stood next to the platter. A steaming pot of yellow and dark pink *biryani* was placed on the stove. The aromatic vapour emanating from the pot reached my nostrils. The visually satisfying scene sharpened my senses. My taste buds were aroused, as were my smell buds. My eyes were glued to the orange platter and the pot of *biryani*. I felt like a fawn in the clutches of a tiger. Then the inevitable happened. Greed, all-pervading greed, enveloped me completely.

I rushed back home. I had noticed a counterfeit two-anna coin that had been lying in a container for quite some time. I picked it up and hurried to the neighbourhood mosque. A blind beggar used to come there every day. He sat with folded knees in an attitude of prayer, both his hands clasped over his chest. With his brown hair and beard he looked like a dervish. There was a bamboo staff by his side. Lifting his face to the sky he kept pleading, '*Ek paisa is andhe ko dogay to malik tumko lakh dega*' – If you give a paisa to this blind man God will give you a lakh. The small tin container in front of him had a lot of small change – pais, paisas, half paisas, even a few annas. They sparkled like freshly minted coins from the dark interior of the can. In the growing dusk it was hazy all around. I took advantage of the situation and dropped the counterfeit coin into the tin can. It fell with a jangle somewhat like the combined sound of cymbals and the *ek-tara*. The old beggar prayed to *Khuda* for my welfare and that of my children. Casting a surreptitious look around, I picked up a few one-anna coins from the can and ran back to the tempting food-stalls of Babur Bazaar. People are capable of doing just about anything for the sake of these heavenly delicacies. I ate to my heart's content. It was out of this world. So satisfying to the palate! No words can describe the pleasure. This experience left an indelible impression on my mind. It has lingered in my memory with a vividness that is still intact.

It is a sunny *Sravana* afternoon, a special day. Wherever you turned, on the streets, terraces, balconies, porches, doorways and window-sills, street lamps and roadside trees, there were black dots, an ocean of human heads. The entire town of Dhaka was tense with excitement for the *Janmashtami* procession – a spectacular float celebrating the birth of Krishna. Perhaps nowhere else in this subcontinent can a scene of such huge proportions, grandeur and surprises be seen. The hands that had produced the world famous muslins were also the creators of this artistic float. For two consecutive days the float, rainbow-coloured and ever-changing, swept past, as if an enormous *kantha*, exquisitely designed, was slowly unfolding itself. It created the impression of looking through a kaleidoscope. Though the active participants were Hindu, the procession was quite literally for everybody.

The afternoon sun moved to the western sky. Through the dusty cloud a dark form emerged, setting off ripples of excitement among the crowd. The towering hill-like form moved forward at a snail's pace. 'It is coming, it is coming', roared the crowd. Its echo rose from Babur Bazaar, went up and floated to us in the form of a sound wave. Oh, the thrill and the joy, and the jostling and pushing! A tide of colour greeted the eye, rows and rows of colour. Behind the elephant came galleries about thirty feet high supporting a platform with Vaishnav idols on silver and gilded thrones. The platforms were being pulled by bullocks. In front of the idols was a dumb charade of mythological stories or devotional songs and dances, very often just plain bawdy dance. It was an extraordinarily rich spectacle. Like the traditional frame supporting the Durga image, there were many decorated bamboo and wood structures, decked with tinsel and *shola*. Various live figures occupied the centre of the frame, gaudily dressed female figures. Their glittering beads and zari ornaments dazzled in the garlands of light provided by the mobile carbide lamps.

Next to arrive were the comic dancers, rows and rows of them. They sang devotional songs, satirical songs, patriotic songs and ballads to the accompaniment of cymbals and tambourines. The symmetry was so perfect that they seemed to be singing in one voice, the instruments too were synchronized. Then came the horse-riders, dressed as Rajput soldiers, brandishing swords. They were flanked by people holding flags, moving fans, large velvet umbrellas, spikes and other paraphernalia. They galloped to the tune of drums and bugles, even an army band. The marching music electrified the air. It seemed as though a hundred *pakhawajes* were being played in perfect unison. More clowns came dancing, followed by more horses, elephants, floats – a rich show of endless pageantry.

Once the procession ran into trouble. As it was crossing the mosque in our area, hundreds of Muslims armed with sticks and brickbats attacked them. People fled in panic like chicken, afraid of being run over by the speeding carriages. Many Hindus were injured, but they were all from other localities. We were a handful of Hindu families living in the Muslim neighbourhood. No harm came to us. Needless to say, the attack was well planned and steered by the government. Our Muslim neighbours provided all the basic necessities, like rice, oil, salt, milk and so on, till the situation returned to normal. This experience restored my faith in the basic goodness of human beings.

After the three-day pageant came another *Janmashtami* spectacle, the *Bara Chauki* or 'Big Stage' event of Nawabpur. Like the pageant, this too is an extraordinary visual experience. That stage was another expression of the aesthetic spirit: seekers of beauty showing that there can be no limit to their creativity. In decoration, design and synthesis of the Hindu and Muslim styles, the platform displayed an excellent sense of proportion. And what a riot of colour! With gold and silver work on a base of coloured cloth, paper and foil, the platform transformed the mouldy ancient buildings of Nawabpur into a fairyland. Set against the backdrop of the dark sky the stage stood out, lit by many-coloured lights. On the stage were larger than life-sized puppets acting out scenes from the epics and mythology. It went on all through the night, night after night. The way these puppets were made, the way they were made to move their limbs, the colour scheme, the technique, the aesthetic ideas and the restraint were of such superior quality that one was obliged to pay homage to the unknown artists.

The episode being enacted that day was the slaying of Ravana. It was a terrifying scene. Ravana brandishing his sword in the air seemed to be a perfect match for his swift adversaries, Rama and Lakshmana, flinging deadly weapons at him. Light from Ravana's *kharga* flashed across the dark sky like lightning. Rama and Lakshmana were about to be scorched to cinders in the terrible flames. I was petrified; my heart started pounding wildly. It was an experience I was not likely to ever forget, so vivid, so memorable. To this day the impressions stay with me, as though the whole thing happened just the other day.

No sooner did the excitement of the *Janmashtami* pageant fade, than a new thrill gripped me. The memory of the last Durga Puja, the happiness of those days, filled my heart and I looked forward to another joy-filled experience. A surge of happiness took me to our ancestral village Beltali. My cup of joy was full to the brim and overflowed. How wonderful life was, so lovely, so free! There was water everywhere – canals, ponds and tanks. The houses surrounded by greenery stood like islands. Such a wealth of birds, of fragrant flowers! Bengal, beautiful Bengal – so hypnotizing, so bewitching! It was as though God had been more than generous in providing our Beltali with all the flora and fauna at his command.

One afternoon I rowed the boat and sailed along the canals and marshes. Coming back to our ghat, I tied the boat and stretched myself out on the stern. A beautiful shady nook, sunlight filtering through the bamboo groves – a perfect landscape of the Chinese school of the Tang dynasty. My eyes were dazzled by the scattering sun; I turned over and lay on my belly.

A strange watery world greeted my eyes. Through a criss-cross of light and shade on the quiet water's surface nature's wonders revealed themselves. It must have been the same feeling that the famous scientist Mendeliev experienced when he examined a drop of water under his microscope and was awestruck by the spectacle of millions of germs in that drop of water. Swarming in that tiny space were hundreds of germs, insects, hordes of shrimps and tiny fishes like the *puti*, *banspata*, *mourala*, *tangra* and god knows what else, fighting for space. I turned my gaze upward, to be greeted by the same picture on land. Crowding in a one-square metre area were crawling creatures – earthworms, all sorts of tiny ants, grasshoppers, caterpillars, even baby snakes. An endless variety of life-forms!

While I was pondering over nature's secrets a frantic cry broke into my thoughts. It was the voice of our family priest. What could have happened to him! I rushed in that direction, as did others. From a hole at the foot of a pillar a black and shining young cobra had raised its hood and was charging the priest. It was still hissing, swinging in a slow rhythm, waves of ripples travelling across the entire length of its body. Though barely ten inches in length the cobra exhibited a terrible rage and looked absolutely frightening. The sheer beauty of its body took my breath away.

Strangely enough, none of my cousins was scared. The way they reacted made me feel that they were dealing with an earthworm, not a cobra. There were quite a few young cobras in the hole, they were certain. One of them quickly made a syrup with sugar and water and poured it into the hole. In no time, rows of red ants appeared, marching in single file towards the hole. My cousins found a crack in the foundation wall which they declared was the only escape route for the cobras. Armed with sticks, they waited expectantly, many pairs of eyes glued to the crack. Some time elapsed. Suddenly some ants emerged from the crack, scurried about and disappeared into the crack. Scouts, scouts, my cousins shouted excitedly. Now it was time for the black beauties to emerge. I was struck by their tremendous confidence. Soon enough, a flat head like a teaspoon was seen. As it came up we could see hundreds of ants sticking to its body like leeches. From a distance it looked like an embroidered black tape. How dangerous can these poison-ants be? I had no idea that they never let go of their victim even after it dies. The young cobra was writhing in agony from thousands of ant-bites. Already it was in no condition to lift itself up. One blow from my cousins and the black tape collapsed limp on the ground. One after the other, fifty-six cobras met their end in this manner. The entire operation took about an hour.

Dusk fell. Men, women and children assembled in front of the Puja platform. The drummers started beating their drums in full force. Cymbals and bells joined the clamour. Firework displays began. Excitement ran high. It had been a hectic day. I was unable to ward off sleep. My eyelids felt heavy. I quietly left the *pandal* and sneaked off to the western porch to flop down on the community bed. I felt a little scared because everybody else was at the Puja scene, at least three hundred yards away. Shutting my eyes tight, I tried to sleep, when somebody else crept in under the mosquito net. In the dim light of the lantern I could make out that she was a relative, a young woman in the full bloom of youth. A few minutes later a brother by relation crept in quietly too and lay down close to her. The rustle of clothes, jingle of bangles and heavy breathing made the stuffy night even more unbearable. Some more unfamiliar noises reached my ears. Outside, the steady chirp of the crickets went on and on, increasing in slow crescendo. Soon the noise reached deafening

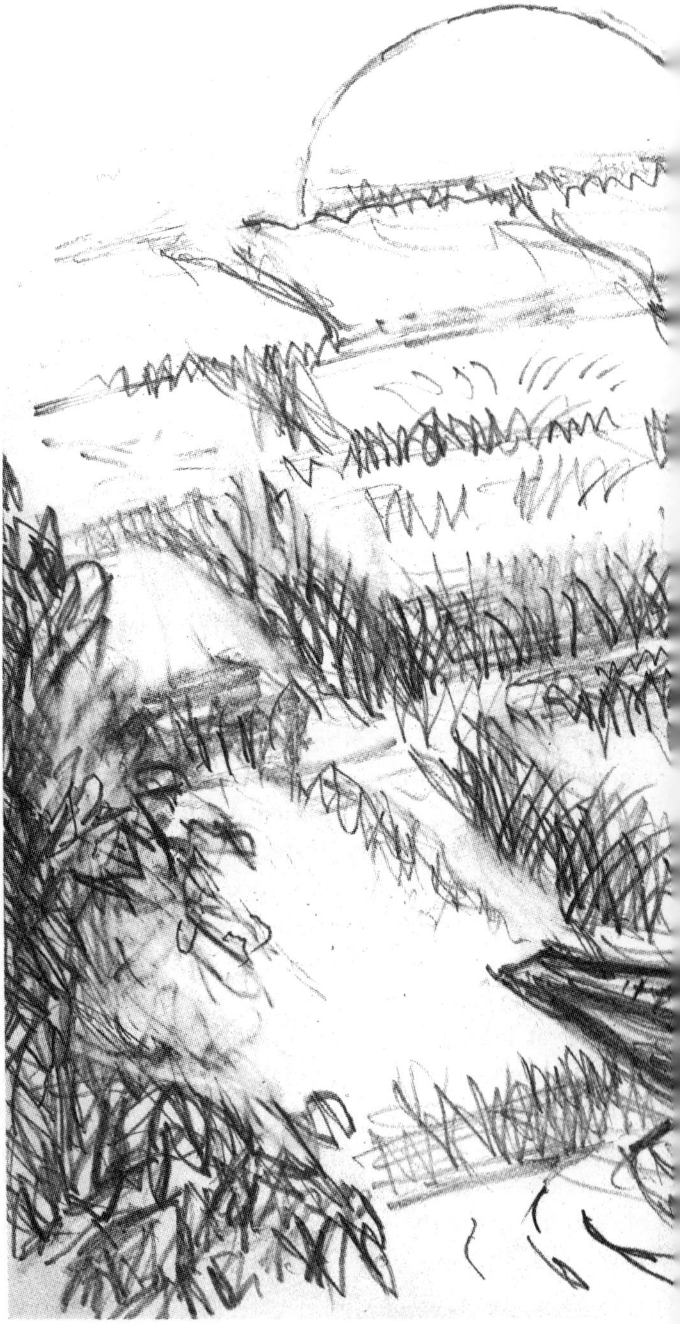

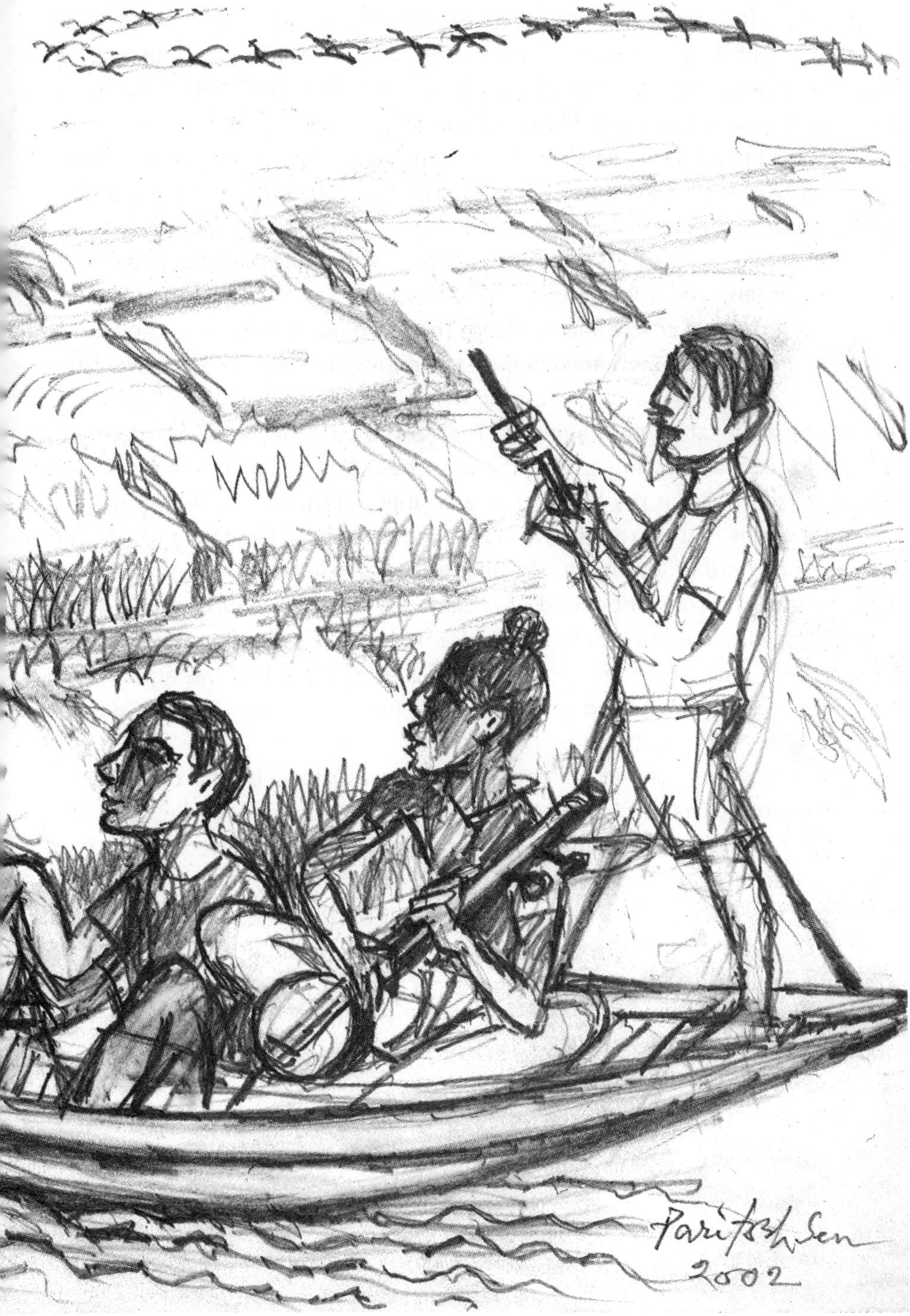
Paritosh Sen
2002

proportions. Then abruptly it came to a stop. I must have fallen asleep, I do not remember when.

In our Beltali home three large brick buildings served as community bedrooms. After dusk scores of mosquito curtains would come up everywhere – to your right, to your left, on cots, on the floor. It was a jungle of beds. There were fixed beds only for married couples and the elderly. Others were free to flop down on any bed after dinner was over.

In this game of musical chairs one night I found myself next to the young lady of the earlier episode. In the middle of the night I was woken by a gentle push. She had to go out to relieve herself and I should accompany her, I was informed in a soft whisper. It was not an unfair request as the area marked for the women's toilet was a little away from the building, in the middle of a thick overgrowth of *chalta* and bamboo. The place was infested with god knows what, one could hear owls and chameleons during the day. The story went that the spot was haunted as well. Turning her back to me, she took off almost all her clothes and sat on her haunches. Then came a steady whistling sound as if a spring wind was blowing among the branches of an *amlaki* tree. An unknown thrill coursed through my body. I felt a strange sensation, my legs grew limp. The light of the lantern revealed a round smooth part of her bare body glistening like the gourd of a *tanpura*. The silence of the bamboo grove, the darkness of the night, the constant sound of crickets and the dim light of my lantern – everything combined to create a truly dramatic scene. Not that I had not seen parts of the female body earlier, in chance glimpses, but this was an unforgettable occasion. I was obliged to have a good look. A *tanpura* indeed! So lovely to look at, so sweet to listen to.

It was the *kojagari* full-moon night. I was sitting by the tank steps. It was my favourite haunt. I loved to watch the fishes plop above the surface of the water. From the back wafted the monotonous tone of the recitation of the Lakshmi *panchali*, and from time to time the aroma of *luchi* and brinjals being fried. The huge shadow of the Arjuna tree fell on the water in the northeast corner. One could not make out where the tree ended and the shadow began. From beyond the shadow a faint silver glow gradually became visible, turning the liquid shadow into a brush stroke typical of Chinese artists. The moon was about to rise. My nephew Pacha, about my age, appeared and forced me to go to the ferry ghat.

We climbed into a small boat and proceeded towards the half-submerged paddy fields. Madhusudan Bhatiyal, one of our ryots, was also in the boat. He turned his *do-tara*. Across the bamboo grove a village woman could be seen doing dishes by lantern light, her head covered by her sari. From somewhere nearby a chorus of *ulu* rose and faded among the *jamrul* and *jeol* leaves. The glow of a lamp swam into view, it was from the *tulsi* platform in the house of Kamakhya Sen of Dakhinpara. There was no sound, not a soul anywhere. All of a sudden a swishing sound was heard from far away. I looked up to find a flock of birds, most probably ducks, flying in a single file under the canopy of the sky. They were headed for the southern horizon. Their wings glowed in the faint golden light of the *kojagari* night. Madhusudan, moved by the sight, sang out loud. We cheered him. The choice of song was really apt.

Oh how the golden bird flies.
Oh bird if you are flying east,
Tell my beloved,
How am I to spend the sad nights?
Oh how the golden bird flies.

I brought my gaze down from the sky. A beautiful scene greeted me. Stretched before me was the soft paddy field half-submerged in water. Sheafs of corn glistened with dew as if a light silk veil was spread over the entire landscape. The blue-green reflection of the paddy field looked back from the dark gray surface of the water. The sky vaulted over the scene in a large circle of copper, gold, silver and mercury. Later in life I have had occasion to witness many moonrises. But they pale into insignificance, like common *tagar* flowers before magnolia. I seem to lose myself every time this scene comes back to me. It transports me to a faraway world of pure beauty where life opens up a fountain of sheer joy.

Translated from the Bengali by Enakshi Chatterjee

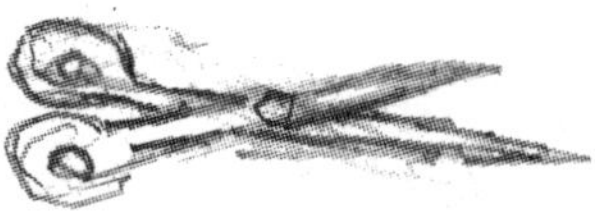

Hafiz Mian tailor par excellence

Our neighbourhood in Dhaka was predominantly Muslim, the Hindu ratio to them being one is to two. Except for a handful of professional middle-class families, the rest were small traders. It has been about half a century since I last saw them, yet my life in Dhaka was inextricably linked with them. Half my childhood and adolescent memories are of the Muslims of Dhaka. They were very special and distinctive and each very different from the other. Some of them, with their clownish features, could have stepped right out of the pages of the nonsense verses of Sukumar Ray.

There was Hafiz Mian the tailor, who was particularly bad-tempered. Jabbar Mian of the dry fruits store, who looked like a ferocious bandit. Owner of the horse-carriage stable, Mirza Saheb, who was perpetually tipsy. Dentist Akhtar Mian, who was dark, hairy and enormous. Fruit-seller Asgar Mian, who had a fat belly, like a ripe watermelon. Kallu Mian, the tobacco-seller, who had a bald head, shiny like a freshly scrubbed brass *dekchi*. Then there was Karim Khansama, sporting a line of thin moustache. He owned a restaurant. I also vividly remember Ustad Jhullur Mian, the magician. His tortoise-like slow gait, with the two legs wide apart, gave the impression that he had to drag himself with effort.

Within ten yards from our house, on the other side of the road, stood the tailoring shop of Hafiz Mian. The sight of him sitting cross-legged with his scissors, intent on cutting out segments for a coat, reminded one of a fasting Buddha in meditation, reduced to skin and bones. One could have taken him for a statue of the Buddha in slate stone, in the Gandhara style. His ribs jutted out of an emaciated body, the stomach below resembled an empty jar of curd. Instead of a head-dress, he had close-cropped hair of the colour of rotten jute. His vague moustache of the same colour bore no likeness whatsoever to any style common among the Muslims. His likeness to Lord Buddha ended there. He perpetually suffered from stomach ailments and had been reduced to such a state that his liver revolted against whatever food he ate. Nevertheless, nothing less than very strong tea of the colour of liquid tar, *kaleja ka salan* with

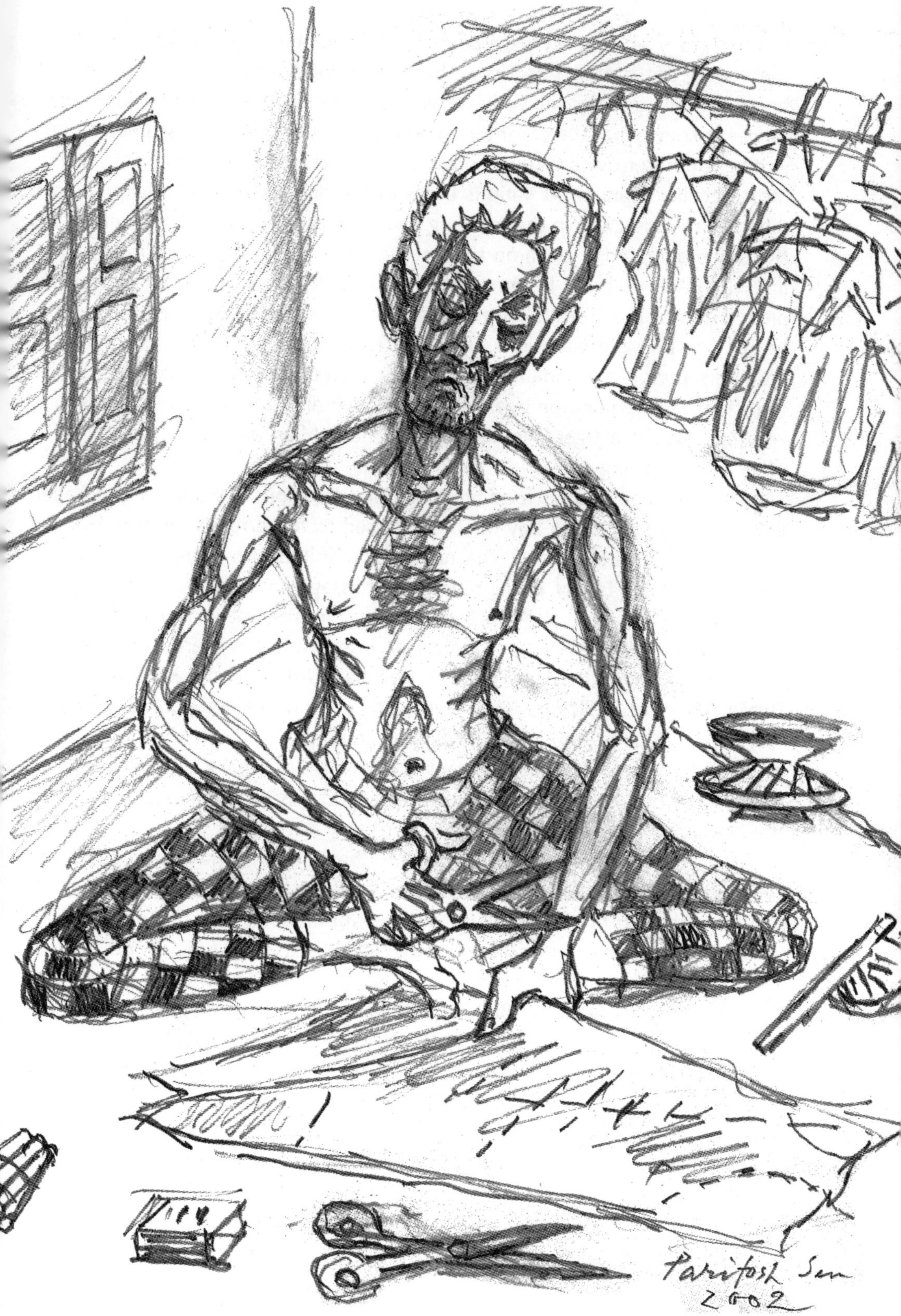
Paritosh Sen
2002

red-hot gravy and greasy *parathas* would do for him. He would raise hell if these were not supplied on time. The mutton gravy used to be the colour of bright-red *abir* powder mixed in water. When we heard his shouts from a distance we knew what the commotion was about. Along with the stomach problem he suffered from a chronic cough and cold. This had affected his voice in a most peculiar manner. At various times of the day his vocal chords produced different sounds. Early in the morning it was *Sa*, the first note of the octave. As the day progressed, it became shriller. His voice modulation had no apparent link with daylight, but it became softer towards the evening, though it changed pitch if he was provoked for some reason. When angry, his vocal chords exhibited all the possible variations of sound, each note coming out with greater emphasis. It would sound like a quarrel between the two celebrated fighters of that time – the champion wrestler Kikkar Singh and the famous Shyamakanto who had fought a tiger. We used to call Hafiz Mian *papad-tor pehelwan*; in other words, strong enough to crush a *papad*.

The Mian had his food brought from the shops of Islampur and Babur Bazaar by turn. A young boy of thirteen used to run errands for him. He was very poor and dark-skinned. The name Kallu suited him perfectly. Kallu was Hafiz Mian's Man Friday, giving him an oil massage on the scalp, massaging his body, getting him *paan* and *bidi*, even handing him the water-filled *badna* when Hafiz did his morning ablutions – for everything Kallu was there. They spoke in a mixed language, a curious mixture of Bihari Urdu and the Kutti dialect of Dhaka. The Mian bellowed his orders in the style of a Delhi *badshah* and the way they were executed would have done an emperor proud. After all, he lived in close proximity to the palace of the Nawab of Dhaka. Though not the Nawab's tailor, he used to stitch dresses for dozens of people claiming to be the Nawab's nephews. He could very justifiably put on airs.

On days when Kallu informed him that the shops had run out of mutton curry – '*kaleja ka salan khatam ho gais*' – Mian used to literally blow his top. It was as though no food was left in the world. What was he to eat? Kallu would try to console him in his own way, '*Salan nahin hains to kya hoois? Biryani hains, shik aur shami kabab hains, chup hains, mutton chop aur cutlis hains, mutton curry aur keema hains.*' But no, that was not good enough for Hafiz. He must have *kaleja ka salan* at any cost. He would threaten Kallu with the handle of his hand fan, expressing a desire to skin his back. Kallu would cringe in fear – he had to get hold of the dish, by hook or by crook. He was even ready to go home and ask his mother to cook it, for him it was a question of life and death. But Kallu was resourceful. He usually managed to get hold of the mutton curry by foraying into the food-stalls of other localities. The sight of his favourite dish would bring a subtle smile to the Mian's lips but he was careful not to show Kallu that he was pleased lest Kallu take advantage of his generosity. On the very rare occasions when Kallu failed to bring the dish he was mercilessly thrashed. I used to get infuriated. How could a human being behave like an animal? Why could not this old man exercise a little restraint?

Actually, there were sound reasons for these outbursts. The Mian was a sick and lonely man ever since he had lost his wife. But he was tremendously proud of his professional skills. He was not just a high-class tailor, his expertise extended to other fields as well. This included pigeon-flying and breeding superior quality pigeons. I will come to that later. The title *ustad* was probably reserved for the likes of him in the nawabi regime.

I witnessed an interesting event one afternoon as I was idly watching the street from our balcony on the first floor. A Ford Convertible with a tarpaulin hood pulled up in front of Hafiz Mian's shop. Cars were not a very common sight in those days. Barely a couple of cars would appear on our Zindabahar lane during the course of a day. I was curious about the passenger under the hood of the car. The sight of the visitor brought Hafiz Mian to his feet. He hurriedly did a respectful *Aas salaam alaikoom*. A fair-complexioned young man in a bright red fez cap and ghee-coloured silk *achkan* got down. He was carrying a length of woollen fabric in his hand. In spite of his brown beard, the young man had a somewhat feminine look. He handed the fabric to Hafiz. 'I want a coat made for me', he said. Hafiz happened to be down with his stomach ailment that day. This coupled with an attack of the common cold had played havoc with his vocal chords. This happened quite often – his coughing bouts would wake me up even in the dead of the night. He was also in a particularly foul mood, as was evident from his day-long tirade against Kallu. When the young gentleman spoke to him Hafiz put on his best manner and answered politely, 'Please leave the material and come back after three days for a trial.' The *nawabzada's* cap almost fell off in astonishment. 'But, but . . . ,' he stammered, 'but you have not taken the measurements yet, how can you talk of a trial?' Hafiz spoke again, trying to keep his voice as sweet as possible. 'Come after three days, then we will see.' The *nawabzada* was nonplussed. This tailor is trying to pull my leg, he must have thought. However, without saying anything more he got into the car and drove off. The tailor's voice, though feeble, had the authority of long experience and expertise. There was something in it which had obviously suggested to the *nawabzada* that Hafiz Mian wanted him to leave because he was feeling out of sorts.

Early the next morning I found Hafiz bending over the fabric which was spread on the floor before him; with a flat piece of coloured chalk he was drawing straight and curved lines on it with infinite care. From time to time he closed his eyes and seemed engrossed in deep thought. Perhaps he was trying to visualize the figure of the *nawabzada*. His fingers, which were as slender as the *topshey* fish, clutched the piece of chalk. The way he wielded it had a small boy like me marvel in wonder. Was he just a tailor or an artist, I wondered. He stood up after every couple of minutes, closed one eye and examined the chalk markings. Then, very carefully, he applied his scissors along the chalk marks. How bold of him, I could not help thinking. In fact I was getting nervous lest he made a mistake. The sleeve might be shorter than needed or the back might be a little too tight. What would be the consequence then? I was panic-stricken. All kinds of ominous possibilities began to haunt me. Was it possible to stitch a coat without taking measurements, and that too for no less a person than a *nawabzada*? How could an important person like him accept it and pay for it? Was this some divine bliss acquired through performing *Milad shareef* at the shop every *Jumma* day? Or was it just plain madness?

On the third day I was up at the balcony, determined not to miss the fun, though with trepidation in my heart. It felt as though it was I being put to a difficult test. What if the coat did not fit the *nawabzada*? But Hafiz Mian was not the least bit bothered. Clad in his blue and brown *lungi* and a dirty pink vest, he sat leaning against the door, discussing incomprehensible details of the pedigree of pigeons with another person. During such discussions he forgot all else; even the presence of a *nawabzada* would not have made any difference.

The Ford drew up in due time. I was almost bursting with excitement. Hafiz Mian greeted his client and stood up to retrieve the coat from a hanger inside the cupboard. He did not seem worried at all, but the *nawabzada* was frowning a little. In fact, he looked a little apprehensive. He was made to stand in front of a mirror while Hafiz put the coat on him. Wonder of wonders! It was a near-perfect fit; the sleeves, shoulder, armpits, everything! There was only a tiny fold on the back. The *nawabzada* was so surprised that he could not believe his eyes. He stood frozen, like a statue, in front of the mirror. For me it was the eighth wonder of the world. Meanwhile, Ustad Hafiz Mian drew some signs like algebraic symbols on the coat and placed pins on the marked spots. Then he gave some instructions to his son. The *nawabzada* was still too stunned to speak. Finally he proceeded to the car. Just before getting in, he paused to turn to the master tailor. A faint smile played on his lips as he mumbled to himself, '*Kamaal, kamaal, gazab, gazab*.' After a couple of hours the coat, neatly folded and pressed, was sent to the Nawab Palace through the Mian's son. What a wonderful craftsman! Completely bowled over by the skill and expertise of this illiterate man, I continued to stand on the balcony, as overwhelmed as the *nawabzada*.

Though stitching was his profession, Hafiz Mian was more devoted to his favourite pastime, pigeon-flying. In fact his entire heart and soul were consumed by the pigeons which lived on the roof of his shop. It was an addiction, like opium. The first thing he did every morning was to climb up to the roof. He was then a very different man from the listless, feeble Hafiz who had been

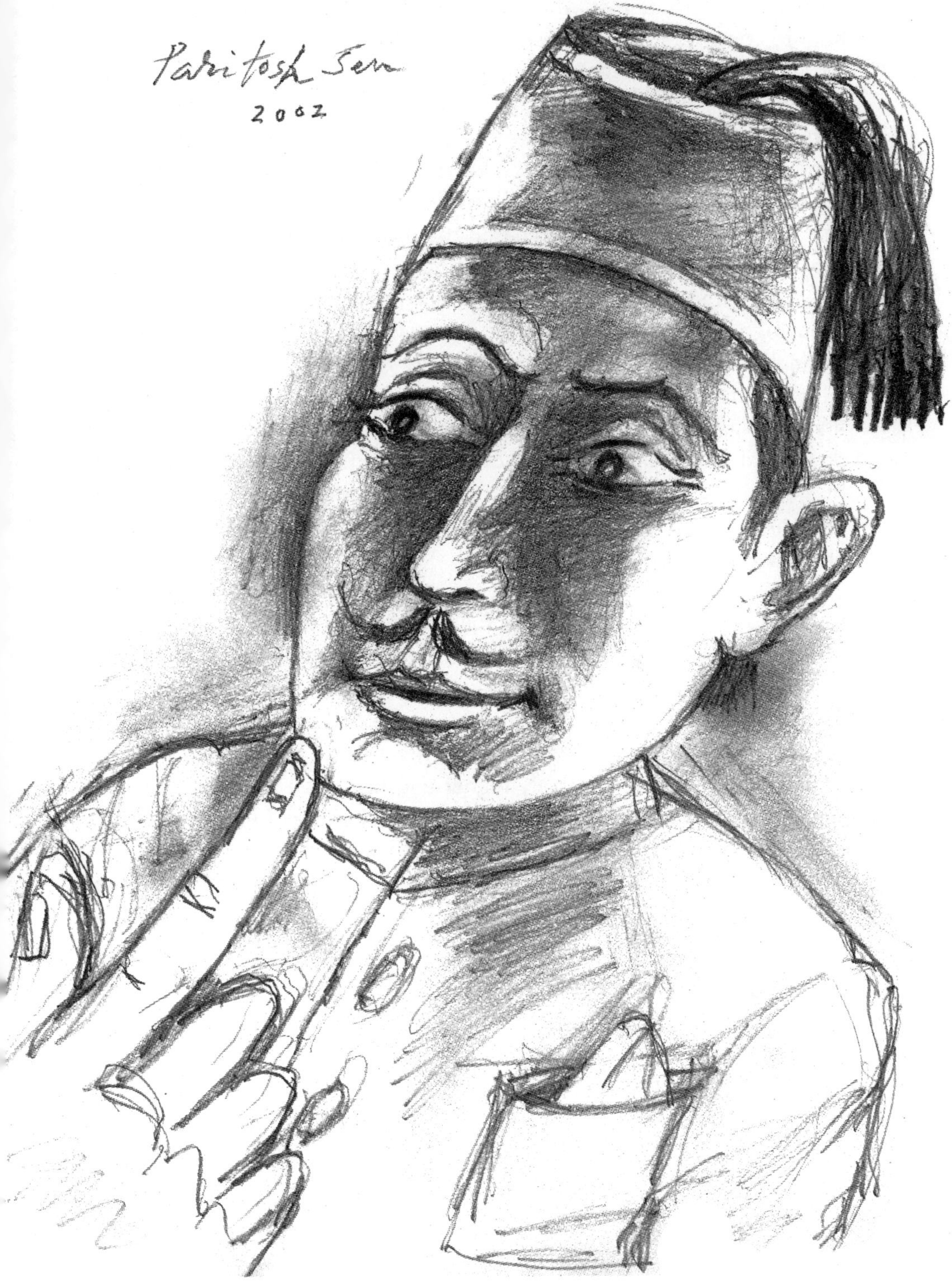
Paritosh Sen
2002

stretched out on the mat the previous night. All traces of lethargy or sickness would vanish for the time being. A wave of activity and excitement seemed to possess him. On seeing him the pigeons would start pushing against the cage door to come out. A lot of pushing and jostling would go on, like among children who had caught sight of long-lost parents. Hafiz would scatter fistfuls of paddy on the floor and open the cage. At once the pigeons dashed out like flood waters. But they must have the last bits from the master, perched on his hand. Like a man petting his dogs, Hafiz caressed them lovingly. A truly touching scene. He was completely devoted to those birds.

The meal over, Hafiz chased the pigeons with a bamboo staff, on the top of which was tied a piece of red cloth. The entire flock fluttered up to the sky. I wondered at their astonishing vitality, their sheer exuberance, like horses galloping without reins. Was there anything comparable to this in the entire world of winged creatures? Each and every feather in their wings was charged with electricity and the speed of lightning, packed with restless excitement. At first the pigeons went straight up like rockets. The very next minute they dived downward in a straight line. They flew off in different directions at the flicker of an eyelid and came back with equal speed. Meanwhile Hafiz continued to sway his bamboo flag with one hand and pressed his lower lip to the upper to produce a shrill whistling sound.

What a flurry of activity everywhere! The sky, the air pulsated with the tremendous commotion. This was followed by a scene of extraordinary beauty. About fifty pigeons of good Gerobaj stock went round and round rhythmically, circling the air and turning somersaults as though it were a bird ballet. In the early morning sun their wings and feathers flashed pink like rows of roses shot from a rocket. My heart wanted to fly with them. I felt restless all over. They kept flapping their wings to fly higher and higher till they disappeared from sight. Perhaps no other bird enjoys the sheer pleasure of flight like the pigeon. Kites and vultures too float high for hours together, but their wings seem to lack the vitality and abandon of flying pigeons. Even so, the sight of these birds too making wide circles held aloft by dark storm clouds is a thrilling experience. It is both visually pleasing and soothing to the eye. You feel your taut muscles relaxing, the mind gets a release from the everyday worries of urban life. No wonder Gagan Thakur was inspired to draw some sketches of such a scene in Chinese ink.

Unlike other pigeon enthusiasts, Hafiz Mian was not interested in using this sport as a form of gambling. He was snooty about it. For him associating money with this sport made it an inferior pastime. The way he taught the birds to fly in a pattern and other skills was almost army-like in technique. He played the role of a sergeant major training fresh recruits. And yet, he elevated this hobby to the level of a fine art. This was acknowledged even by his arch rivals, though they would never admit it to his face.

He had a few snatcher pigeons in his flock, who could be compared to the Casanova type among humans. I was amazed at the skill with which they enticed the she-pigeons from other flocks. Hafiz produced these various types by mixing different good stocks like the Banarasi Kagzi with the Bengal Kagzi, or the Subdum with Nasra, or the Sabchinia with Kagzi. Nazri pigeons had the keenest sight, according to Hafiz. They were unparalleled in performing the most difficult tricks. On the other hand, the plain variety could remain in flight for the longest period. People hovered around him, hoping to benefit from his knowledge obtained by long years of experimentation. They would do anything for him, from pure flattery to washing his feet. But the sole owner of this expertise and skill, Hafiz Mian, would not share his knowledge so easily. He would give all sorts of excuses, like 'I do not feel well today', 'Some other day perhaps', and so on, to get rid of them. In this he was like the celebrated musician Faiyaz Khan who, it is said, used to refuse to oblige his admirers using similar techniques.

But no addiction is enjoyable without company, be it opium or *ganja* or pigeon-flying. Hafiz Mian, who kept himself busy flying pigeons the entire morning and with his professional work the rest of the day, was basically a lonely man. He had lost his wife some years ago. His family consisted of just one son who assisted him in the shop but did not share his passion for pigeons. After working hours he would go away to be with his friends, leaving his father to himself. Poor Hafiz found the long nights unbearable. All his physical ailments would begin to bother him then and this was when he needed the services of Kallu most. Under the stern exterior, the prominent ribs of his chest, breathed a warm heart. Like any other person, he too had stories to tell and he always looked for a close person in whom he could confide. This after all is a primary necessity, like having two meals a day – confiding in somebody, particularly if that person happens to be a loyal admirer. My elder brother was a loyal fan of his and Hafiz Mian gladly accepted him as a junior partner. Hafiz treated him with the same affection he showed his own son, and talked to him about his pet pigeons and also of his joys and sorrows. My brother was the only one with whom Hafiz shared his innermost thoughts. They had long sessions, often extending to eleven at night. By and by the addiction caught on; it could be very infectious, as we were to realize soon enough. Before I knew I too had joined this charmed circle.

In our house too we had some ordinary pigeons dating back to my grandfather's time. Soon my brother and I were involved in the business of breeding and flying pigeons. It was an all-absorbing hobby, which kept us very busy. We had no time for meals or studies. The hobby took complete hold of us in a way that is difficult to explain to the uninitiated. But in my case the obsession did not last long; it was replaced by a stronger addiction.

One afternoon as we came back from school, we were told by Hafiz Mian of a pigeon race from Narayangunj, at the extreme end of the city. About thirty flocks would take part in the race. Most importantly, their orbit would be right over our neighbourhood. The Mian was determined to capture the best pigeons as they flew over our sky. He would do it at any cost. He needed our help in this venture. Needless to say, we were more than willing. In fact I was so excited that I could hardly sleep that night.

The next morning we were awake before the earliest crow. We found Hafiz Mian already up and about, supervising the grain and water for the racing pigeons. His son was posted on the second-floor terrace of the adjacent building, and Kallu was asked to climb up the dome of the nearby mosque from where the daily calls for prayer were sent out. We were given orders to keep an eye on the eastern sky, the direction from which the flocks were to come, flying from east to west.

Our eyes were fixed to the sky, scanning it with the seriousness of gazers looking for the Eid moon. A very light mist spread over the entire city like a muslin cover. Beyond the mist the winter sun bathed the sky, making it shine like a freshly fashioned copper sheet. The entire sky was spotless except for some tiny specks made by distant crows and mynas, and resembled the bare canvas of an artist before he applies the first dab of colour.

Suddenly a sound from the direction of the mosque's turret made us prick our ears. '*Aa rahis, aa rahis*', they are coming, shouted Kallu. We stared at the eastern horizon, beyond the houses, the dome on the gate of the Nawab Palace and Jagannath College. But no, nothing could be seen, not even a common sparrow. As we gazed on, a thin smoke-like spiral became gradually visible. Could it be from the jute mills of Narayangunj, we wondered. It could also be from kitchen stoves, the most natural thing in the morning. Whatever be its source, we did not take our hawk-like gaze off the spiralling smoke. The smoke soon darkened and moved towards us like a black cloud of *Bhadra*.

The Mian sprang into action, opening the doors of the cages one by one, releasing all his pigeons. Then he chased them with the bamboo pole the way long-distance runners are flagged off. A series of long shrill whistles followed. We too joined in the chorus. The still morning now pulsated with excitement and activity. The black cloud by now had broken into fragments and was spread over the entire eastern horizon. It was moving fast, we could hear its approaching sound quite clearly.

Meanwhile Hafiz Mian's pigeons were circling in their own orbit. Hafiz began moving the red flag like the top of a betel palm tossed by a violent wind.

He was sending out signals, as if to an advancing army. Like an enemy attack, the competing pigeons were moving fast in formation. As they entered our territory, Hafiz Mian's trained pigeons penetrated their line like paratroopers. They were aiming at catching the birds from the advance flocks. Mian kept whistling, sending them various signals. Very soon his paratroopers soared high above the rest with some of the racing pigeons in tow. They seemed to vanish into thin air. My brother and I were terribly worried but Hafiz seemed unperturbed. He sat on the low wall of the terrace and lit a *bidi* as though nothing had happened. After a few puffs he threw the *bidi* away and sprang into action once again. With incredible swiftness he swept the entire terrace and scattered paddy on it very liberally. Earthen bowls filled with water were placed at regular intervals. He kept looking up from time to time. After a while he signalled to us to leave the terrace, as though he had received some wireless message. His son too came down from the terrace of the next house. We ran to the lower balcony. We could see the Mian hiding behind the door leading to the terrace. The flock was returning.

That was the beauty of Hafiz Mian's training. Just as the racing pigeons were getting exhausted with thirst and fatigue, the trained robber birds directed them to the terrace. The timing was perfect. The unfamiliar surroundings frightened the new recruits at first and they tried to escape, but the robbers did not allow them to get away. No wonder the Mian was increasingly becoming friendless, for such acts of robbery are not likely to attract friends. The work of the robber pigeons was now over. Hafiz took over to complete the operations. The pigeons were hungrily pecking at the grains and dipping their beaks in the water containers. Taking advantage of their concentration, Hafiz tiptoed to the cages to open the trap door just wide enough for the birds to enter. The cages too were equipped with plenty of pigeon-feed. Once the paddy out in the terrace was finished the trained birds pushed the newcomers into the cages. It was an amazing strategy which they accomplished with perfect skill. The credit for this of course went to their training. The pigeons were crowding the cages, all was confusion. This was the perfect opportunity. Hafiz was now sure that the right moment had arrived. He crept with the gait of a tiger moving towards its prey and in a swift movement closed all the cage doors.

Watching him with admiration I said to myself, like the *nawabzada*, '*Kamaal, kamaal, gazab, gazab*.'

Translated from the Bengali by Enakshi Chatterjee

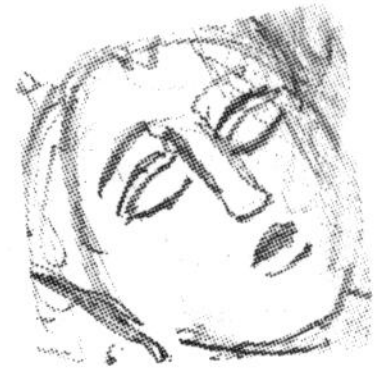

Scene painter Jiten Goswami

Just south of our ancestral home in Dhaka, there was a Kali temple. The busy arterial road that extended from west to east connecting Babur Bazaar and Islampur passed before this temple. Across the road stood a Portuguese church. It was famous for being the oldest place of worship for the Christian community, although the whites of the city regarded it as a church of the natives and gave it a wide berth. Adjacent to the church was a mosque. It was hardly surprising, therefore, that such a multireligious place should attract members of all kinds of dubious professions. Whenever religion manifests itself as a source of material gain, greed and other temptations are bound to take root. This is true everywhere, not just in our country. No wonder, therefore, that within a hundred yards of the various shops that had mushroomed on both sides of the road there flourished a colony of prostitutes – two in fact, one on the north and the other on the south. The first catered to upper middle-class clients, the second to the lower rungs of society. Although the thoroughfare was known as an arterial road, in reality it was like a marketplace: rows of fruit shops, *dhabas* displaying mouth-watering *kababs*, chops, tandoor-cooked cheese-*parathas*, sweetmeat shops, dimly lit liquor shops selling both country-made and foreign brands, tobacconists dealing in *tambaku*, cigars and cigarettes, shops selling household and other goods of daily consumption, kite shops selling kites of all hues and patterns, pharmacies stocked with allopathic, ayurvedic, unani and homeopathic medicines, florists, grocers, jewellers, shops for repairing musical instruments, and a lot more.

On the left of the entrance to the Kali temple was the famous tea-stall of Akshaya babu, which also served as a meeting place for the local people. Next to the shop was a narrow strip – just six or seven feet wide, but nearly twenty feet deep. The interior of this strip was manned by a single person. It was as different from the neighbouring shops as an ultramarine peacock among a host of ravens and crows. The owner of the shop was as unique as his occupation. In his early sixties, he was and firmly built. His complexion was fairer than that of the average Bengali, and his skin was as taut as the strings of a tennis racquet. Under his long and sharp nose was a thick growth of moustache. He always wore a severe and moody look. Long and wavy salt-and-pepper hair crowned his head and cascaded down to his shoulder. His attire was a short-sleeved, unwashed vest and a *dhoti worn salwar*-style, over which he tied a red checkered cotton towel. Unless it was absolutely necessary, he would not venture out of his narrow shop. On the rare occasions that he stepped out, in a freshly laundered shirt and proper *dhoti*, and with an umbrella in hand, people were likely to mistake him for a judge of the courts – his appearance was that impressive and distinguished.

Jiten babu, or more correctly, Jiten Goswami, was a scene painter by profession. He drew scenes for theatre and other stage productions. A huge stretch of virgin canvas made of unbleached cotton hung from the ceiling of his shop to the floor, like an oversized scroll. It was attached to two bamboo poles to keep it taut. The floor was littered with dozens of small and medium clay cups and other containers, and sheets of soiled and crumpled newspaper. Two large terracotta vessels filled with water and with a few brushes dipped in it were always to be seen. Clean brushes of varying sizes stood arranged on a stool close by, including two shoe brushes. At the far end of the room, some empty, unlabelled bottles stood on a shelf. Obviously they were not medicine bottles. On the window sill, adjacent to the shelf, were some old dog-eared books, arranged asymmetrically. They were mostly historical novels and plays in Bengali.

Apart from painting scenes, Jiten babu also got commissions to make stage props, such as thrones for kings, swords and shields, flowering plants to suggest a garden, sometimes even a small hillock. Over a wooden frame he would nail thick cardboard cut to shape and paint it with the right colours at the right places, such that an onlooker would be completely taken aback by the verisimilitude.

While painting a large scene he would dip a shoe brush into the clay pots filled with colours and cover areas of the canvas with sweeping strokes. But when painting a throne or a sword and its scabbard, he would use extra fine brushes to render the intricate patterns. His handiwork was so precise that he could create the finest of impressions: of gems studded here and there with light reflecting from their surface, for instance. So refined and controlled was his craftsmanship that it could easily pass off as that of a master goldsmith rather than a scene painter. Whether working with a shoe brush or an artist's brush, Jiten babu would be completely absorbed in the act, in a trance-like state. It was as though an unseen power guided all his actions. His concentration was so total and his respect for his work so intense that any attempt by stray passers-by to strike up a conversation would be rudely rebuffed. In his baritone voice he would ask the man to 'get lost'. At the sound of these unusually stern words, most people left promptly. Those who did not were sprayed with colours. Solitude and silence were very precious to Jiten babu; he would go to any length to gain these.

Often, I would give my studies or games a miss and quietly watch him working with great wonder. I could keep doing so for hours. What was astonishing was that this god-gifted man, who so fiercely guarded his solitude, was indulgent towards me. And his subtle, unspoken affection was reciprocated by me. Perhaps he was aware of my silent admiration for his art. There was a silent bond of communication between us.

One Sunday, after having completed my homework, I decided to go and see what Jiten babu was doing. I found him sitting cross-legged on a stool and nervously smoking a *hookah*, his gaze fixed on the milk-white canvas in front. What was he so intensely deliberating upon, I wondered. What kind of scene he was going to paint – whether it was to be human figures or a landscape with trees, houses and animals? An outdoor scene or an indoor scene? His eyes were so focused on the canvas that my presence at the door went unnoticed. Cups containing colours and brushes of different sizes had been carefully laid out on sheets of newspaper that were spread out on the floor. Meanwhile, the puffs at the *hookah* became faster and faster. His right leg, resting on the left knee, began to shake. His thick eyebrows were knitted, resembling a pair of hillocks. His fixed stare grew sharper. Smoke filled the room, like a thin veil of rising autumnal mist. There was every hint that something was about to happen.

Jiten babu finally put the *hookah* aside and sat very still, with eyes closed, as though in meditation. He whispered something to himself. Was he chanting a *mantra*? He remained still for a few more minutes. Then, suddenly, his eyes opened wide as if he had just woken up from deep slumber. He stood up, and with one of his hands picked up a bowl of yellow ochre, and with the other a long brush. He stood perfectly still for a while again, like the lull before a storm. Then the long brush started moving. It first made lines in the air around his right knee where his hand rested, raised itself and drew more lines in empty space. Then the brush moved to the canvas and Jiten babu started drawing some bold straight lines, first to the right, then to the left, followed by some curved ones on top. Next, he quickly climbed up on the stool to draw a few equally bold horizontal lines above these. His movements were as fast as lightning. He then jumped down, put the brush and colour aside and started to prepare his *hookah* for a smoke by lighting a few flat cakes of powdered charcoal from the open *chulha* outside Akshaya babu's teashop and arranging them over the lump of sticky *tambaku*. He took a few deep and quick puffs which bore testimony to the tension that was gripping him. With each puff a gurgling sound, 'phrut, phrut', emanated from the *hookah*. Silence and sound, light and colour, action and actor charged the atmosphere with great drama.

All this while, Jiten babu's gaze had not strayed from the canvas, which by now looked like a jungle of lines. He soaked a piece of cloth in clean water and rubbed out the superfluous lines. This was done to impose some order so that definite shapes could emerge from the jumble of lines. He picked up the brush again and drew some fresh lines here and there. Then he proceeded to join two vertical lines with a curved one on the top to suggest an arch. More such arches were created in quick succession. Through one of them there soon appeared a *jali*. He then painted another one, as if to maintain symmetry. Between the two he painted a door. He picked up another bowl of colour and a hard flat shoe brush. The quicksilver movements of his hand, his sure strokes and impeccable sense of proportion could have put artists even half his age to shame. Jiten babu dipped the shoe brush in the bowl held in his left hand and, with sweeping strokes, filled up the space between the two flaps of the door. With the same colour, he created two openings in the centre of the *jalis*. An azure sky now shone through the door and the *jalis*. What imagination, what technical skill and fiendish energy this silent, mysterious man was gifted with! Just minutes ago the canvas had looked like a blank, white-washed wall. Now, it was filled with a many-arched hall, through which not just a deep blue sky but also a clear suggestion of a distant landscape with water and trees was visible. This was indeed magical!

Jiten babu lit his *hookah* again to take a few quick puffs: puffs which were indicative of a suppressed excitement. As always, he kept his gaze fixed on the canvas. What new configurations was he going to introduce into the scene? What kind of colours – cold or warm – would embellish them? For what class of people was this arched hall being created? Judging by the shapes of the *jalis*, the door and the columns with their floral designs, it was evident this was no ordinary room for an ordinary person. He put the *hookah* aside and picked up a longish piece of wood, somewhat like an over-sized foot-rule. He held it horizontally and drew lines using it from the right to the left of the canvas, covering the foreground. He repeated the exercise holding the piece of wood vertically, and soon a checkered board emerged. With the help of new brushes he went on to fill up every alternate square with black. To simulate the veins of a marble slab, he drew light-grey lines on both the black and white squares. In order to achieve perfect verisimilitude, he then softened the edges of the lines with a water-filled brush.

Suddenly he turned and shot a question at me, which frightened me so much that my heart began to beat fast. Why had he chosen to ask an ignorant and immature boy like me? After all, there were other people around, like Akshay babu, Vraja babu, Sattar mian and Akhtar mian. Pointing to the canvas, Jiten babu asked, 'Tell me, what do these squares stand for?' On the face of it the question was simple and straightforward. But coming as it did from a serious man like Jiten babu, I was petrified. He repeated the question impatiently, and with a touch of admonition. I was alarmed. As I pondered, two words escaped my mouth like a bird accidentally freed from a cage. 'Chess board', was my hesitant reply. 'Why a chess board?' he posed a counter-question. 'Why not a straightforward black-and-white marble floor?' He paused, then asked again, 'Who has ever seen or heard of a chess board of such gigantic proportions?' In the narrow room his booming voice resounded like a stentorian roar.

His counter-questions both humbled and intimidated me. Why did I have to parade my ignorance and stupidity? Surely silence would have been a better answer. Or simply, an 'I don't know.' By trying to be smart, I had made a fool of myself. My sense of frustration had begun to give way to anger, when Jiten Babu put a stop to it. Turning towards me he gently said, 'Your answer is correct.' Having said this, he quietly turned back to his *hookah*. Correct! I was completely taken aback. After having dismissed my answer just a few moments ago? Was he trying to trick me or was he pulling my leg? Jiten babu stopped smoking and declared dramatically, 'But this is no ordinary chess board. Do you know who the players are? One is no less a person than the *Badshah* of Delhi. And it will be played with real-life elephants, horses, even ministers and soldiers. You see, the *Badshah* has challenged his own *Wazir-e-Azam*. If the latter loses the game he will not only be relieved of his job, he will lose his head as well. So, you see, it's not going to be an ordinary game of chess.'

Good God! What a terrible prospect! I was deeply alarmed. In the game of dice Yudhisthira had lost only his kingdom. Here a human being's life was at stake. Waves of sympathy for the *Wazir-e-Azam* started to well up inside me. Profoundly concerned, I started asking Jiten babu, 'And if . . .'. He interrupted me, 'And if the *Badshah* loses the *Wazir-e-Azam* will be rewarded with a hundred thousand gold *mohurs*.' Needless to say, I sent out fervent prayers for the *Wazir's* victory. Suddenly Jiten babu looked at me and declared, 'You will shine.' What will make me shine, and how? Men of few words such as Jiten babu are always apt to express themselves in the form of puzzles. What did these mysterious words really mean? What kind of promise or possibility had he discovered in me? His brief remark kept circling in my mind for some time.

The next day I rushed to Jiten babu's place, for I was keen to find out how far he had progressed with the chess scene. What I saw when I arrived there was mind-boggling. All the columns, arches and walls had been decorated with enamelled inlay work, as is found in most Mughal interiors. Huge chandeliers were hanging from the ceiling. Soft beams of many-coloured light radiated from the crystals. In front of the door a raised platform had been set up for the emperor's throne. Just above it was a trellised balcony, probably meant for the *Begum*. When had Jiten babu managed to put in such a supreme effort? He must have worked through the night. Had he not felt the need for even a wink of sleep? Or to go home to rest? It seemed impossible to me that he could have completed such a complex scene overnight. My respect for and wonder at the old man's genius grew in direct proportion to his love of his work and perseverance.

Jiten babu laid a few pieces of thick cardboard on the floor and drew some lines – both straight and curved – on them with a pencil. He cut the pieces of board along the lines, using a pair of tailor's scissors. Then he primed their surface with a coat of liquid chalk and nailed the pieces on the frame of a wooden chair kept in one corner of the room, the largest piece shaped like a heart being fixed to the back. I wondered who the seat was intended for. Will the *Badshah* of Delhi issue his *firman*s from this seat? Taking quick puffs at his *hookah*, Jiten babu fixed his gaze on the seat. The gurgle of the *hookah* slowly faded till there was no sound at all. What was it that was demanding such total concentration? In its present state, the chair looked like nothing more than a seat made of cardboard. Briskly, he mixed gold and silver powder with glue and water in two separate cups and kept them by the side. With a fine brush he painted floral designs on the chair, introducing tiny birds here and there. The legs of the chair were shaped like falcons, to give the impression that the seat rested on their heads. A globe was painted in between two birds. '*Jehanpana*': didn't the word mean Lord of the World? Without doubt, the seat now looked fit for royal occupation.

The floral designs were touched up with gold and silver at the right places. Pearls, emeralds, turquoise, cobalt andother gems found their place in the overall design. They sparkled as though in the reflected light of a chandelier. What marvellous simulation of light and shade! What extraordinary knowledge of colour, harmony and proportion! Most of all, what wonderful craftsmanship!

The following evening I went with my brothers and sisters to watch the *aarati* at the Kali temple, as usual. On my way back, as I passed by Jiten babu's shop, I would always look in to see what was going on. That day, I found the door partly shut. But his voice, angry and loud, emerged from within. There were dramatic ups and downs in the tone. What was the matter? Was he quarrelling with somebody? I could not stop myself from peeping in. What I saw was so strange and incredible that no less a pen than Shakespeare's could do justice to it. A thin column of smoke rising from the incense-filled *dhunuchi* trailed upward, hit the ceiling and drifted down. I could smell the fine aroma of the incense from outside the door. By the light of the naked electric bulb hanging from the ceiling I saw Jiten babu, in his usual soiled vest, dhoti tucked over his knees and a red *gumcha* tied on his head, reclining on the *Badshah's* throne.

He held a glass in his right hand and a bottle containing some opaque liquid in the left. Gazing at the wall with drowsy eyes he was talking to himself – I could not quite make out what. Had the good man gone crazy? I was genuinely alarmed.

'Do not for a moment think that this throne is my reward', Jiten babu was saying. 'On the contrary, this is my punishment. It is no throne but a heap of explosives.' Was he really sitting on explosives? I was scared. My heart missed a beat. As if in answer to my thoughts, Jiten babu coughed a few times to clear his voice, and then went on: 'I herewith remove my royal crown and leave it under the throne.' As he pronounced these words he placed the bottle and the glass on a stool. Then he removed the red *gumcha* from his head with elaborate care, as if it was a crown studded with jewels and the Kohinoor and he was voluntarily giving it all up. The *gumcha* now lay at his feet. Jiten babu paused and took a sip from the glass. His eyes were red and moist. His voice seemed to tremble. Some indistinct words emerged at first. Then he said, more clearly, 'I wish to abdicate and hand over the reins of the kingdom to him and proceed to Mecca. As I sit here my mind turns in that direction – during my waking hours, in my sleep, in all my meditation, I am forever pining for that most sacred place.' A deep sigh emanated from within him that seemed to split the incense smoke down the middle. After pausing for a minute he resumed in a low voice, 'You need have no worry on my account.' As he finished the sentence two teardrops rolled out of his eyes, stopped momentarily in the folds below and travelled down his cheeks before disappearing altogether.

The next thing Jiten babu did was to put away the empty glass and pour the opaque liquid straight from the bottle down his throat. His eyelids drooped and his head lolled to the right. For a while he continued to mutter to himself. Then there was absolute silence. Thinking he was asleep, I was about to leave when he suddenly came back to life. Turning towards the door he shouted out a question, 'Tell me how are things out there? . . . Everything going on as before?' Startled by the suddenness of the question, I was prompted to instantly reply, 'Yes, yes, of course Jiten babu. Please don't worry. Everything is fine. Sleep in peace.' But how could he be aware of my presence in his present state of mind? After all, I had been watching him through a half-shut door. By now, Jiten babu had poured whatever was left in the bottle down his throat. His eyes took on the colour of a red hibiscus, the lids drooped and his head slumped forward. Pointing his forefinger in the air he spoke again in a surprisingly clear voice, 'I ask you, o sky, why is your colour blue? And you, o sun, why are you still shining in the sky?' Then, adopting a tone of severe admonition, he continued, 'Come down, I say, come down, you shameless ones!' With these words his head drooped once more to rest on his left shoulder.

This was the only way his body could get some rest. Like birds awaking

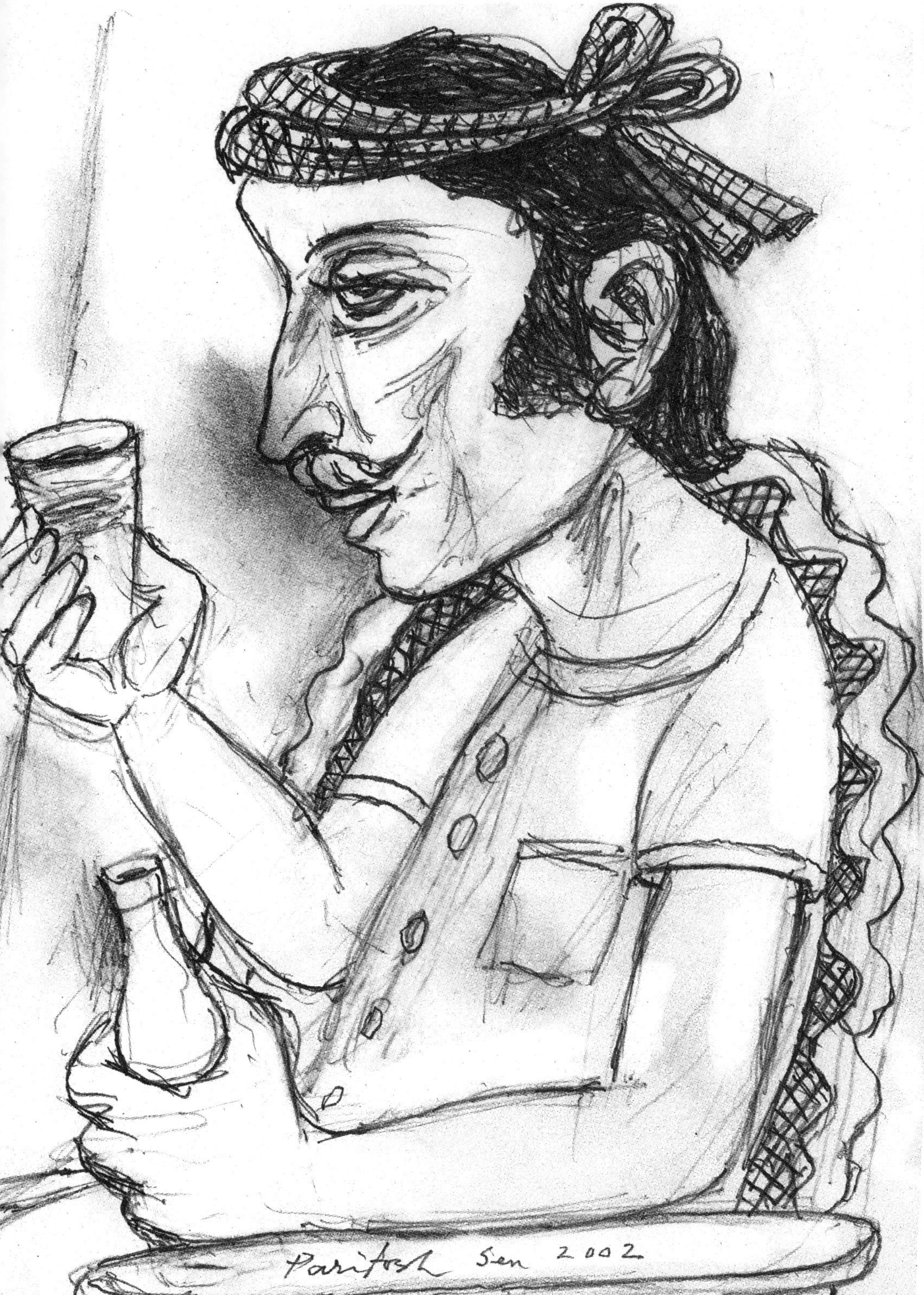
Paritosh Sen 2002

with renewed vigour at the crack of dawn, Jiten babu too was invigorated after such restful intervals. Between bouts of surcharged activity the little time he spent in smoking and in the worship of Bacchus were all he allowed himself by way of leisure. What he earned from the painting of scenes hardly did justice to his genius, yet he kept accepting one commission after another. I have yet to see a man more indifferent to money and more unaccustomed to leisure. He was as restless as a child if he did not have a canvas hanging before him from the ceiling. It had to be there three hundred and sixty-five days of the year. This was the regimen he was used to for almost every day of his working life. To him, wasting time was tantamount to sin. A man who has found his life's purpose in work does not require company or small talk to keep him going. Work for him is a philosophy, it provides him with the true joy of living and saves him from the agony of loneliness. The greater part of Jiten babu's working life was spent in a high tide of activity.

One day, when I peeped into his shop on my way to school, I found him seated on his shaky stool and smoking away as usual. He was gazing beyond the damp walls at some unknown place. The huge chess board scene and its accompanying props had been delivered. A roll of unbleached canvas lay on the floor, evidently meant for a new scene. Jiten babu was by nature a reticent man, I was aware of that. Yet, unmindful of the consequences, I asked him an insolent question, 'Jiten babu, how many scenes have you painted so far?' He did not bother to turn towards me, nor did he stop smoking. Since he did not keep accounts like usual shopkeepers, a question like this may not mean much to him. Perhaps he had not heard me properly. All these thoughts crossed my mind, but I was wrong. He muttered in reply, between puffs, 'A few hundred.' It was a vague answer, yet it assumed the shape of something awesome and reverberated in my brain. My success in extracting a reply from this man of such few words emboldened me to fire another question at him, 'Jiten babu, don't you feel upset to part with your work?' 'Rubbish', was his brusque reply. Perhaps in his scheme of things there was no room for attachment or emotion. Pondering over this, I went on my way.

The window at the far end of Jiten babu's narrow room faced the southern wall of our house. I was sitting up with my books after dinner the next day in order to prepare for my imminent annual examination. Suddenly I heard Jiten babu's voice and I paused in my studies. I pricked my ears. He was singing. This unusual event prompted me to go downstairs, to his shop. For once I found his window open. The canvas roll which I had seen lying on the floor the previous day was now filled with a beautiful scene representing flowering trees and birds, flowing streams and human figures. What fiendish energy even at this age! I was stunned. Hiding behind thick foliage on the canvas was the figure of a handsome young man wearing a crown and an impish smile. Some

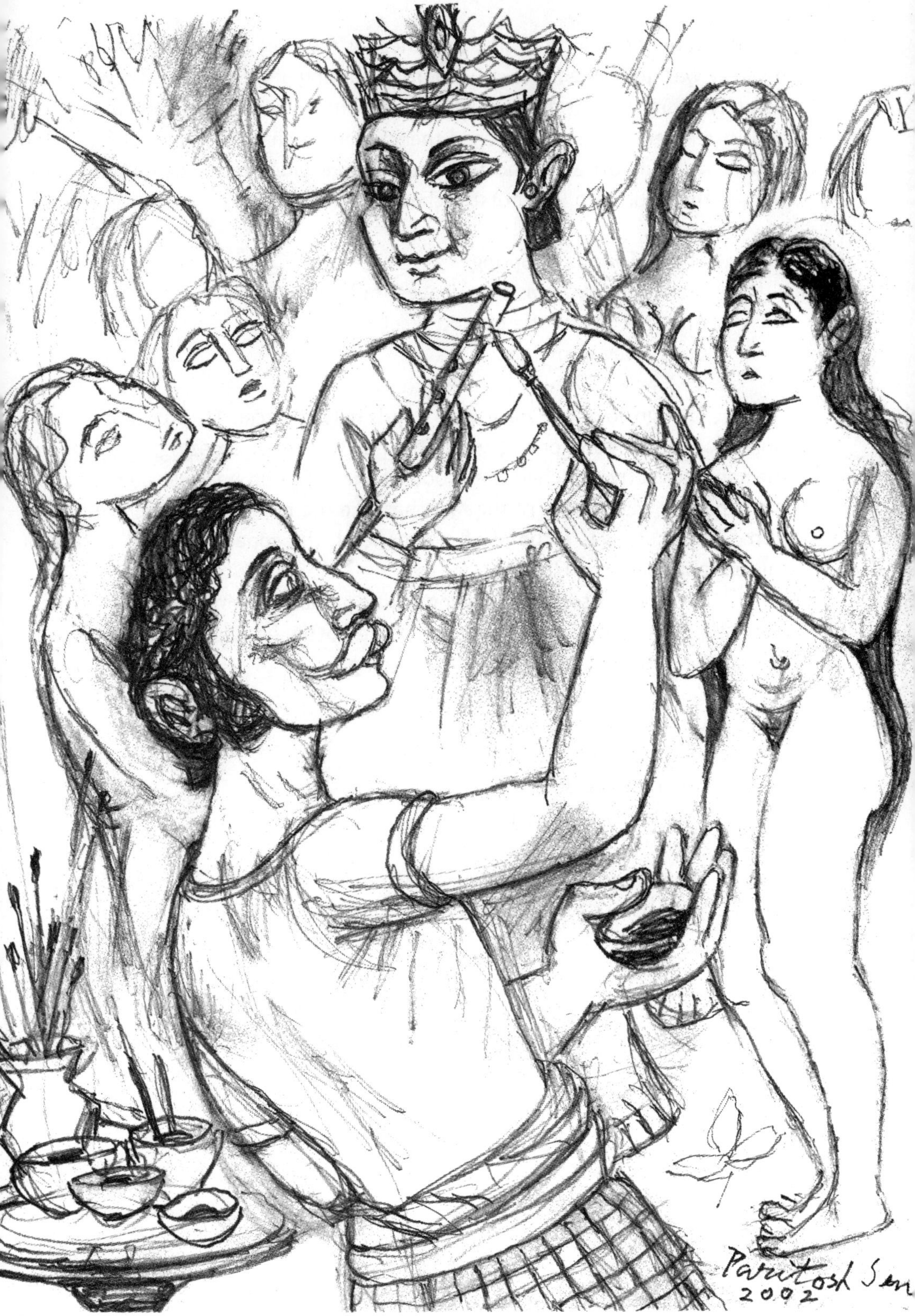
Paritosh Sen
2002

clothes were hanging on nearby branches. As my eyes travelled downward the mystery was unravelled. Beautiful women bathing in a pool of water were desperately trying to hide their naked bodies with mixed expressions of coyness and love. Their gestures increased their feminine charm a hundred-fold. Jiten babu, glass and bottle in hand as usual, and eyes glued to the painting, was sitting on the floor with legs outstretched and singing away:

The evil winds of Spring
Blow o'er my breasts an' leave 'em bare
And that rascal of a cuckoo
Coos away in my ear.

Though low, his voice was surprisingly musical. So Jiten babu was a singer too, and a good one at that! The man was really amazing. The mood of the song perfectly matched the mood of the scene he had just painted. How many people were aware of the fact that, like the honey-filled beehive hidden from view, there was a cupful of *rasa* beneath the apparently hard surface of this extraordinary man?

Jiten babu's song was getting a trifle garbled. Having noticed that there were still a few drops at the bottom of the bottle, he was holding it close to his mouth, upturned. He resumed his singing,

Wait for me, my sister
My drapes are struck in the brier
And that rascal of a cuckoo
Coos away in my ear.

The last words of the song grew muffled as his body went limp. Within seconds Jiten babu's exhausted body lay slumped on the floor like a creeper.

Translated from the Bengali by Enakshi Chatterjee

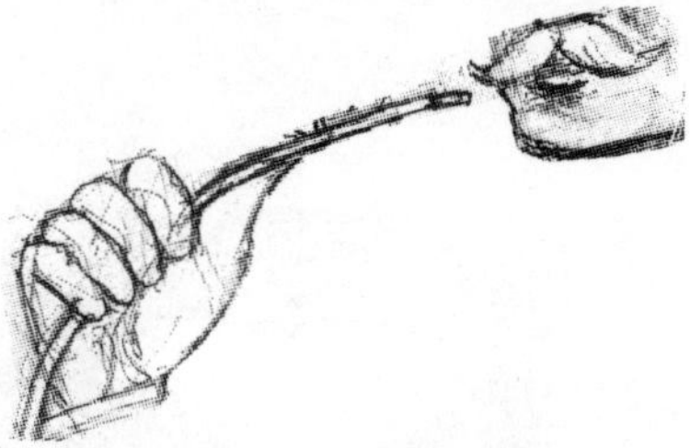

Prasannakumar

An old-fashioned mirror stands in front of the threshold, surrounded by shaving paraphernalia – a folded English razor, soap, brush and some black liquid resting in a bowl. On a low stool sits a hefty gentleman, strong in build though advanced in years. The morning sun lights up the entire scene, giving it a kind of transparent sheen. With the help of a paint brush which looks like a miniature tooth brush, the old man is applying finishing touches to his well-kept whiskers and well-groomed hair. The make-up done, he dons a *nayan sukh*, a delight-to-the-eye *dhoti*, a product of Manchester, and a very fine *kurta*, the sleeves artistically creased. Then he picks up a robust walking stick with a carved handle from the corner of the room, ponders over something and puts back the stick. Evidently, he is in no hurry. Perhaps he has forgotten something. Sure enough, it is the perfume. He opens an old wooden almirah, brings out a bottle of *attar,* dabs some on to a piece of cotton and sticks it carefully behind his right ear. At last his grooming is complete. Casting another look at the mirror, he picks up the stick again and walks out of the room, and down the stairs to the outer room. The caged parrot from the left of the courtyard sets up its usual squeak of delight. The gentleman crosses the courtyard and makes for the cot in the sitting room. He reaches out for a fat cushion and leans back in style.

Soon the entire house reverberates with his booming call, 'Gopal!' Gopal, his loyal Bihari attendant, rushes to him with the hubble-bubble, blowing at the *tikia*; the aroma of quality tobacco hangs in the air. A little later the gentleman goes out in his horse-drawn carriage to attend to his patients. His day has begun.

The man I am talking about is Sri Prasannakumar Sen, the eldest son of Sri Kalikumar Sen, a *kaviraj* of repute, known all over East Bengal. It was the Dhaka of 1925 or 1926. The Sens had been practising their profession there for more than two centuries. The founder of the family had migrated to East Bengal from Kasidham.

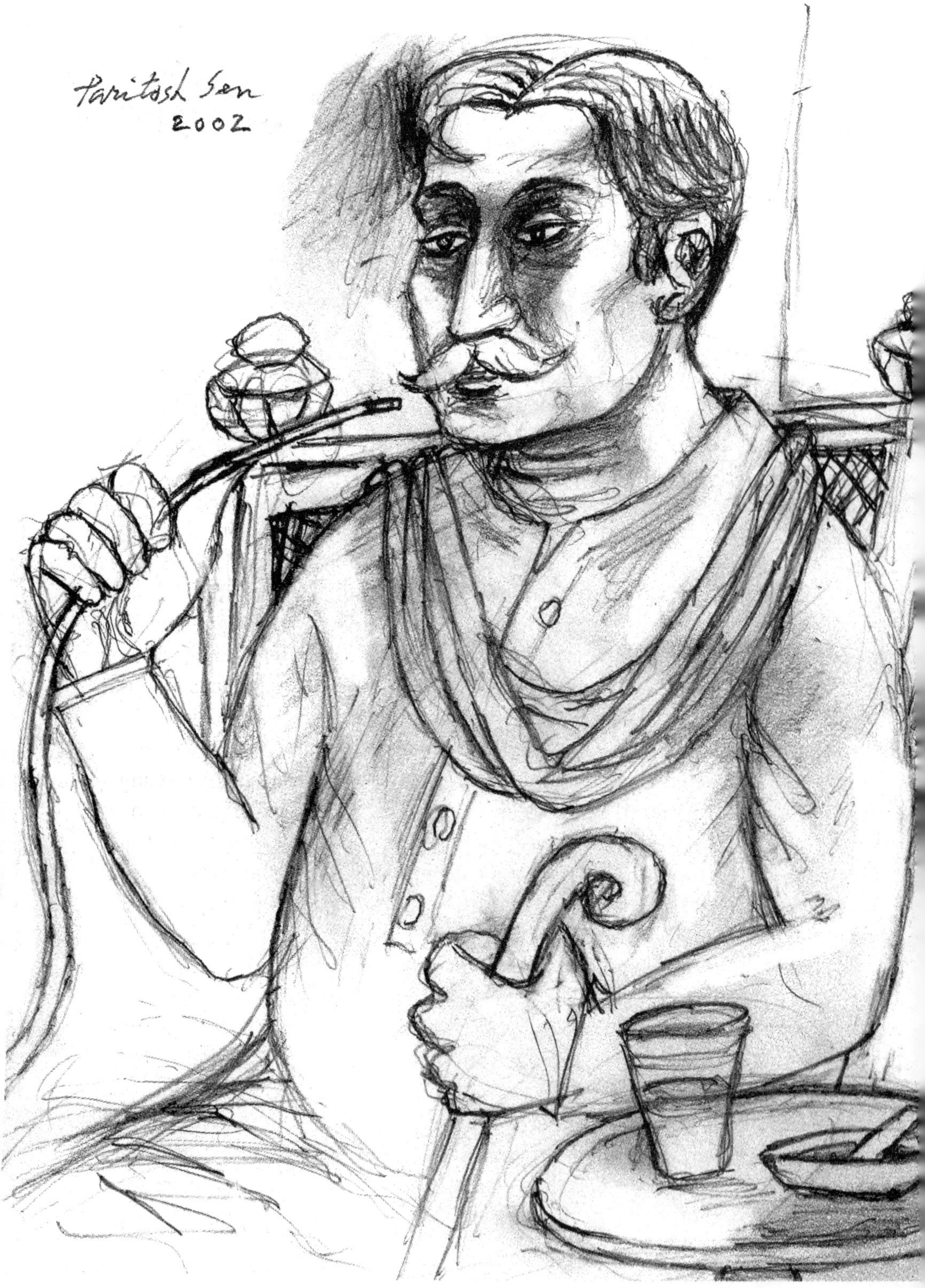
Paritosh Sen
2002

Prasannakumar had five daughters and three sons from his first wife. He married again after her demise and had twelve more children by his second wife – seven sons and five daughters. Twenty altogether. That such a man, in spite of his girdle of fat, would be tiger-like was only to be expected. He was often mistaken for a zamindar, though, truly speaking, there was no blue blood in his veins. Six feet in height, ample in proportions and with a large face like a red radish – he was a man to reckon with. My position was that of the seventeenth child in this large family.

Prasannakumar enjoyed a good medical practice, partly inherited from his father, partly built up by his own ability. Fifty years ago, the cost of living in East Bengal was unbelievably cheap; it was almost as though we were living in the time of Sher Shah. A big two-and-a-half *seer hilsa* used to cost only four *annas*. For two *annas* one could get twenty eggs, and fine parboiled Burma rice for three rupees a maund. In winter twenty *seers* of milk could be had for just a rupee. Gold was sixteen rupees a *tola*. A house with six rooms, a verandah and courtyard could be rented for less than twenty rupees, at least on our Zindabahar lane in the Islampur locality. So maintaining such a big family presented no problem for Prasannakumar.

Not much was known about his general education. Nobody had ever heard him speak English. But he knew the *Ayurveda* by heart, which was all in Sanskrit. While examining a patient he would freely recite from Susruta, Charaka, Banabhatta, Chakrapani Dutta and other masters. He had the entire Ayurvedic system on his fingertips. I have seen cases where, when all other systems had failed, he completely cured the patient.

One morning a horse carriage drove up to the outer room where Prasannakumar usually sat in the morning. A sick boy was carried out of the carriage by two *lungi*-clad men. Prasannakumar went up to the sick boy and helped him up on to the cot. He muttered a Sanskrit *sloka* as he looked at the patient. The boy looked like a skeleton. His ribs bulged through a dirty vest and his head was disproportionately big, like a coconut on a stick. He was weak and emaciated. He was having trouble breathing and could hardly keep his eyes open. Judging by his bloated stomach and swollen legs it seemed fairly certain that his days were numbered.

Without even going into a routine examination, like checking the pulse, inspecting the eyes and the tongue, Prasannakumar dictated a prescription to one of his compounders. Of the various medicines prescribed one still rings in my ears. It was quite a mouthful: *Bijay patpati* – a mixture of pearl, gold, silver, mercury and *pokhraj*. The patient was not to have any food except milk in increasing doses, from half a *seer* to five *seers* a day. He asked the patient to come and see him after a month. He would be able to come on his own, he was assured. I was hugely impressed by Prasannakumar's tremendous self-confidence.

During lunch I hovered around, wishing to ask him a question that had been bothering me all day. Prasannakumar sat cross-legged before the large brass platter on which his food was served – a neat little heap of fine *govinda bhog* rice topped by a bowl of ghee. It looked like the Sanchi *stupa*. A number of small bowls sat on the plate, each containing a different dish. All the brass utensils, including the large water tumbler, had his name engraved on them, glistening in the reflected light of the sun. But I had to get an answer to my query. When he finally looked my way, I mustered up all my courage and asked, 'Father, will that half-dead man be all right?' He muttered in the affirmative through a full mouth. 'Hmmm', he said. He was certain the man would respond to his treatment. I was so stunned that I stood rooted to the spot.

A few weeks passed. I was at the upstairs balcony one day, idly watching the world go by. It was the height of the hot season – the month of *Jaishtha*. Prasannakumar had moved from the sitting room to the porch outside and was sitting with friends, their palm-leaf hand fans, looking for all the world like elephant ears, moving from time to time. There were not many patients that day. Our Zindabahar lane was alive with the noise of passing carriages, calls of hawkers and other traffic sounds. Prasannakumar chatted relaxedly with his friends, in between puffs of the *hookah*.

I spotted a sprightly young man, a Muslim, in a kingfisher-coloured vest and bright checked *lungi*, at the corner of the lane. He was carrying a basket of bright red mangoes and a ripe jackfruit on his head. What fascinated me most, however, was a fluffy baby parrot perched on his right forefinger. I raced downstairs to take a better look. The young man had come to a stop before our house, and he was bowing at Prasannakumar's feet. Before Prasannakumar could draw back his feet the young man held them in a vice-like grip: 'You possibly haven't recognized me, Babu, I am your most obedient servant Samsuddin. I had almost died due to an enlarged liver; it is only through your kindness that I am back to good health. I am even able to work in the field now. If you accept this insignificant gift your servant will be much obliged.' Prasannakumar was well known for his love of birds. He picked up the little bird tenderly and gently caressed it. 'This is not really necessary', he mildly remonstrated. Then he asked Gopal to bring a cage. Such expressions of gratitude were not infrequent. A flicker of satisfaction passed across his face as he murmured, 'As God wills.'

It was twelve noon, and the last of his patients were gone. Prasannakumar tied his red checked *gumcha* around his waist and got ready for his bathing ritual, which he observed with religious regularity. A small container was taken out of the almirah. Seated on a low stool, Prasannakumar picked a small grain-like tablet from it and gulped it down with a glass of water. Taking leisurely puffs from the tobacco pipe brought by Gopal, he gazed at the western sky, beyond the house-tops, from the *bel* tree to blue infinity. He was a picture of calm resignation as he sat still, very still, like the sculpted statue of an Egyptian pharaoh. It looked as though he was taking a temporary respite from the worries of the large household, its problems of domination, anger, everything. But not for long. Soon Gopal appeared again, to remind him that the bath water was getting cold.

Taking opium in tiny doses was a regular feature in our family. I have seen my grandmother take it. She lived to be ninety-five in perfectly sound health. My maternal grandmother too had the habit and she too died at a ripe old age. Till the end she was as strong as a bamboo stick, had all her teeth intact, and used to cook her own meals. They were fortunate people indeed. According to the *Ayurveda*, a little opium taken with milk guarantees long life and sound health. Incidentally, when my youngest brother was born, Father was seventy-five years old.

I have already talked about Prasannakumar's impressive personality. He was reticent and grave before his children. Even my older step-brothers and sisters were afraid to speak to him, and I was but small fry. An invisible wall stood between him and the rest of the family, that he was not aware of; so overpowering was his tremendous ego and authority that all of us were extremely careful not to do or say anything that might incur his displeasure. Nobody knew what might provoke him; and if that were to happen, god help us!

I remember one summer afternoon. I was sitting by the window sill, doing sums on a slate and peeping out through the shutters once in a while. The world outside was so fascinating that I was soon lost in it; suddenly the slate slipped out of my hands and landed on the street outside with a crash. My father was having a nap. The noise woke him up. 'What is that?' he thundered. The doors and windows of the house seemed to rattle with the sound. I was struck dumb with terror. The room melted in a mist of tears. Which boy would dare tell a lie to such a father? When he came to know the reason for the crashing noise that had disturbed his sleep, he was so angry that it was as though flames were coming out of his eyes and nostrils. A few harsh words would have sufficed, but he was so furious that he brought out a cane and gave me a few good lashings across my back. Usually mothers come to the rescue of the child in such situations, but my mother did nothing of the sort, perhaps because she was overawed by Father's sudden outburst. In actual fact my father had a very loving nature beneath the harsh exterior. This apparently insignificant event remains etched in my memory because I felt it was very unjust. After all, a slate did not cost more than a couple of annas. My punishment was too heavy, considering the offence. I felt hurt and humiliated. For a long time I nursed the grudge, like a hidden iceberg.

The relationship between Prasannakumar and his wife Hemangini Devi was neither that of love nor friendship. There was no question at all, of course, of equality. In spite of that, he tried to spend time with her in his own way, particularly when he was in no hurry to visit patients. Let me tell you about one such occasion. One morning, Prasannakumar proceeded to the kitchen where his wife was busy stirring a huge, boiling pot on the stove. She promptly drew the *aanchal* of her sari over her head as she saw her husband approach. 'What is the menu?' Prasannakumar asked. What followed was rather amusing: the gentleman, dressed in formal attire – an old-fashioned coat with a collar, a folded *garad* shawl hanging over his back, the front end of his fancy *dhoti* trailing on the ground, polished brown shoes – this formal attire the gentleman sat down and started cutting vegetables with the deft touch of an experienced housewife.

His wife's attitude towards him was one of awe mingled with respect. She addressed him as *Karta* in front of the children and others. He was indeed like a feudal lord in every way, and much older than she was, by about thirty-five years. I believe Hemangini Devi was hardly sixteen when she got married to this man. Some of his children by the first wife were older than she was. She came from a family of simple means and little education. The responsibility of a sprawling household and the role of step-mother was quite unnerving. Small wonder, therefore, that she suffered from an inferiority complex. She was introverted by nature, probably a natural consequence of having a domineering husband.

It was afternoon. Clad in only a red-and-white checkered *gumcha*, Prasannakumar sat on a low wooden seat in the western verandah. A bucket of water stood by his side, in which floated a brass *lota*. This was another of his regular habits, like the grain of opium before bathing. He was so meticulous in his habits that I could tell the time without looking at a watch. It must be half-past four. The sun shone above the *bel* tree like a bright gold ornament. After lunch Prasannakumar had suffered from excess acidity and had not felt comfortable till he threw up. This done, he seemed to get renewed energy and had continued with his daily chores of visiting patients, finding time to exchange gossip with neighbours in between.

To the right of the divan-like seat stood a rack of *hookahs* ready with a *kalke* on top. To me they looked like a row of palm trees against a background of white. Gopal or one of the compounders would light them when necessary. The *hookahs* were marked according to caste and class. The first one was to be used only by brahmins, the second by Prasannakumar and his very special friends. The third was for the low castes and the fourth for Muslims. Usually he was the one to direct one which was to be given to whom. When he was preoccupied the compounders exercised their discretion.

Not that no mistakes were made, some with dire consequences. I shall come to that later. The regular visitors would bring out small pipes from their pockets as a prelude to the smoking. I found this ritual rather amusing, as if a game of cards or chess was about to start. One of them, Sitanath Mukhtar, always brought with him a pipe made of banana leaf. I always waited it to give out a whistle like the usual banana-leaf whistles. The hookah would make its round, with each visitor putting his own pipe on the hole. The aromatic smoke would spiral up, filling the entire house. Whatever the topics discussed, usually not of any great significance, the booming sound of the conversation would reverberate throughout.

One day an inadvertent mistake was committed by the junior compounder Akrur. Rupchand Saha, a rich merchant of the low-caste *gandha-banik* community, had come to get medicine for his ailing wife. As Prasannakumar listened to the report of the illness, he ordered the compounder to serve tobacco to the visitor. Akrur lit the *hookah* and offered it to the gentleman. Within seconds Prasannakumar's eyes were glowing with rage. He gave Akrur a sidelong glance. The red tinge spread from one corner of the eye to the other. His eyebrows came together in a vicious scowl. Poor Akrur, realizing that he had committed the unpardonable crime of placing a *hookah* meant for brahmins in the hands of a *gandha-banik*, began to shake in fright. He quickly tried to make amends by reaching for the correct *hookah*, but Prasannakumar stayed him by merely lifting his right forefinger. When the gentleman had left Prasannakumar stood up. 'Stupid pumpkin!' he roared. It was like a shot from a cannon. The medicine bottles in the cupboard rattled. The sound of horse carriages in the street faded.

Prasannakumar believed that his presence was the only thing needed for the smooth running of his large family, as though it were a clock that would keep on working mechanically if given proper clothing and food. It was against his nature to show any tenderness or make any concessions to family relationships. He never talked to the children and made no attempt to understand their problems; even showing intimacy to his wife was out of the question. In the evening, after the patients were gone, Prasannakumar would go upstairs, change into more comfortable clothes, wash and then recline on the bed. This was the time set aside for his wife Hemangini Devi to fan him and press his legs if necessary, and talk about family matters. While he leaned against the huge side pillow, *hookah* in hand, Hemangini Devi would hand him a glass of cold drink and try to assess his mood before broaching subjects involving various family problems – books to be bought, clothes to be made, school fees to be

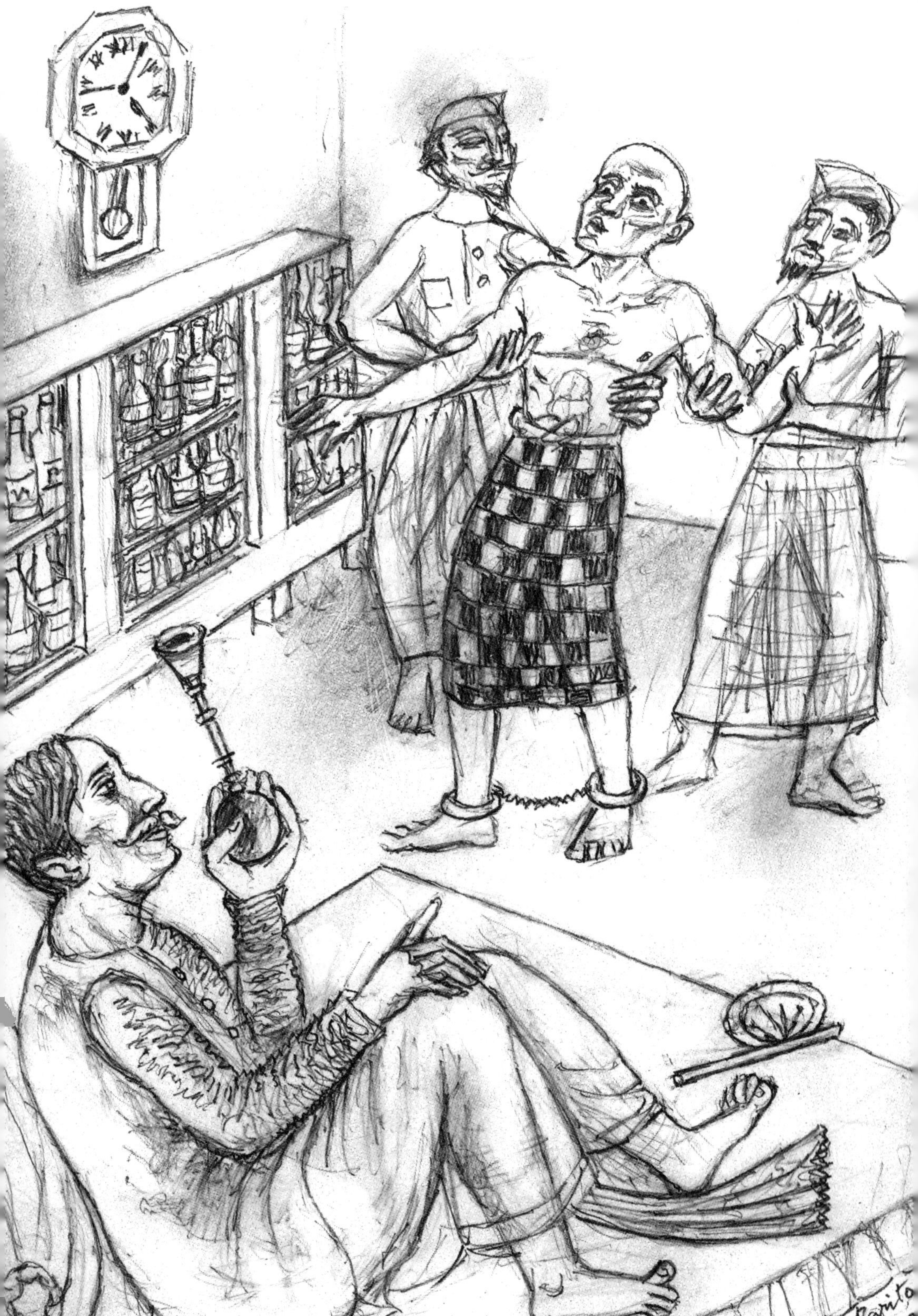

paid and so on. Prasannakumar would give her a patient hearing with just a noncommittal 'hmm' now and then. Soon it would be time for his frugal dinner – a bowl of thickened milk and two *chapatis* rolled in a wet cloth. That was all he had. Hemangini Devi made the arrangements. Then it was time for Gopal to bring the smoking paraphernalia. After a few puffs he would feel drowsy. Hemangini Devi would tuck in the mosquito net and depart. She had various chores to finish before having her own dinner.

It was the height of summer. Prasannakumar called out to Gopal: 'Put some crushed ice and rose water in the hubble-bubble.' Rangada, his fifth son, appeared before him proudly clutching a big shield. His older children very rarely had the opportunity to meet him. Only the young ones like me enjoyed that privilege. The shield had bright silver decorations on a black wooden background. It sparkled in the light of the lantern. I was particularly fascinated by the engraved figure of a handsome athlete in a running posture. It looked like a royal treasure to me, with its intricate and beautiful ornamentation. Dada was all puffed up with pride. He displayed the shield before Father, declaring that he had won it in the sports competition at college. Prasannakumar paused in his smoke, gave the prize a glance and continued smoking. 'I hope you are not neglecting your studies', he said to my brother. Without another word, Rangada beat a hasty retreat.

Sometimes, in a rare show of fatherly emotion, he would call me and my elder brother, pat our backs fondly and supervise our homework. We would take advantage of his mood and ask for things which normally we would not dare raise. On such occasions, though rare, he would look exactly like the father we used to dream about, his face glowing with love and affection.

At a quarter past nine in the morning, dressed in his outdoor clothes, Prasannakumar set off to visit his patients. Before leaving he fed the pigeons and the parrots. At his call the pigeons swarmed the courtyard, and he scattered paddy for them. It was wet gram for the parrot. The parrot repeated 'Hare Rama Hare Krishna' after him. The parrot in the next cage relished the green chilly offered to it. Prasannakumar offered a second one, whistling happily. True to his name, he was the very picture of contentment. Still whistling to himself, he proceeded to the sitting room. I was just about to start having my breakfast along with my elder brother when a deafening howl brought us rushing downstairs. We saw a young man, his hands and feet tied with a strong rope, standing before our father. There was another rope tied round his waist. He was bare-bodied. His head was shaven, and it glistened like a green *bel* fruit. His bloodshot eyes seemed to pop out of their sockets. Three people were struggling to keep him in check, one holding on to the rope round his waist, the other two clutching at his hands. The young man was trying his best to free himself; the muscles on his shining black body stood out. During the struggle he kept up a barrage of obscene words, complaining against everybody, even God. His loud voice mingled with the others' shouts to create quite a cacophony. People passing by were being drawn to the scene.

In the midst of all this, Prasannakumar sat unperturbed. He put down his *hookah* and asked Gopal to bring some food and a glass of water. He placed the dish and the water before the young man. The man stared at him for some time. Slowly the flicker of a smile appeared on his face – as if the early morning sun had risen. When Prasannakumar took the dish to his lips he lost no time in gobbling up its contents. How long has be been in this condition? Prasannakumar inquired of his companions. He had various other queries. Then he told them what medicines were to be given – snuff of a particular kind, Ayurvedic concoctions, a wet bandage to keep him cool, and so on. One thing he insisted on – under no circumstance should he get excited. They must take care of that.

About three months later I and some of the boys of the neighbourhood were sitting in the porch chatting, when a well-built young man came and stood before us. He was handsome in appearance, with a crop of wavy hair, and was dressed in a sky-blue *lungi* and white *kurta*. He smiled bashfully. I noticed that he was carrying a shopping bag. He walked in, touched the raised platform on which Prasannakumar sat with his forehead, and placed the contents of the bag on the floor. It was a *rohu* fish, freshly caught. As it moved, its scales glistened as though they were a glittering dress. The young man revealed his identity. He was the same person who had been brought in that day with his hands and feet tied. Recognition dawned at last. Prasannakumar drew a deep sigh, pointed upwards and said, 'It is His will.' Nobody in his wildest imagination would have guessed that this was the same person!

It was early morning. A ray of orange light touched my face and I woke up. I saw Prasannakumar applying dye to his hair and moustache. Gopal entered, blowing at the *hookah*. 'Open the windows', my father ordered. He paused for a moment, looked up at the sky and sniffed the air. Meanwhile Gopal had placed a bucket of water for him to wash his hands and face. He called out. 'Will you go and see if the lemon tree has sprouted blossoms?' Soon Gopal returned with a fresh flower, its four petals as white as the froth of milk. At its centre was a faint tinge of violet. 'How many days are left for the *puja*?' Prasannakumar asked. 'Let me go and ask Ma', answered Gopal as he went downstairs. His toiletries over, Prasannakumar proceeded towards the sitting room. His eldest son Prafullakumar, who was in his fifties and a father of six, was summoned. The son stood obediently before the father, eyes cast down. Prasannakumar gave him instructions for the *puja*, adding that the festivities should be on a grander scale this year. 'Very well, sir', said Prafullakumar respectfully and went inside the house.

The autumn sky looked like a watercolour in copper hues. One morning the entire family set out for our ancestral village in large passenger boats, led by Prasannakumar. Their sails, puffed up by a steady north wind, sped the crafts as if towards some unknown destination. Oh, the sheer delight of sailing under the open sky, away from the congestion of the city! A spirit of freedom filled my entire being. The horizon on the other side of the Buriganga river formed a hazy green and blue outline. Soon we left the main river to enter a crisscross of canals, among flooded paddy fields. The swamps and ponds through which we negotiated were filled with water hyacinths. They brushed against the bottom of the boats. The eerie sound of jostling water and weeds gave rise to a strange sensation. Through the thick foliage of the *madar*, black berry, *geol* and *jamrul* trees, sunlight flickered. The boats came out of a long canal to enter another inundated paddy field. And the towering *arjun* tree which stood at the bank of our pond came into view. A chorus went up. 'Here we are, here we are.'

In no time a festive atmosphere set in. The *puja* preparations were started, with Prasannakumar at the helm of affairs. With drums and bells, the blowing of conches and *ulu*, our Beltali village came alive. As dusk descended, a man holding a stick slowly walked up to the dais where the *puja* would be performed and settled down on a chair facing it. A light aroma of *attar* mixed with the smell of incense filled the air. In his fine *kurta* and crinkled *dhoti*, the man looked so distinguished that all eyes were upon him. The end of his *dhoti* which trailed on the ground looked like a Japanese hand fan. He leaned back in the chair with the pipe of a *hookah* in his hand. His strong magnetic personality had an instant effect on the congregation. Some of them came up to him. The drummers tied the *dhak* on their back, and were impatient to start. As the priest stood up, ready to begin the *aarati* ritual with a lamp-stand of five lamps, the drummers struck. The accompanying song echoed through the entire area. The *dhunichi* dancers increased their tempo, not to be outdone by the drummers. Meanwhile the fireworks started a brilliant display, having received a signal from Prasannakumar. The dancers, the players, the spectators, all were highly excited. After watching the celebrations for some time, Prasannakumar made his way to the inner house.

It was *mahashtami*, the eighth day of the fortnight. The entire village was assembled before the dais. Prasannakumar was seated on a chair in the porch of the outer house. Stacks of *dhotis* and *lungis* were placed next to him. Usually frugal in his habits, he was a different person during the days of the festival. He would become benevolence incarnate. The ryots of both communities came to pay their respects. As they came up one by one and touched his feet, he handed clothes and some earthenware to each. Some were fortunate to get monetary gifts as well. Then they were treated to a sumptuous feast. During such days, Prasannakumar assumed the role of a zamindar of sorts, though strictly speaking he was not one. The village folk went home happy, all praise for the *Karta*, the master.

It was afternoon, Prasannakumar sat by the side of his mother's memorial. A long canal stretched out in front of him. Behind him was a pond. Paddy fields, half-submerged in water were visible beyond the canal. Between two paddy fields a slender skiff raced ahead, propelled by bamboo poles. Piles of clouds in the eastern sky glistened like snowclad mountain peaks in the rays of the setting sun. Branches from *madar* and *jeol* trees leaned towards the pond. A few boats were tied to the trunks of the trees – boats which had brought people from other villages hoping to benefit from Prasannakumar's free treatment. There were all sorts of people – from chronic malaria patients to people suffering from asthma, heart trouble, dysentery, even tuberculosis. Prasannakumar prescribed various herbal remedies to them – roots, leaves, barks of particular trees, green coconut water, light *moong dal*, pickled *amloki*, baked *bel* and what not. Some of his most difficult patients, now completely cured, came to thank him, to express their gratitude. They brought him gifts, such as a huge pumpkin or a bunch of bananas or some other farm produce. They were eternally obliged to him. Feeling reassured at having met him, the patients returned by boat.

The sun set behind the bamboo grove, lighting it up with the colours of a peacock's plume. Our village took on the air of a fairyland, dreamy and mysterious, with its thick foliage and trees. Prasannakumar stood up, leaning on his walking stick. He touched his forehead to the threshold of his mother's memorial temple and slowly proceeded towards the western verandah. The slightly stooping figure of the handsome old man disappeared in the shadow of the enormous *jamrul* tree.

Translated from the Bengali by Enakshi Chatterjee

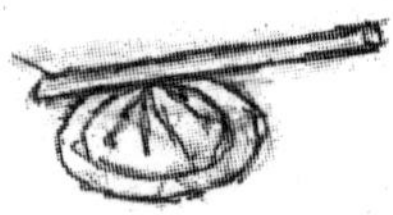

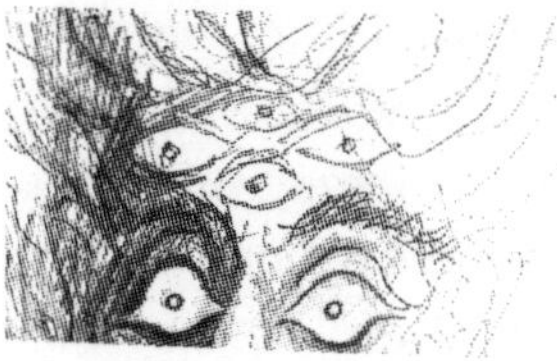

Fire

It was the afternoon of Vijaya Dasami. All the women in the village, including my sisters, sisters-in-law and nieces, had assembled in our *puja* pavilion; my mother too was among them. Most of them wore in sparkling white saris with wide red borders flanked by embroidery work in *zari* that enhanced the brilliance of the red. Looking down on this play of red and white were the large lotus eyes of the Devi, her face golden yellow, her eyeballs like two black pieces of the Kohinoor.

I was transfixed. The fresh dots of *sindoor*, which all the married women wore on their foreheads, looked like big *karamchas*. Matching these were their *alta*-lined feet. Their *aanchals* circled their faces, and were weighed down with the heavy bunch of keys tied at the end of the sari, so that the outline of their faces stood out. The unmarried girls looked no less charming with their hair combed straight down, highlighting their slim waistlines. Younger girls stood around in coloured frocks, gazing up at the idol. The sparkle of the lamps bounced back from their lovely *kohl*-lined eyes. The diamond and pearl nose-rings of the married women reflected the light as well.

The comely good looks for which Bengali women are famous were on display in good measure. For all the world, the scene was like a masterpiece executed by the expert *pata* painter of Kalighat, Nibaran Ghose. My mother was among the ladies conducting the farewell ritual for the goddess. The frenzied beats of the *dhak* and *dhol* indicated that the climax of the festival was approaching.

My mother pinched a dab of *sindoor* from the silver container and extended her arm so that her forefinger could touch the forehead of the Devi. All of a sudden there was a flash from the sword of the devil lying under the feet of the Devi, or so it seemed to my mother. It must be an illusion, she thought, and refused to dwell on such evil thoughts; nor did she confide to anyone what she had imagined she saw.

Four days after the *Kojagari* full moon my father was taken ill. At first it was nothing serious, but the fever showed no sign of remission even after ten days. The senior members of the family, *Mejokaka*, *Baba* and *Ma*, began to look worried. There was general apprehension in the air. All the treatment that was available in the village was tried.

It was a couple of hours after midnight when I was violently shaken out of my slumber. Get up, get up, quick, somebody was shouting. I sat up, still groggy with sleep. *Chhordi* stood before me, tears streaming down her cheeks. 'Come, if you want to have a last look at Father.' She dragged the four of us, me and my younger brothers and sisters, to the westside verandah where a wailing crowd had already gathered. As my eyes scanned the room slowly, I saw my mother bent over Father's chest, sobbing like a child. I too felt a sudden urge to cry. Everybody there was in tears. But why, for heaven's sake? What was the fuss about? Father seemed to be fast asleep, a white sheet over his body, and looked serene and peaceful. I don't remember when I withdrew to an adjoining room and fell asleep.

I was alone in the room when I woke up. I dashed out in alarm. The eastern sky was taking on the colour of red. Where was my mother? She was in the courtyard, where a group of women had formed a ring around her, trying to console her. I moved forward. Men were standing huddled together near the tank. A light blue column of smoke spiralled up, slowly turning into a shade of violet. I crept up and peeped through the crowd. Now I could see my father's body laid over logs of wood, with only his face visible. The pyre must have been lit some time ago. Suddenly a branch from an adjoining *madar* tree fell into the dark green water of the tank. A bunch of watercress detached from the main mass drifted away like paper boats till they hit the low branch of the *madar* and seemed confused about which way to go. A dragonfly was about to land on the island of watercress but a sudden gust of wind carried the latter away. A couple of boats, polished and painted in black tar, lay in anchor, the reflection of their black bodies making the green water seem greener. The boats formed a lovely pattern of convexes and concaves in black.

The flames from the pyre went up slowly, like lazy caterpillars. It was a wonderful play of colour – the zafrani red of the flame against the cold green of the tank. I had never seen anything like this before. People moved about like thin shadows, red *gumchas* wrapped round their waists. Somebody from the crowd uttered a muffled cry – *Bolo Hari, Hari Bol*. Meanwhile, the smoke had changed colour from blue to the dull black of a buffalo's skin. Parrots fluttered in panic from their nests and sat on the spire of the Shiva temple to the south. They had patches of red on their throat and chest.

Soon the flames rose high till they soared above the crowd. What a spectacle! I had seen fires of various kinds, in lamps and candles, in stoves and camphor containers. But this one was totally different. It looked different, it sounded different, it even smelt different. How terrible it looked! Its eyes glowed red like the red-hot iron of a blacksmith's kiln – the irises were like the ruby-blood eyes of a goat just slaughtered. Rays of light, like spikes of silver, leapt up from the sparkling, diamond-like centre of the pyre, rushing upward like a *kash* forest on fire. The ugly pouches under its eyes were like the swollen flesh of drunkards. Its mouth was yawning wide, like a hungry baby crow, creating a chasm deep and horrible as a fresh sore. Its tongue flashed like the dangerous Kirtinasa river out to gobble up more land. Occasionally it withdrew its tongue noisily, revealing guillotine-like teeth, ready to crush everything – whatever came its way – trees, hills, people. Like a hydra-headed snake, the many tongues of the fire swirled and twisted till they formed not one but many whiskers. Huge rings dangled from its ear lobes, studded with stones that resembled the eyes of a vulture – eyes that scanned the entire world in search of bodies to devour.

Somebody stirred the fire with a stick. Had it gone off to sleep, like the mythological Kumbhakarna, that it had to be pierced to wake up? The fire came to life in great fury, gnashing its guillotine teeth. The earth trembled, the ground beneath my feet shook. In utter fright, I put my hands around a pillar for support. I was scared to death, the fire looked so terrible. Was this the fire that had destroyed the Khandava forest, its heat sending thousands of animals screaming in flight only to be scorched to death? Even eagles and vultures soaring high above had caught fire and come circling down to the great fire raging on the ground. Duryodhan must have had this great devastation in mind when he decided to set fire to *jatugriha*, intending to burn the five Pandavas and their mother to death. My eyes strayed to my father's face. I felt as though I had been struck by a huge stone. His powerful countenance was painted black and it had shrivelled like a baked *bel* fruit. No, I couldn't stand it any longer.

Mainamagne vidaha mabhishocha masya tva che
Chikshipo ma shariram . . .

Please, Fire, I beg of you, do not turn this dead man to ashes, do not hurt him. Do not reduce him to nothing. This fire reminded me of hell fire – a scene that had never ceased to haunt me in my dreams was one of sinners being boiled in huge cauldrons and evaporating within minutes. I could almost hear the splutter of the hot oil.

My eldest brother poured some ghee on the pyre. Instantly the fire erupted, like a wounded tiger. The ferocious beast lurched towards its victim. Boom, boom, went the logs. Had they mixed explosives in the wood? Sparks

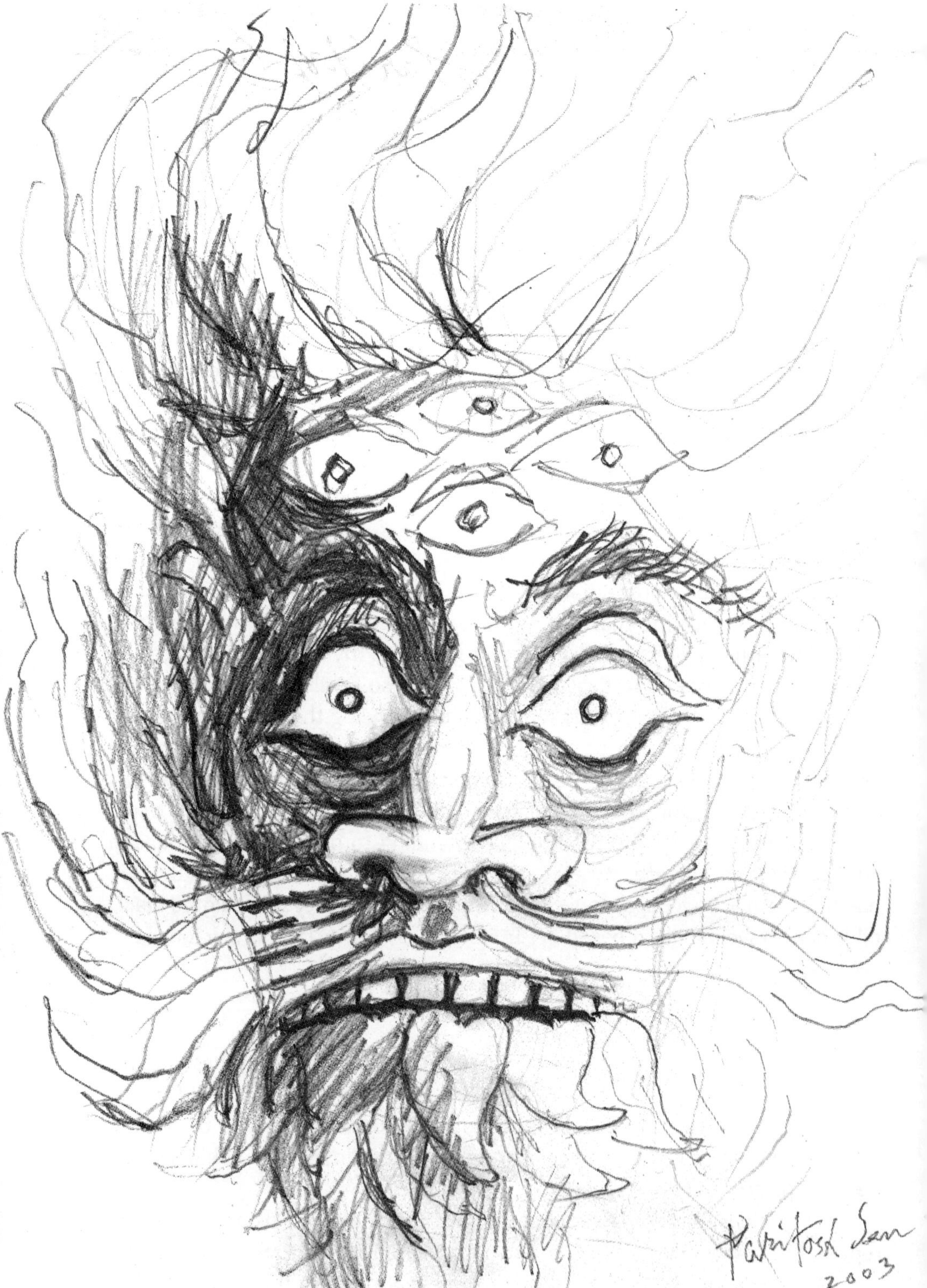
Paritosh Sen
2003

flew off in all directions, forcing the people around to cover their faces. The crows resident on the mango trees to the south of the tank flew about in panic, their frightened cries of *crowah crowah crah* sending out a danger signal to their kin. The earth-shattering sound – boom boom crash – bounced back from the trees and sent echoes all around. By now the flames had become long and narrow like sugarcane leaves, bending and swaying in the light breeze and chasing the trees which stood to the south of their domain. Panic-stricken cries of birds filled the air as crows, mynas, sparrows, cormorants, kites, vultures, magpies, robins started flying about.

The stories I had heard from my grandmother of how Hanuman set the kingdom of Lanka ablaze came to my mind. And of how the fire had swallowed up hundreds of elephants, horses, peacocks, parrots and birds of many hues. Was this fire going to do the same to the birds of our village? Please God, I prayed. Don't let this happen. Spare these poor creatures. My heart was beating like a kettle-drum. Unable to bear it any longer, I flopped down on the porch.

My eldest brother poured more ghee into the fire and it turned into a huge glowing pit, as though it was a volcanic crater. The splendour of the shooting red flame with black smoke dazzled my eyes. I dug my face between my knees. When I shut my eyes the red of the fire turned into a cool green. It was an unforgettable feeling. Often in the early morning I have stared fascinatedly at the lush green of the rain-soaked banana groves on the other side of the tank. A flying insect would occasionally get into my eyes and I would close my eyelids. But I had never seen the green of the banana trees change into the colour of fire!

The colour red can produce a strange sensation on the optical nerves. In my long career as an artist this powerful hue of the rainbow spectrum has always played havoc with my imagination. I cannot wipe it away from my palette – it seems to have a magnetic hold on me. That childhood spectacle of the fire from the funeral pyre of my father has left a deep impression on my sensibility as an artist. Once, later in life, while trying to paint the colour of fire something happened to me; my head reeled and I lost consciousness. No wonder this colour is associated with danger, devastation and revolt. I know of two other artists, Rufeno Tamayo of Mexico and Ben Shan of the USA, who have been obsessed with fire and have painted monstrous pictures of it.

The use of various kinds of red in the paintings of Tamayo – the red of wine, the red of burnt brick, the red in the fall colours of trees like the birch, dogwood and maple – have fascinated art lovers as well as children. Shan, on the other hand, prefers the terrible and mystic beauty of fire – its bright glaze so dazzling that one has to look at it through a black lens, like one watches a solar eclipse. Often fire takes the shape of a primeval beast, drawing on the blood of all possible earthly animals, with waving tongue, terrible facial features, legs, tails – in fact the entire body seems to be painted with the rays of the setting sun, the body a bare chunk of raw flesh. Even the claws are red with deadly poison. Shan was caught in a blaze in his childhood, an experience which he never got over, and his paintings are unusual expressions of that experience. They have a terrible charm.

Fire signifies not only colour and beauty, but also light, an important ingredient in painting. Its strange manifestations as experienced by me can be felt by only a few. The experience has remained vivid in my memory.

When I finally opened my eyes, the sun had reached the top of the *madar* tree. Like freshly moulded steel spikes, its beams hit the surface of the tank and broke into a thousand pieces. The tank was like a huge mirror. In the reflected light from below, the branches of the tree were tinged copper, the shade of the chest feathers of a *munia* bird. The people standing round the pyre looked like Japanese masks, the tips of their noses and high spots on the cheeks glowing. As they squinted, their eyes receded into their sockets, exactly like the empty sockets of skeletons. Their features took on grotesque shapes in the reflected light. Much later when I saw the work of a European artist, I recalled those distorted, mask-like faces I saw in my childhood. I am talking here of the famous Spanish painter Goya, who used reflected light with great success in his series on rebellion.

There is a world of difference between direct and reflected light. They evoke totally dissimilar reactions. In Dante's *Divine Comedy* the greatest being is presented as a dazzling source of light – the poet himself was blinded by its brilliance. Can any mortal stare at a thousand suns?

> And suddenly, as it appeared to me day was added to day, as if He who can had added a new sun to Heaven's glory.

It is a curious coincidence that the divine experience related by the Indian saint Sri Ramakrishna is almost identical. By the grace of *Mahamaya*, he had seen a tiny lamp-light expand till it swept across the entire universe. He went into a trance as the magical light entered his body and surrounded him like a halo. What could it have possibly been – fire or light or a lightning flash? Sri Ramakrishna was in this state when he touched Naren's chest with his toes and his favourite disciple was completely knocked out. Naren was then Narendranath Dutt, he had not yet become Swami Vivekananda. In the *Mahabharata* we have the great hero Arjuna stunned for a moment when Sri Krishna reveals his real self. It makes Arjuna cry out in panic:

Drishtwa adhutam rupam ugraam tavedam
Lokatrayam prabyathitam mahatwan

Not just Arjuna, but all three worlds also tremble in fear. At last God takes pity on his disciple and grants him the divine vision. But the terrible spectacle of the flaming mouth and monstrous teeth so unnerves Arjuna that his head is in a whirl, he can bear it no longer. He appeals to Krishna to withdraw the vision and so Krishna assumes his usual self.

But I had no gods to oblige me, no Krishna or Ramakrishna. Why was this terrible vision of fire revealed to me? Who had done it? There was nobody I could appeal to, pray to, to withdraw, to spare me the sight. The scene was more than just terrifying, it was overwhelmingly artistic. The sound of the fire growing from a soft murmur to a sudden explosion was for me like the hypnotic spell of a chanted *mantra*.

Sada*kaka*, one of my uncles, emerged from the crowd – a thin dark man, his hair dishevelled. He poked at the fire with a bamboo pole. *Barda* sprinkled some more ghee from the clay container. In the twinkling of an eye the flames burst forth once again, like carved swords hungry for blood – they soared towards the top of the *madar* tree. The bark of the trunk and its branches were gutted, patches stood out like burnt coke, blisters formed like molten tar on summer streets. The leaves, brown from the heat, displayed an intricate lace-like design. Who knew that the solid green of a leaf contained such wonderful handiwork, rivalling the finest work of a skilled goldsmith? It struck me dumb, much in the same way as Arjuna was overwhelmed by Krishna's revelation. Later, I read in a biography of the great artist Paul Klee that, impressed by the fine structure of leaves, he had preserved a few in a jar. Inspired by nature, he had also attempted some very fine lace-like designs.

Our woodcutter Kartikchand and our *mali* dragged some big logs and shoved them into the pyre. Spirals of dark smoke shot up, hiding the trees, the sky, everything, under a smoke screen. The blanket of smoke was studded with sparks of fire, like stars on a moonless night. Through the cracks the transparent blue of the late autumn sky peeped out, as the voices went up: *Bolo Hari, Hari Bol*.

Sada*kaka* and one of my brothers again poked at the fire. Like a drowsy snake awakened, the flame hissed and stood poised to attack. With renewed vigour the fire shot up hundreds of fireworks, shaking its terrible head. How ferocious! Twenty maneaters would have paled into insignificance before its savage rage. My heart began to beat fast, gripped by an unknown fear.

The clay pot of ghee was overturned, offering its last drop to the pyre.

The fire leapt up in a final burst of rage, destructive, terrible and all-pervading. Its eyes looked to me like the molten iron of the lake of Baikal. Its mane danced in mad glee, the locks shaking like huge red chillies, as though a giant was on a dancing spree waving flaming torches in wild rhythm. Is there anything else in nature that can break into such a frenzy at the slightest touch of a breeze? This was a cosmic dance of the wildest kind. Even the flares emanating from the Bajrapani of Tibetan *tankhas* were nothing compared to this. From its dark deep cavity protruded not one but seven tongues, like seven bloody waterfalls. Its terrible countenance, from the hair to the tip of the tongue, contained all the possible shades of red the earth could offer – the red of the hibiscus, *karabi*, flame of the forest, *shimul, gulmohar, rangan*, rhododendron, *bakul*, banyan-fruit, litchi, walnut leaves in winter, watermelon, *abeer, alta, sindoor, makaradhawj*, the tuft of a cock, the beak of a parrot, all kinds of red. It was as though a concoction of red was being brewed in the furnace of a steel factory. I could not take my eyes away. I was in a dream, half-dazed. The fire kept growing. It kept expanding like the fairy-tale giant who puffed up like a balloon with each breath till he covered the entire sky. Was this fire going to spread to the entire village, reducing the trees and huts to cinders? A chill went down my spine; beads of perspiration stood out on my forehead.

I had experienced a similar sensation while watching an animal film once, in which a hungry lion was chasing a herd of zebras. The zebras were fleeing for life. The last one looked back. Instantly the lion's eyes pinned him down, so magnetic was its gaze. The poor zebra stood hynotized. This was exactly the same. I was the victim struck motionless by the fire. My heartbeats grew louder and louder like a rail engine. I was breathing hard. My eyes were fixed as though nailed with a screw. Was the hungry fire going to devour me like the African lion? Oh Fire, the greatest of the great, the bright one, the wise one, the remedy for all sin, the destroyer of enemies – I know you are merciful to your worshipper. You are benevolent, you shower your worshipper with wealth and happiness. You are kind and helpful. I will make a *puja* platform for you, make a seat of *kusha* grass, and offer ghee thrice a day. You hold the universe in the palm of your hand, you nurture and preserve the world. Please, please, forgive this small child. Put your soothing touch on me, let me go back to my mother.

Panic-stricken, I wanted to run, but my legs refused to move. A heavy weight seemed to be holding them down. They were rooted to the spot and my arms were numb. My throat felt parched. Would this terrible fire consume all the people I loved – *Barda*, Sada*kaka*, Chinu*da*, Kartikchand, Bhui-*mali*, all the friends of the family gathered for the last rites, and most of all, my dearest pet dog Bhola? And me too? The fire had been staring at me all this while, frowning and gnashing its teeth. It was after me! I trembled like a sapling caught in a storm. I must get away, I must. I have to get back to my mother. A tingling sensation gripped me. Where are you *Ma*, where are you? I felt utterly helpless, I could not speak. It was as though I was being pressed under a heavy roller. Let me go, let me go, I struggled.

From somewhere far away I heard my mother wailing in a sad monotone. To me, though, it was not sad but just the opposite, the voice of hope. My heart began to dance like a peacock. Freedom at last! Wait for me, *Ma*, I am coming.

I reached her exhausted. I collapsed, my head on her lap. The fire had gone, so had the darkness. I could see the moonlight. A few drops of *Ma*'s warm tears fell on my cheek, a welcome shower on parched land. she was softly crying while breast-feeding my ten-month-old baby brother. She put one hand on me, caressing me. How wonderfully comforting, how soothing her touch was!

Translated from the Bengali by Enakshi Chatterjee

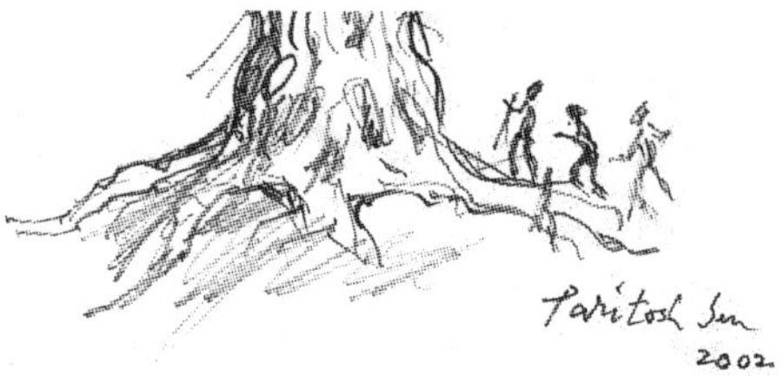

Arjuna – a tree in my village

Our village in East Bengal was dotted with numerous ponds, lakes and canals. Rivers were not far either. During the monsoon, every home became an island. We had to row our little dinghy to visit neighbours and to buy provisions from the marketplace. This abundance of water, the strong sun and the intensely humid climate during most of the year, are what make Bengal a great showpiece of nature's munificence. The astounding variety of its lush tropical flora and fauna is like a vedic hymn in praise of creation.

Whenever my mind travels back to my boyhood days in the village, an abstract picture, painted somewhat in the manner of Mark Rothko, appears before my eyes. Slabs of all possible shades and tints of green, ranging from the silken blackish green of the margosa leaves as the morning light filters through them, making them gleam like the green crystals of a chandelier, to the turquoise green of the floating water hyacinths in the evening. It was such an all-pervasive sea of verdure that I often felt as if the whole village had just had a dip in a pool of green light. Indeed, the sun itself appeared green in some unconscious moments.

On the northeastern bank of the large pond situated at the far end of our house, where we did all our bathing and washing, stood a giant Arjuna tree (*Terminalia arjuna*), rising nearly a hundred feet up to the sky and dominating the entire landscape. It was so huge, so dense, that it seemed like a small forest in itself. Its thousand branches spread like outstretched arms in all directions. Its majestic height dwarfed every other tree in the village. Its powerful build, magnificent proportions and statuesque three-dimensionality were reminiscent of the monolithic ninth-century Jaina figure of Sravanabelagola in Mysore – one of the great landmarks of Indian classical sculpture.

Did anybody in our village have any idea of the age of this Arjuna tree? Did the murmur of the future forest that arose from the molten mass on the day of creation predetermine its birth? Who knows! Looking at it, one got the impression that it was as old as the temple of Rameses the Great, erected on the golden sands of Nubia nearly three millennia ago. It had an air of eternity about it and it seemed to proclaim, 'I was, I am, and I shall ever be.'

The Arjuna tree was a world unto itself, as alive and eventful as the human world, if not more so. It gave shelter to countless birds, reptiles and insects of every description. They seemed to be so happy living in it that they would not exchange it for any other place in the world. I was however amazed to discover a complete social hierarchy prevailing from the top to the bottom of the tree. For example, the big buzzards occupied its crown. Immediately below nested the kites and the falcons. Then came the ravens and the crows. On the next rung lived the green parrots, the kingfishers, the common mynas, the robins, the tailor birds and so on. The tree had an uncanny resemblance to a modern, high-rise building, in which the more affluent own the highest flats, enjoying the light and air and the best view of the surrounding landscape. On days after a heavy downpour, when the sky cleared and the sun shone brilliantly, these birds would spread themselves lazily, row after row, on the horizontal branches, to preen themselves and to dry their colourful plumage. It was a sight of extraordinary beauty, reminiscent of a rainbow over a freshly drenched, green landscape.

At the bottom of the tree, the innumerable branches of its root, just before they entered the earth, intertwined to form dozens of sockets and holes. In these lived hundreds of iguanas, chameleons, snakes and lizards, not to mention the teeming insects that constantly crawled up and down the smooth gray trunk of the tree. In fact, the 'traffic' was so heavy both ways that it rivalled the rush hour in a city. The pressure on living space was so great that it seemed to be the most densely 'populated' tree in the whole world.

What was a source of constant wonder to me was the acute sense of territoriality among the denizens of the tree. This would often result in fierce individual or group fights, especially during the hour of homecoming. At such moments the deafening cacophony that ensued – *pi, pi, pi, ikui-chung, chri-chiri-chiri-chr-r-r-r-rh, mir-r-r-r-rah, mir-r-r-ah, biter-bit, biter-biter-it-bir-r-r-r-hr, nikhar-kich, nikhar-kich, uiti-uiti-uiti-uiti, tuia-tuia-tuia* – rose to such a crescendo as to sound like the blaring hi-fi speakers of a jazz band gone berserk. Such fights frequently ended up in a bloody mess. Sometimes I would discover a badly injured myna or bulbul gasping behind a shrub that grew around the trunk of the tree. I would gently pick it up, carry it home and bandage its broken leg tenderly with a hot paste of white lime and turmeric. Or I would carefully clean the wound on the head with absorbent cotton and apply the healing juice of marigold leaves. I would then feed it with earthworms and Bengal gram and nurse it back to health.

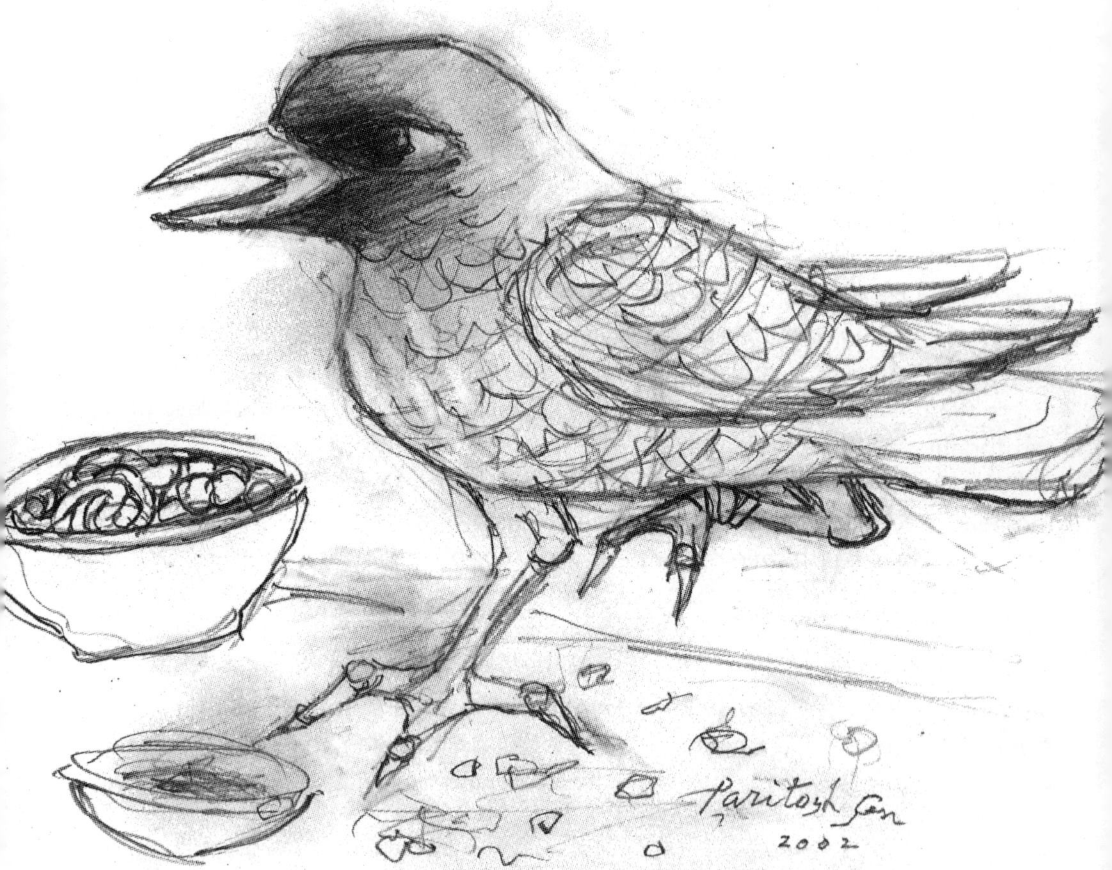
Paritosh Sen
2002

One morning, an unusually loud noise woke me up. I opened my bedside window to find hundreds of birds flying helter-skelter. Their combined cacophonous calls left me in no doubt that they were some kind of danger cry. As I approached the tree, I was surprised to see two black-faced langurs jumping from branch to branch like Tarzan and swinging from one part of the tree to another by holding on to the many creepers that entwined it. The monkeys were like two expert trapeze players in a circus. What a wonderful place for fun and frolic! Why not occupy it? Probably with this in mind, they launched into an act of wanton destruction, ruthlessly pulling down scores of nests and scattering eggs and young ones on the ground below. Meanwhile, alerted by the cry of their terrorized kith and kin, birds from the neighbourhood hed gathered. They flew round and round the tree as though in a battle ritual, and suddenly, like a thunderous black cloud, they swooped down on the two langurs. The way seemingly innocent and harmless birds, driven by their instinct for survival, transformed themselves into fury incarnate, filled me with awe. I was astonished to see the two aggressive langurs, now with their long tails straightened out, jumping madly from branch to branch, fleeing for their dear lives and trying to take cover behind the dense foliage. But the birds did not stop their assault until the wretched monkeys were lacerated all over. With great difficulty they managed to run to the safety of a thick bamboo grove nearby. Quite a few small birds lay dead under the tree.

The quality and direction of light inevitably bring about a change in the appearance and mood of an object. The transformation of the Arjuna tree during different hours of the day fascinated me endlessly. For example, when it caught the first rays of the sun, it looked like a great yogi in deep meditation facing the east, his right hand held in a gesture of compassion, as in the figure of Gautama Buddha, with flocks of common blue pigeons circling it as if in obeisance. During high noon, when the sun was overhead, the harsh mercury-white light and lamp-black shadows so accentuated its three-dimensionality that it not only looked much larger than its actual size but also fierce and aggressive, ready to take on legendary demons like Sumbha and Nisumbha, Taraka and Puloma and others, who had rocked heaven itself. And in the light of the setting sun, the tree assumed the form of a royal charioteer ready to set off in his many-splendoured vehicle towards the western horizon.

Early autumn afternoons in the village were hot and sultry. There was such stillness in the air that not a blade of grass moved. It was siesta time for humans, birds and animals alike. But the world of insects and fish would be wide awake. Their ceaseless activity amidst this all-pervading silence engrossed me. I spent hours watching them. I heard sounds that I did not normally hear at other times of the day. Besides, the dark shadow of the Arjuna tree and its proximity to water made the ground under it the coolest spot in the entire area.

Richly patterned butterflies flitted from one hyacinth flower to another. An orange-hued dragonfly tried to balance itself precariously on a vividly purple water lily at the pond's edge Through the still, transparent olive-green water, in the shadow of the tree, I saw myriads of tiny fish and various other forms of aquatic life, jostling nervously as if in fear of losing their territory to impending marauders. Water beetles, earthworms, grasshoppers, caterpillars, centipedes, fish-eating spiders, black and red ants, and many other known and unknown living beings moved about busily, foraging for food or yearning for companions of the opposite sex, but ever alert to fend off the sudden attack of hidden or camouflaged predators.

It was under the Arjuna tree that I first became aware of the mysteries and wonders of creation. It was there also that I learned a fundamental truth – the inalienable right of all forms of life to coexist. This right was commonly respected, except at moments when hunger and the instinct for survival drove them to acts of aggression.

One afternoon I witnessed a group of black ants carrying a lifeless beetle towards their home at the root of the Arjuna tree. Immediately above, in the dense foliage of one of its lowest branches, lived a colony of big red ants. I saw some of them rush down the trunk and encircle the smaller ants. Within minutes others joined them. Soon a battle royal ensued over the possession of the beetle. Sensing danger, a new army of several hundred black ants recklessly threw themselves into the fight. Although each red ant was six or seven times larger than a black one, its physical advantage was neutralized by the sheer numbers of its diminutive opponents. There was a veritable tug-of-war for the dead beetle between the two groups and for a while it seemed as though the red ants would succeed. But by the force of their numbers the black ants overpowered their enemies and ran home with the booty, despite suffering heavy casualties. Military tactics apart, I was also impressed by their keen collective intelligence.

On another occasion, a crisp late morning shower had left small muddy patches around the root of the tree. In one of them lay a dead moth. It was as delicate as an object made of the finest silk. Some ants, who were evidently foraging, suddenly discovered this unexpected food. In their excitement a few of them rushed towards the moth, but got stuck in the mud. Seeing this, the others turned back one by one sending some inaudible, coded message all down the line, and promptly retreated from the scene. I was surprised to see them return in a short while with miniscule grains of sand. They dumped these on the mud patch until, in about an hour's time, a 'bridge' had been built right up to where the moth lay. Then, within seconds, they transported the beautiful silken creature to their home.

One evening, as was my practice, I sat on the bench above the steps that led to the pond. There were two such flights of steps situated at two ends of the pond. One was used for bathing and the other for washing. The steel-blue light of dusk on the surface of the water and the sound of big fish diving deep always attracted me. The quivering reflection of the Arjuna tree in the pond looked like the sweeping brush stroke of a Japanese Zen master calligrapher. As I watched with deep fascination, I noticed a faint silvery light appearing behind this black mass, making its contours sharper and sharper until it resembled the corona of an eclipsed sun. As I looked up to see where the light came from, I saw, rising behind the tree, a huge moon that seemed to fill the entire horizon. The silhouette of the tree made the light so brilliant that it felt as though several moons had appeared on the same horizon. It was one of the most gorgeous sights I have ever seen. In fact, even in subsequent years, the experience of watching an impressive variety of moonrises in different lands and climes has not dimmed my memory of this unique visual experience.

This was, however, in sharp contrast to the experience of a cousin of mine a fortnight later. At this point I think it is necessary to inform my readers that our living quarters and the Arjuna tree were separated by a distance of at least a hundred metres. But we had to walk up to it every day because, in the absence of an underground sewage system, or a septic tank, the 'water closet' was situated right under the tree, this being the farthest point from our house. It was a small, unplastered brick structure, dark and damp, a place that created an eerie feeling even during the day.

My cousin Tapan – Tapa for short – was a voracious eater. He would sometimes consume incredibly large quantities of food if egged on, especially if it was based on a wager, however small. It was a festive day in autumn, when good food was *de rigeur* in every middle-class Bengali family. Tapan had eaten as much as could fill the bellies of at least half a dozen people with good appetites. It was no wonder then that in the middle of the night he had to rush to the brick structure under the Arjuna tree. What followed, I shall now narrate in my cousin's own words.

'It was well past midnight and it was particularly dark, being the end of the fortnight of the waning moon. With a paraffin lantern in one hand and a brass water pot in the other, I proceeded towards the Arjuna tree. On such occasions, our pet dog Bhola would normally accompany me. That night, for some reason best known to him, he refused to budge. As I approached the small structure, I was startled to see the Arjuna tree assuming the form of Kali, the Goddess of Darkness, who roams over cremation grounds. She had long tresses of tar-black hair cascading down to her heels. She looked terribly fearsome, to say the least. A thin diaphanous veil of autumnal mist rose from the pond and covered the bamboo grove nearby. Through it, a shadowy form attracted my attention. I held up the lamp to see what it was. I saw a skinny female figure with a white sari drawn over her head sitting on the bank of the pond with a fishing rod in hand. On closer examination, I was startled to see that her head was missing. But I wasn't the type to be easily unnerved. With a sudden jerk of her lean hand, she brought up a huge fish that landed with a thud on the soft mud. It was an awesome creature. It had three heads with whiskers like those of a walrus. It had enormous tongues dangling from the mouth, like three fearsome Alsatian dogs. Its eyes were like pools of fire. Most curious of all was its long serpentine body with countless joints in it, as if it had been made by putting together scores of oversized pineapples. Its scales consisted of thousands of tiny mirrors, somewhat like a traditional sequinned Gujarati fabric. As they caught the light from the lantern, they threw brilliant beams in every direction. Suddenly, a gigantic version of a hatchet, the kind used by fish vendors in this region, came floating down, followed by two equally huge brass plates. The shadowy figure grabbed the fish and, like a flash of lightning, brought down the hatchet on its neck. Huge jets of blood flowed in every direction, filling the dry pond to its brim. These strange goings-on by now had terrorized me, and I decided to run back home. But just as I was about to turn back I felt an icy hand on my bare shoulder. In an even monotone, a gravelly voice whispered into my ear, "We are having a picnic tonight. It is going to be an all-fish dinner. Do you know who is the cook? Poltu Ray's wife, of course (a woman who was famous for her delectable fish dishes). Won't you join us?" The mention of this woman sent a chill down my spine because she had died a week ago.'

The next morning, my cousin was discovered by our woodcutter lying unconscious under the Arjuna tree.

Another time, our village folk singer, Jogesh Bhatial, was returning home alone in his dinghy after a performance in a neighbouring village. He was singing aloud, as was his habit. As soon as his dinghy entered the canal that flowed behind the Arjuna tree, his song stopped abruptly. He has not been seen or heard since, although, in the dead of the night, his song sometimes comes wafting down from the crown of the Arjuna tree.

Such stories notwithstanding, the Arjuna tree always appeared to me as a unique creation full of wonders, a living monument to the unity of life; and its music, an epic poem of universal love.

I wonder if this magnificent tree still stands. It is nearly fifty years since I last saw it. Like many other beautiful things which are thoughtlessly sacrificed at the altar of so-called progress, it too, perhaps, has inexorably vanished.

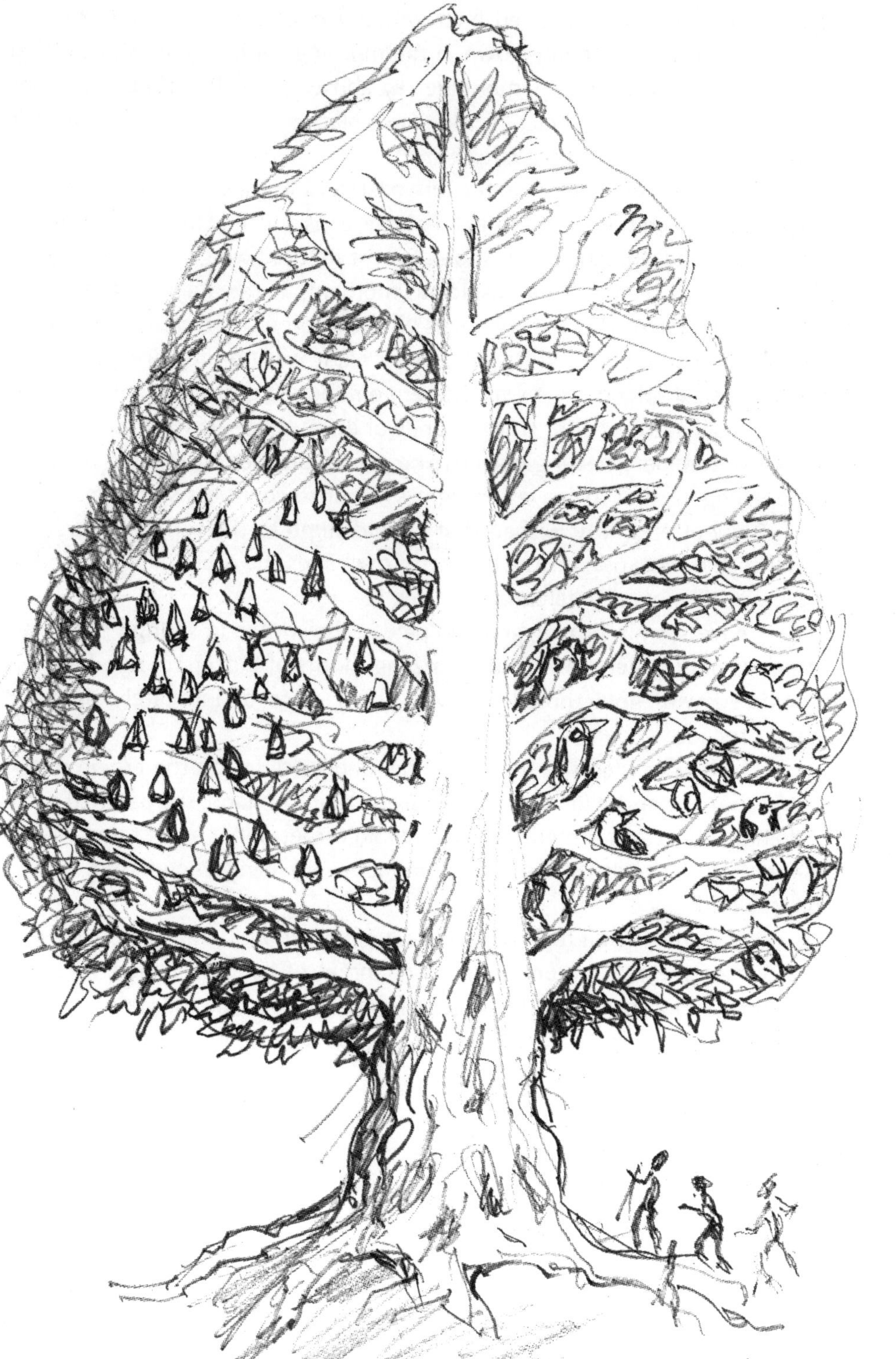
Paritosh Sen
2002

Maybe a new highway has been built where it once proudly stood. Where I once saw the tree's glittering crown in the morning, with a greenish halo that gradually merged into the enamel-blue sky above, one will probably now see beastly factory chimneys belching clouds of black smoke, curling up into the sky like a hydra-headed king cobra.

One summer evening, in the dim past, a violet-hued teal, on its way to distant Siberia from the cinchona-rich Polynesian island, had landed on the soft grass of our pond's northeastern shore, to rest its tired wings. Unknowingly, it had left behind a seed. At that auspicious moment, all the stars sang in unison to proclaim its birth. The ancient sages who wrote our medical treatises conferred on it a name befitting its glory. After all, it was no ordinary tree. Apart from its physical splendour, it was the very embodiment of piety and compassion. It not only gave shelter to thousands of living things, it was also a repository of extraordinary healing powers. The golden powder of its dried bark and the life-giving juice of its leaves brought succour to countless sufferers.

How often I have wished that I could climb to the top of the tree: to experience the sensation of touching with my hands the azure blue sky, and to see the world below as a falcon would see it.

I have seen it look rugged and pale in the winter. In spring I have seen it attired in satin greenery with the dazzling motifs of butter-coloured flowers embroidered with gold thread all over, like a piece of intricately designed Banaras brocade.

I have also seen the first rain-laden indigo cloud hit the crown of the tree and soak the entire landscape. As if by a sleight of hand, the parched earth was dramatically transformed into an emerald carpet. What a sight and what a sensation! All the birds, all the insects, in fact every living thing in and around it, danced with joy.

No wonder I still feel its heart beat in my blood. Living as I do in a city where human feelings are under constant threat of being devalued, I haven't yet become so insensitive as to forget the Arjuna tree. The memory of it still lifts me to a region where a thousand locked doors of the joy of life are opened up.

Translated from the Bengali by Paritosh Sen

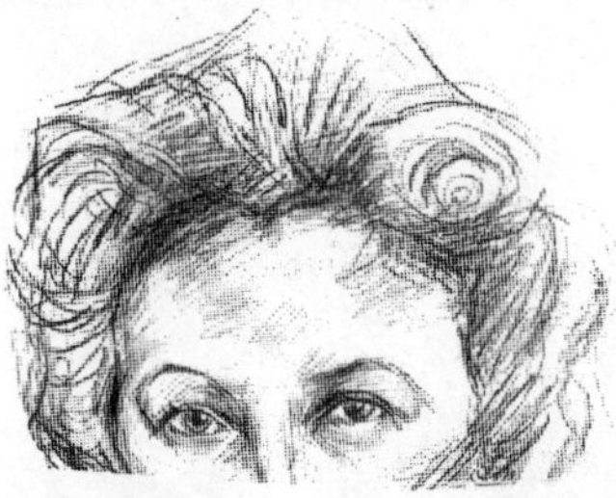

Helen of Lancashire

The beauty of nature, the company of pleasant people, good food and drink – this is an irresistible combination for someone as travel-crazy and sociable as I am. Here I shall relate one of my most enriching experiences during my long sojourns abroad.

It was 1953. Summer was on its way out, and autumn about to set in. In the twilight hour between afternoon and evening, I was on my way to Carnforth, a five-hour journey by train from London. The second-class compartment had no other occupant. I had several newspapers and magazines to keep me busy, and the undulating green of the English countryside – fresh, dense and moss-covered – was a feast to the eye. But after a while I began to feel a little bored. The three or four stops we made on the way had no trace of the vitality or extraordinary blend of colour, sound and smell that make our Indian railway stations so special. Even a big industrial town like Bristol does not have the bustle we associate with such railway stations. At each station a couple of people got off quietly, some got in. No shouts from vendors, no appeals from persistent beggars, no unseemly jostle to get into the compartment. Everything was so very orderly, so very civilized.

Carnforth, where I was headed, was a small village in Lancashire, in the Lake District of England. In keeping with the size of the village, its railway station was tiny, with just one man serving as station master, post and telegraph master, ticket-seller and porter. Moreover, he had to help old and infirm passengers into the train, throw the mail bag into the van and do various other odd jobs.

As I got down I saw Helen come towards me. 'Welcome to Carnforth', she said, and planted two wet kisses on my cheeks. The station master insisted on carrying my suitcase. 'After all, you are Mrs Reynold's guest', he said. I was the only passenger to alight from the train, which soon started out for Glasgow. Helen drove me in her station-wagon, a fairly old model, along narrow alleyways. 'I hope you had a good journey', she said. 'It was lovely', I replied. 'Your

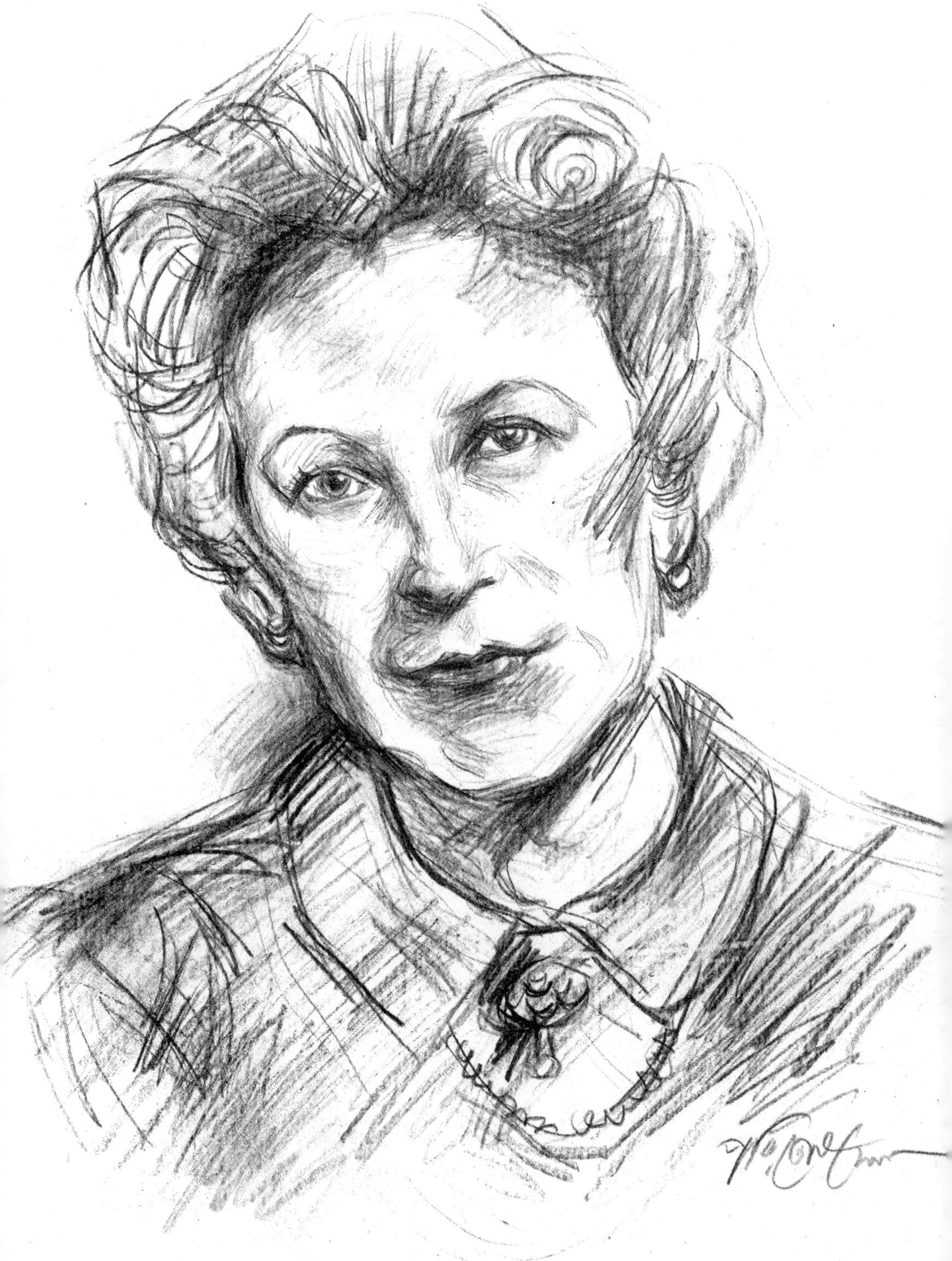

countryside is so green, so lush, a pleasure to the eye.' Huge oaks, birches, poplars and other trees flanked our way, forming a guard of honour. The upper parts of the hills were covered with pine and fir and various other trees which looked unfamiliar. Beyond these trees I could see cottages, though they were few and far between. Nature presented itself in all its glory. 'You aren't feeling tired, are you?' Helen asked. 'Do I look as though I'm tired?' I replied. 'Actually, a very good friend of mine has asked me for dinner and bridge. You too are invited. Are you game? Liz is an excellent cook and she loves people.' I am always attracted by food; I happen to be both a gourmet and gourmand rolled into one. 'Of course I'm game', was my prompt response.

The house stood on a ridge, about four hundred yards from the main gate. A giant of a man in a coarse sweater and tall boots emerged from a cottage to open the gate for us. Instantly, Leighton Hall, Helen's ancestral home, swam into view.

She led me to the second floor, opened the door to a corner room and declared, 'Here you are. This is your room. Freshen up and come down in half an hour. We'll have a drink before starting for Liz's house.' She marched away, whistling a merry tune. The room was huge, with an equally imposing four-poster bed with gilded ornaments on it, fit for a king. It was large enough to accommodate a number of women. And here I was just by myself. Bad luck indeed!

Briskly graceful in her movements, Helen exuded vitality in her high-heeled steps, loud laughter, constant humming and whistling. Unlike our usual idea of the British, she was warm and friendly. She was also exceptional in being a Roman Catholic in a predominantly Protestant country.

I had come across her in Brussels. I was having an art exhibition there sponsored by the Indian embassy, in January 1950. The bargo-master, the equivalent of our mayor, was to open it at 6.30 pm. A young American acquaintance named Peter Scot, better known as Scottie, rang me to ask if he could bring along a girl friend of his, an English artist. 'Please do', I told him.

The spectators started coming in quick succession. Soon enough Scottie arrived, accompanied by Helen. 'Can I buy this painting?' She was interested in a landscape painted in an Impressionistic style – sunlight streaming through banyan trees, creating a kind of magic of light and shade.

'I will send you the cheque tomorrow', Helen said. When it arrived I was surprised to find it was for fifty pounds instead of the declared price of thirty. I sent it back with a note. A little later the phone rang. 'Helen speaking. I thought your lovely painting was underpriced. It should be fifty, at least. Please accept the cheque, will you?

Was she insane? I could not make out if she was being generous or just showing off. Since there was no way of ascertaining the truth I concluded that she was noble of heart. Very soon I found out that my assessment was absolutely correct. We met several times after that. She took me to operas and ballets, and to excellent restaurants. Before leaving for England she gave me her address, saying, 'We must keep in touch. You must come to Leighton Hall.'

For the next four years I stayed on in Paris, one among forty thousand struggling artists belonging to every possible colour and creed. Helen and I corresponded, though not very frequently. In every letter she expressed the hope that I would pay her a visit, which would be inspiring and profitable for her. It was not that I did not want to visit her, but I was in no position to afford a trip. Every year I received a new year gift from her – a cheque for fifty guineas. This year was no exception. The note said, 'Haven't heard from you for a long time, I hope you are well and painting to your heart's content. When can we expect you at Carnforth?' Her reiterated invitation could not have come at a better time. I was down with anaemia. The doctor had advised a change of place and plenty of nourishing food. When I wrote to Helen about my state of health she promptly sent me a money order and a telegram which read: 'Make a beeline to Leighton Hall.' This, in brief, is the background to my visit and month-long stay in Carnforth, one of many expressions of Helen's generosity and affection.

I freshened up, changed and went down to find Helen waiting with a drinks tray in a trolley laden with whisky, port, sherry, gin and other excellent beverages. I poured myself a small glass of port and sank into a couch of huge proportions. It seemed to have been made for a man like G.K. Chesterton. White velvet curtains were drawn uniformly back from French windows to reveal a lily pool and a garden. The late summer sunlight peeped from behind the clouds. It hit the water like a spike and lit up the hilltops like a spotlight. I found the light in England somewhat opaque, as though mixed with white chalk powder. The entire landscape was reminiscent of the paintings of Constable, who was the first to raise rural landscapes to the level of Turner and Wilson. Constable has shown great skill in capturing the essential English atmosphere, the play of light and shade, nature and people at work under the English sky.

I was interrupted by Helen. 'Let's go', she announced.

Our station-wagon drove through a narrow village road just wide enough for two cars to pass. The road was flanked by a low boundary wall of loosely kept boulders to keep the cars from going down the slopes on either side. The evening light, meanwhile, had turned into a kind of dark gray with a mixture of copper and silver. I saw cattle grazing in silence in the nearby fields, no cowherds seemed to be around. 'They graze by themselves all through the night and are usually home by daybreak. If some of them get lost the dogs are there to bring them safely back', Helen explained.

Contrary to the information gathered from newspapers, England did not seem to be more populated than Europe. Cottages were few and far between. The countryside was lush and green. In the darkening twilight I did not miss the lovely flower gardens with roses, lilies, hollyhocks, gladioli and other wild flowers. The ivy-covered walls made a delightful picture. Spiralling smoke from chimneys was the only sign of movement in an otherwise still landscape. There was a wet nip in the air, heralding the approaching autumn.

I had kept my eyes on the roadside milestones while talking to Helen. About an hour later I found that we had covered fifty miles. After another ten miles I could not hold back any longer and I asked her how far we had to go.

'Not far,' said Helen, 'we are almost there.'

'Do you have many friends to play bridge with?' I asked.

'We are eight altogether. We take turns to hold bridge parties. We meet twice a week if the weather is good; the host provides dinner, needless to say.'

The station-wagon raced along, leaving the ninety-mile post behind. There was no sign of habitation yet, not even a spot of light. 'You know, Jimmy, my husband, is coming down from Liverpool tomorrow for the weekend. You will like him, he is very friendly and easy to get along with. You will also be meeting my mother, my younger sister Mary, and our paying-guest Judith at breakfast. The four of us form the permanent population of Leighton Hall. But my cousin Peter drops in every day to look after the old ladies and the estate. And next week two young Spanish girls are coming for a week, intending to learn English. They visited us last summer too. Very nice girls, with charming manners.' This was welcome news. 'I hope you can stay for a long time', Helen went on. 'I want to paint a lot while you are here. I have a lot to learn from you.'

Meanwhile, we had raced past the hundred and tenth milestone. As the headlights lit up tall rows of cypresses, Helen announced, 'Here we are.' Soon we entered a beautiful driveway and came to a stop under a portico. Liz rushed forward to take Helen in her arms. I was introduced to her. She shook my hands. 'Pleased to meet you. Come in, please.' As we entered the room two fierce-looking dogs – a Doberman and a Labrador Retriever – almost pounced on me. But a stern command from their mistress sent them back, and I was able to breathe normally.

In the enormous hall two middle-aged women sat sipping their drinks. A bridge table stood near the fireplace. Both the women seemed to be in their forties, tall, as is usual with the British, though they lacked the grace and charm of their French and Italian counterparts. But their lack of sophistication in dress was amply made up for by excellent manners.

After a general round of introductions Liz offered me a choice of drinks. I hadn't had good whisky for a long time, so I opted for one. Since I was totally ignorant of the game, I made a polite pretence of watching them for a while before retiring to a spacious couch, a book and a glass of whisky in hand. I looked around the oak-panelled room to the vases of roses on sixteenth-century marble-top Italian tables. Fortified by the whisky, and with tins of Three Castles, Balkan Subrani and a box of Havana cigars within reach, I was beginning to enjoy myself. As I lit a fat cigar I felt life was really wonderful after all. After four years of deprivation in Paris this was a royal interlude. The experience was similar to that of Omar Khayyam for as long as it would last.

I opened a book at random. Nature and the Gardens of England. Nothing could be more suited to my mood. My eyes fell on a paragraph. 'There is something in the English Soul which rejoices in the work of Nature, or as it would have been called until very recently, of God, more than the works of man. Nature, the English love, and after Nature, Art.'

The English are mad about nature. The art of making a garden, a unique combination of the earth, water and sky, is a special gift they have. They are particularly blessed with a poetic sentiment that expresses itself through the various colours and dimensions of flowers and trees, taking the beauty of nature a step closer towards perfection. No wonder England boasts of so many nature poets and such wonderful nature poetry.

The makers of famous English gardens were inspired by the landscape painters of the seventeenth and eighteenth centuries. They believed in the least interference with nature – a view totally opposed to the French idea of gardening. Gardening for the French invariably means imposing a formal pattern on nature. This view, oddly enough, was not shared by the French landscape painters.

Every time I visited England I was impressed by its countryside. The entire region seemed to be a garden. Nature was bountiful here – a favourable climate, fertile land and hard-working people with a zest for the outdoor life. Over and above these blessings, they have a poetic temperament.

I was deeply absorbed in the book, an album of the gardens of stately homes, of the experiments with exotic plants brought from various other regions. They had created unusual varieties of rhododendron brought originally from the Indian Himalayas and China. This was just one example of their successful horticultural experiments.

Meanwhile my glass was empty. Liz, the perfect hostess, had noticed this even though she was absorbed in the card game. 'Sen, please fill up your glass', she said. I was only too happy to oblige. A middle-aged woman in a black dress with a white lace collar came in to announce that dinner was ready. As far as I remember, the menu consisted of oyster soup, roast duck, baked potato, buttered beans and carrots, and French salad with vintage red wine. This was followed by a delicious cherry pudding. Even after so many years I can still remember the mouth-watering taste of the roast with apple sauce. Then we were offered a variety of after-dinner liqueurs. It was well past midnight when we said our goodbyes. I was feeling so drowsy that I could hardly sit up straight in the car. It was two in the morning when we reached Leighton Hall. The sound of our approaching car excited the dogs and they set up a chorus of welcome. 'Come down as soon as you hear the gong at nine', said Helen. 'Good night. Sleep well.' She marched away, whistling a tune. I began my long walk along the corridor towards the southern staircase.

The corridor was flanked by landscape paintings. Above them on the walls hung stuffed heads of wild buffaloes, barasinga deer and exotic birds. In the dim light the heads took on a weird appearance. The light reflecting from the eyes of the ferocious buffaloes made them look as though they were ready to pop out. The heads suddenly came alive, as if about to make a dive. The dead birds stared at me. I could almost hear them scream. I had to get away from this haunted place. I walked as fast as I could towards the staircase. Time, place and lighting can bring about magical transformations. Stuffed heads are just dead objects, but they had never looked so weird, so uncannily real.

Because of its position on a ridge, Leighton Hall was exposed to strong winds all through the year. The wind turns into a blast in winter. As I lay on my bed listening to the wind beating against the window panes, I found it difficult to sleep. I did finally doze off, through fitful starts of wakefulness.

A little before breakfast a huge gong sounded. Its sound reverberated throughout the house, making it impossible for anyone to stay in bed. I was told that this bronze gong, three feet in diameter, had been brought by Helen's grandfather from China. Weighing 50 kilograms, it could drive even ghosts away. This was reassuring to me, as I am scared of ghosts. Some of the old houses of this region are said to be haunted.

I got dressed and came down to be greeted by the four dogs. Helen was writing a letter. Noticing my discomfiture, she told me that the dogs were harmless. She was about to shoo them away to the next room but I stopped her. 'Let them stay', I said. Pretty soon we got friendly and, during the rest of my stay in Leighton Hall, they kept following me about. There were two spaniels and two pomeranians, and they were called Hamlet, Dandy, Ophelia and Scarlet.

The English are proverbially fond of dogs, comparable only to the French obsession with cats. I find the English sentiment for dogs quite baffling. I will give two examples. One dates back to 1937 in Madras, when I was being trained by Debiprosad Roychoudhury. In dire need of money, my colleague Gopal Ghose and I decided to try our luck with Englishmen, who are supposed to be lovers of art. We set out with rolls of watercolour landscapes under our arms. We drew a blank at the first two houses. The lord and master of the third house, a young and handsome man, was kind to us, but he was not interested in our paintings. If we could make faithful portraits of all his six dogs, he was willing to pay us twenty-five for each portrait. 'You can start work from tomorrow if you like. You can have your lunch here even if I am not at home. But the likeness has to be perfect.' Gopal Ghose made portraits of three dogs, I did the other three. I must admit that we took unfair advantage of the animals because they were not fussy, unlike human models. The master was so pleased that he entertained us lavishly with generous amounts of whisky and other delicacies. He paid us exactly as much as promised. We went back happy with fresh, crisp notes in our pocket.

The other incident happened in Glasgow. I had gone to see a neorealist Italian movie with Helen. There was a scene in it in which a stray dog is run over by a truck. At this Helen let out such a terrific yell that many in the audience rushed up to see what the matter was. 'Let's get out of here', Helen said. 'I can hardly breathe.' We went to a shop nearby and sat there for a long while sipping tea, saying nothing. Back at home, she related what had happened to her mother and sister. They too were stunned and so apprehensive about the safety of their own pets that there was hardly any conversation during dinner.

The dining hall at Leighton Hall was huge. The black, polished dining table was large enough to seat thirty people, suitable for a grand banquet. Two young girls in their early twenties stood on the side in identical clothes, ash-grey with white lace collars. From the way they stood I guessed that they were the maids. They greeted us, pulled back our chairs and asked us to take our seats. I gave the two charming girls a fleeting glance and was amazed by the similarity of their features. Helen introduced them. 'This is Isabella and this is Julietta, from the Ravenna region of Italy. They help around the house and in the kitchen. Nice girls, twins.' The mystery was solved. Almost immediately the three other residents of Leighton Hall made their entrance: Helen's mother, Helen's sister Mary, and Judith. 'Welcome to Leighton Hall', they said in unison.

We had porridge for breakfast, followed by slices of ox tongue, toast, cheese, home-made jam and honey, and fresh coffee with cream. There were bunches of green and red grapes and the famous English apples, as green as the meadows – all products of their own farm.

Helen's mother, Penelope Gillander, sat at the head of the table, a position she would occupy at every meal. Her head and shoulders towered well above the table. She was close to six feet tall and 88 years old, but she looked not a day older than seventy. Her skin was unwrinkled, she had strong teeth, she drove the car herself. She was every inch a lady of aristocratic birth. The way she carried herself and the way she spoke reminded me of Queen Victoria without her regalia.

After breakfast she grabbed my hands and led me to the gate. 'Come with me, darling': though fondly spoken, it was almost an order.

With thirty-six rooms across four floors and a basement, the building was like a castle. It was a queer mixture of various styles of architecture – Elizabethan, Georgian, Edwardian, Victorian. The only thing it had lacked until comparatively recently was a high boundary wall. This was built by Helen's grandfather, who was His Majesty's cabinet-maker by profession. He made a name and soon acquired land and property. But his successors were forced to sell a large part of the grounds to pay the huge death duty which had come into force by then. Even maintaining the house was a problem. Helen and her family had to take recourse to a measure which had been unthinkable in her grandfather's time. For four months in a year the house was open to the public for a fee, like all the hundred and fifty halls in the Lancashire region, many of them much older. Tourists visit these historical houses; they are taken on a guided tour, given lunch, tea and dinner – all for a charge of eight to ten pounds. As a bonus the tourists also get a panoramic view of the visually delightful Lake District.

We went to an enclosed pen in the backyard. Helen's mother was carrying a plastic bag. As soon as the ducks saw her they rushed towards her, cackling loudly. It was feeding time. The lady scattered the grain calling the ducks fondly by their names – Rosie, Susie, Sally, Maggie, Dick, Bill, Harry and so on – and they responded. She made kissing noises and patted their necks. It was a display of sheer love and affection. Their meal over, the ducks made for the lily pond adding splashes of colour to an already lovely scene.

'How about an outing after lunch', suggested Mrs Gillander magnanimously. 'We will take the train. It will take an hour at the most. I'm sure you'll like the fall colours. This happens to be the best season in these parts, even better than springtime. You're sure to love it.'

Helen drove us to the station. The train chugged along a small loop line. 'The rail tracks skirt the back of our home', Mrs Gillander explained. 'There is not much traffic though, just two trains per day. In winter you can get a glimpse of the house through the trees because they are bare. But in summer you can't.' We were travelling past cultivated fields of vegetables – cabbages, beetroots, cauliflowers, all of them of such huge dimensions that my eyes were ready to pop off. The cabbages were like giant footballs, the cauliflowers could have put huge bouquets to shame. The trees all around had tinges of bright yellow, rust and copper, bathed in the soft afternoon light.

We got down at the station, a modest little stop like Carnforth. A tall, middle-aged gentleman came forward, kissed Mrs Gillander on the cheeks and shook hands with me. He was wearing a suit, but from his collar I could make out that he was a priest: Reverend Sidebottom – a somewhat incongruous name, for he was a well-proportioned man. He had organized a meeting to discuss a charity show for the benefit of refugees of the Second World War. Mrs Gillander was one of the distinguished guests. The meeting was followed by tea and snacks. Then we were on the train again.

The train was approaching Leighton Hall when my companion did something quite unexpected. I did not know what to make of it. Mrs Gillander stood up, yanked the alarm chain and brought the train to a grinding halt. As she got down she fished out two twenty-pound notes from her purse. A smiling, rather than scowling, guard approached her. He looked as though he had been expecting this. I was more and more intrigued. Mrs Gillander pushed the two notes into his hand and led me out with the air of an empress. 'You see darling, it is much easier to pay a fine of forty pounds and get down here than to go all the way to the station and drive back home.' So therein lay the clue to the mystery. The temptation of getting down within a quarter of a mile from the house was too great to resist. What was a mere forty pounds to her, after all. The indulgent smile of the guard was ample proof of the tacit support she received for such acts. We walked along the tree-lined path. 'I wanted to walk', she declared. 'It's so lovely out here. I rediscover my soul in the woods.'

After a while I came down from my room to find Helen busy setting up her studio. Our painting sessions were due to start the following day, with us venturing out if the weather was favourable. I was asked to comment on the still-life paintings on her studio walls. I told her what I felt. One coat of colour must dry completely before applying a second: otherwise there is unnecessary thickness and also a loss of brightness. 'If you are not happy with the choice of colour in a particular patch, wipe it clean with tarpin, then start again. That is the best way to retain brightness.'

It was a fairly large room with French windows to the west, through which one had a view of the garden, trees and a slice of the sky beyond. A bunch of rhododendrons stood in a square green vase. This was going to be her subject. My hands began to itch as I breathed in the studio atmosphere and its pungent aroma of linseed oil and tarpin. As I looked at the blank canvases on two easels I could not resist the temptation. Why wait for tomorrow? I asked Helen. Let's start right away. But I had no interest in painting flowers. I requested her to take a seat by the window, paying no heed to her feminine desire to change her dress and hairdo. I almost forced her to sit. When making a portrait I usually take a lot of liberties with design and form, while keeping the basic features of the model intact. I was influenced by the post-impressionistic school of painting. Helen's dress was a dark indigo, the background was the colour of ripe lemon, there was a tinge of pink on her face and hands, and her hair was a rust – these were the basic colours I used, with which I freely mixed others. My work proceeded satisfactorily and in an hour and a half it had taken definite shape. Helen sat with one hand on her cheek and the other on the table right next to the rhododendrons and a pile of books. The style was somewhat like that of Van Gogh's famous Arlesienne. It was getting dark. 'I will finish it tomorrow', I told Helen, and released her. Helen gave the unfinished work a good hard look and said, 'I will reserve my comments for until it is finished.' I was aware of her conservative views on art, more in line with the Royal Academy. In fact her entire family was conservative, not just in matters of art but also in dress, décor, way of life and political views.

The dinner gong reminded us that it was time to proceed to the dining hall. I found everybody assembled in the anteroom. A tall gentleman in a formal dinner jacket shook my hands. 'I'm Jimmy', he said. 'Pleased to meet you, Sen. Helen has told me all about you. May I offer you something? Port or sherry?' 'Sherry please', I said.

I felt a little ill at ease in this company, for all of them were in formal attire. This, I came to know later, was the family custom even if there was no guest present. I found this rather ridiculous. I possessed just two pairs of trousers, a coat and a thick sweater. I had given up wearing ties as superfluous. Naturally, I could not help feeling a little self-conscious.

An impressive row of tall candles at the centre of the table created a festive atmosphere. The silver cutlery glittered. But the light that outshone them all was that from the diamond Helen's mother wore. I have no idea what the famous Kohinoor looks like, but this looked to me like another Kohinoor.

We had roast duck again, though with a different sauce. But I was soon to discover a difference between the roast duck we had at Liz's place and this one. When dinner was over we retired to the anteroom and settled before the fire for coffee. I was ordered by the grand lady to occupy the chair next to her. All four dogs were cuddled at her feet. They were asleep – I had no idea that dogs could snore like humans. One of them moved its legs while it kept opening and closing its mouth. Noticing my astonishment, the grand lady said, 'Hamlet is chasing his father's ghost in his dreams.' Good God, I thought. There really were more things in heaven and on earth than I could dream of. 'Sen, do you play canasta?' Mrs Gillander asked. 'This is what we do every evening.' It did not take me long to learn the rules of the game: it was somewhat like rummy; it was played with two packs and four jokers.

Suddenly a suppressed belch brought back the taste of the roast. 'The duck was delicious', I found myself saying. Mrs Gillander's response made me gasp and all the pleasure of the dinner evaporated. 'Of course, that was Susie', she said. As if that was not enough, she added, 'She was such a darling.' Amazed though I was, it also set me thinking. You call these ducks Rosie, Susie,

Sally and other loving names, and fatten them up only to bring them to the dinner table? Was this not Hedonism, poles apart from the Catholic way? Perhaps she guessed at my dilemma and tried to explain. 'We have to be rational about these things. This is the only way to keep the bird population under control.' Much though I disliked the idea, I had to admit that Susie would have met the same end if she had been sold in the market.

After a few games of canasta it was time for ghost stories – another time-honoured ritual of the family. The stories were either read out or told, and everybody had his or her turn. After the first story I excused myself, saying I needed some fresh air. People of leisure who do not have to worry about making both ends meet are indeed ingenious in their modes of entertainment, most of them quite weird.

I came out of the house on to the gravelled area. Beyond it the ground sloped. Moonlight on the soft, moist grass created a velvet-like effect. Suddenly patches of black and white on the green slope started moving towards me. They grew bigger and bigger as they approached. I was petrified. There was a puffing noise as well. I ran in, and when I recounted my experience they laughed. 'Must be our black and white cows. They come to graze here every night', said Helen. I was not completely reassured. The creepy feeling persisted.

The next day we planned to go out into the countryside to set up our easels. After breakfast Helen and I collected our painting paraphernalia and set out for a village a couple of miles away. It was a small village with only a few thatched cottages. The morning sun shone brightly on the white-washed walls. Cattle and sheep grazed in the field, some farmers could be seen climbing up haystacks. The golden hay against the distant background of the hills of the Lake District made a perfect setting. We decided to paint this delightful landscape. I relished the prospect of doing an outdoor sketch after a long time.

An hour later, three-fourths of the painting was done. I walked back a little away to get a better view. As I lit a cigarette I noticed a car parked close by and a middle-aged woman watching our work with great interest. Our eyes met. She beamed and said, 'Hello'.

Meanwhile Helen was having trouble with her colours. She had put too much on the canvas. To help her out, I wiped clean some of the patches and asked her to apply fresh paint. This time she was more successful.

After the painting was done, as I was beginning to pack up, the observer came up to me. 'Would you like to sell this painting?' she asked. 'If yes, I would be delighted if you let me have it for fifty pounds.' I could hardly believe my ears. Lady Luck was indeed smiling upon me. Besides, beggars can't be choosers. I would have felt happier if she had offered to buy Helen's work as well. But then, my need was greater than hers.

It was already lunch-time, but Helen hadn't yet completed her painting. I told her she could finish it at home and we went back. Jimmy was waiting for us with a huge mug of beer and a just-lit cigar. He offered me a mug of very fine Bavarian beer. Life is indeed wonderful, I said to myself, as I sipped at it.

Lunch was nothing spectacular: spaghetti a la Bolognaise. I was familiar with the dish, but cooked and served as it was by the pretty twins, it had a special taste. In fact, it tasted much better than what I had had in Bologna itself. When I conveyed my appreciation to the sisters they were beside themselves with delight. There was red wine to go with it, followed by a pudding garnished with grapes and apples swimming in home-made cream. To do full justice to the meal I went up to my room for an afternoon nap after the eating and drinking was over.

When I came down I found Jimmy and Peter arranging chairs for a cocktail party they were going to have for their business friends. Isabella brought in a vase of roses. The guests started to arrive, most of them couples. Some had dealings with India, mostly in cotton products. There were about fifteen of them. A few were middle-aged, the rest were pretty advanced in years. I was not too keen to be in such company, but I could hardly offend Jimmy who was such a perfect gentleman.

During the course of a conversation I learnt from an old lady that she had been to India a long time back. 'What was your most memorable experience?' I asked her. Her answer was so ridiculous that for a moment I did not know what to say. Even now I can barely hold back my laughter as I think about it. She said, 'Of course, it was the Agha Khan by moonlight.' This was an image more suited to Salvador Dali – quite surrealistic – Agha Khan and moonlight! I was at a loss to detect the connection. 'Are you sure it was the Agha Khan by moonlight?' I asked her. She was a little irritated, and thumped her hand on the armrest of her chair as she affirmed, 'I am absolutely positive.'

Before I come to the solution of the mystery I would like to remind my readers that the Agha Khan she was talking about was the grandfather of the present Agha Khan, the father of Ali Khan, who married Rita Hayworth. The Agha Khan was the richest person in the world, but he was short, chubby and bald. What could be so fascinating about him in moonlight? Pretty soon the obvious answer flashed across my mind. It was the Taj Mahal by moonlight she was referring to. Perhaps the lady had had a little too much sherry. Hence the confusion.

The next day, as I was painting after breakfast, all by myself – Helen and her family had gone to church, after which they were to have breakfast with the pastor – suddenly a series of gun-shots shattered the peace of the morning. Alarmed, I ran out towards where the shots had come from. It was none else than Jimmy, busy at target practice with four loaded pistols. He stopped when he saw me approaching. 'I love shooting and hunting', he said. 'Next Monday we have arranged for a greyhound meet with friends from our hunting club. It will be very exciting. You must join us.' He handed me one of the pistols and urged, 'Here, have a go at it.' But allergic as I am to any weapon, I refused. 'Thank you, but I have to finish my painting.' Jimmy gave up. 'Sometimes I feel terribly bored here', he confessed. 'What a nice way to spend one's time', I said to myself.

The days passed cheerfully, with eating, drinking, painting, listening to music, taking long walks in the woods. In the words of the poet Jibanananda, I was drinking in the beauties of nature cup by cup. Except for the ghost stories it was a right royal interlude for me, an altogether splendid experience. I regained my health and recovered my zest for living.

Soon it was another weekend. Some guests were expected from Spain. They must have arrived at night, for I met them at breakfast. Two sisters, both in their late teens. One was a blonde with green eyes, the other had black eyes and hair. They seemed to be bursting with youth, in every sense of the word – Melba and Gilermina. They were lovely, cultured, warm and charming – an explosive combination. Helen said that her two sons were also coming down over the weekend, which created a ripple of excitement among the girls.

By lunch-time the sons arrived, driving a red sports car. The entire house soon resounded with the sound of youthful laughter. The boys were here for the hound meet. After lunch the young people lost no time disappearing into the woods. The way they were holding hands was enough to throw me into a fit of despair. The initial expectation and excitement created by the presence of the young girls were replaced by a sense of despair. There was nothing left for me to do but retire to my room for a long nap.

It was already dark when I woke up. I hurried downstairs. Jimmy was busy with the cocktails tray. I enquired about the young guests. 'Yes, they came back, but have now gone to the chapel for confession', I was told. I could never understand this duplicity, so common among Catholics. All sorts of immoral acts can be justified if only you confess later.

Jimmy, Peter and the young people were out of the house at the crack of dawn the next morning. Helen said we would join them at around ten. We drove along the country road for an hour. 'Look, there they are', Helen pointed them out to me. I turned to see a group of riders in white breeches, bright red coats and black caps, whips in hand, were galloping at breakneck speed, jumping over hedges, shrubs and ditches. What a wonderful sight it was against the emerald-green backdrop! Ahead of them ran about twenty ferocious greyhounds. Whether all this was necessary to chase and kill a few innocent rabbits seemed a doubtful proposition to me. Perhaps arguments can be made for and against the question, but I do not want to go into that now. All that mattered to me was the visual richness and excitement of the scene.

The sound of horns was heard. I was told that this meant the greyhounds had been successful in getting the rabbits. It was also a call to all the riders to assemble at the hunting spot. We followed suit. Peter was grinning from ear to ear. Four rabbits had already been hunted down. The poor creatures were reduced to bloody lumps inside a net. The greyhounds were sniffing the ground. It is their exceptionally strong sense of smell that leads them unerringly to rabbit holes. And the riders follow them, regardless of the hurdles. It is a sport that requires perfect control over the horse, and a lust for enjoying the sheer pleasure of riding at breakneck speed. It is not entirely without risk because the dogs do not follow an easy path and the horses could easily trip over fences and hurt their leg, bringing down their riders.

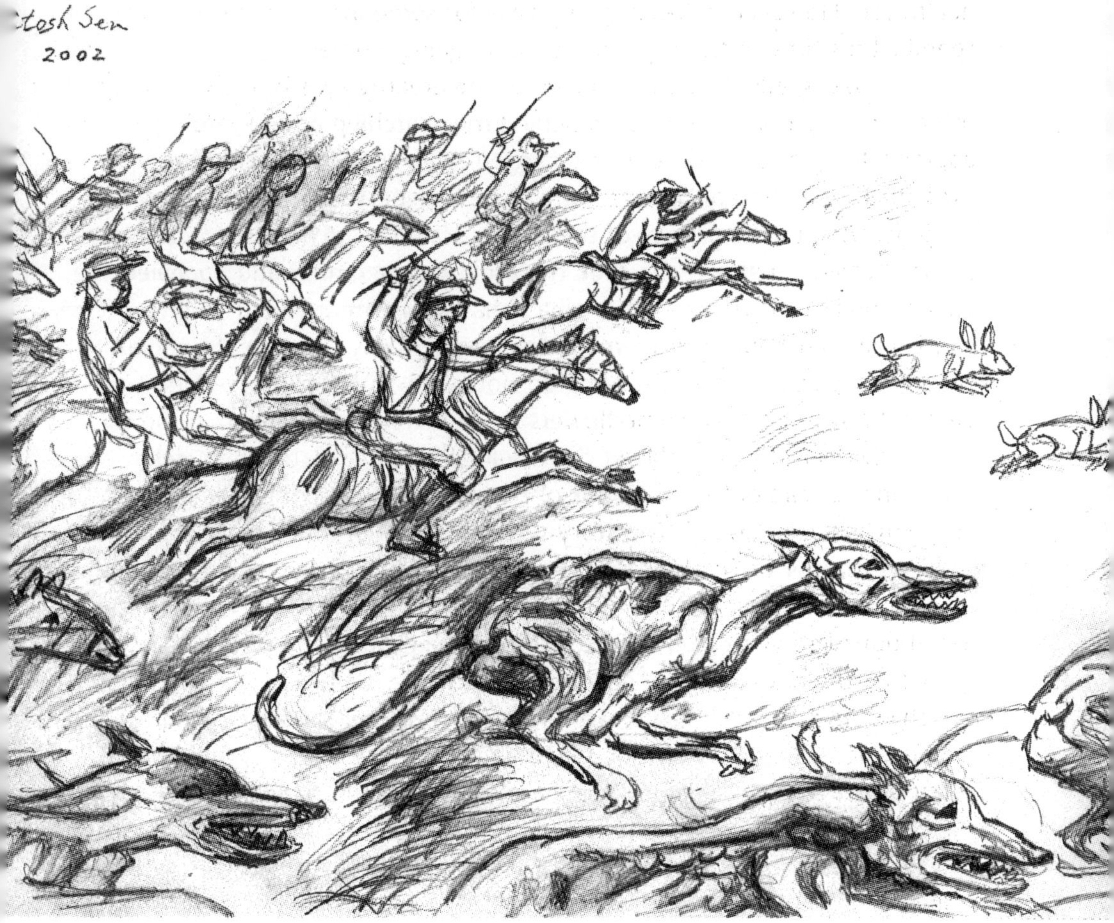

After about a couple of hours the riders returned, bathed in sweat, their chins glowing and shining. After a brief rest and a round of beer Peter blew his bugle, and the hounds and the riders were ready to start again. Peter led them to the woods. Soon they disappeared into the green meadow.

By the time we met again it was around two in the afternoon and both the riders and the horses were completely exhausted. Six rabbits were being roasted over a wood fire. Thick clots of blood lay on a silver platter. The paws of the dead animals were kept on another. We sat around the fire. Peter dabbed a dot of blood on our cheeks. The rabbits' paws would be mounted on wooden frames, he announced, with date, time, place and names engraved. Each person who had been present at the ceremony would be given one as a souvenir. This was an age-old ritual of the greyhound meet.

By the time I came down for breakfast the next morning all the men had left. There was a sudden lull after the flurry of activity. The Hall wore a gloomy and deserted look, but I was enjoying the solitude. It was good for my health too. However, it was not very easy for someone of my temperament to spend all his time in the company of four ageing women.

I was gradually getting drawn to the dreamy eyes of Melba. She would often come up quietly and stand behind me, watching and rewarding me with appreciative glances. We even exchanged smiles. Then I decided that it was time for the next step. Let's go for a walk, I suggested. She readily agreed. As we proceeded to the privacy of the groves, Helen must have seen us. Impelled by her Catholic instinct, she took me aside before dinner and appealed: 'Sen, please don't do anything with Melba.' I had no alternative but to give her my word. This had happened to me many times in my younger days: countless tales of lost opportunities – but I do not want to bore my readers with the details. Suffice it to say, some flowers are destined to be nipped in the bud.

Dinner over, we played our usual game of canasta. Then Helen asked Gilermina to read out from a book of true ghost stories. 'This will also improve your English', she added. The story went like this. In a village at the foothills near the frontier of Scotland and England, a newly married couple, Joarkin and Marguerite, was spending their honeymoon. In the dead of the night they were jolted out of their sleep by the sound of an explosion. They raced downstairs to find all the doors and windows closed. But the room was in a shambles. All the china and porcelain lay broken. They were scared to death. Then the telephone rang. There was no response when Marguerite picked up the phone. She put it down but it rang again. Joarkin picked it up this time. A husky voice at the other end said, 'Hello darling!' Promptly he put down the phone and said it was nobody. The voice was that of his dead lover who had committed suicide by hanging herself from the ceiling. This was the bare outline of the story.

The reading was over. Mary, Helen's sister, exclaimed, 'But this sounds almost like what happened here, at this very house!' 'Really?' I asked, more out of politeness than a desire to know. I had to hear the real-life story against my wishes.

I was told that a couple of years ago a French girl had come to Leighton Hall for a short stay, partly to learn English. While she was there another guest arrived, a rich young man from London, a friend of Richard, Helen's eldest son. Though not particularly handsome, he was young and drove a red Ferrari. His name was Jack Golding. In no time the inevitable happened. Jack was head over heels in love. He was not a man of many words, but a sincere young man. The affair progressed to love. It was soon time for him to go back to London. The night before he was to leave Jack proposed to Chantal, the French girl, only to be refused rudely. She told him she was already engaged.

Golding did not come down for breakfast the next day. They went up to call him, but there was no reply. His locked door was opened with the duplicate key. Jack was hanging from the ceiling, to the utter shock and surprise of the family. 'Which is this room, I may know?' I asked Mary. 'Your room', was her casual reply. A chill ran up my spine, the hair on my flesh stood up. Every so often we come across incidents where life imitates art instead of art imitating life.

No sooner had the story been related than the telephone at the end of the long corridor rang. Helen went to get it, whistling as usual. We heard her say 'Hello', followed by a scream. When we rushed there, it was exactly like a scene out of a Hitchcock film. The receiver dangled freely from its cradle. Helen, all the blood drained from her face, was lying in a half-faint. Her mother shook her. 'Who was it, Helen, who was it?' she kept asking. Mary brought a jug of cold water, sprinkled some on her face and made her drink a little. A muffled sound could be heard from the telephone. 'It was Golding.' Helen somehow managed to utter this. I almost collapsed. A cold shiver ran through my body, my teeth started chattering. But to my great surprise, Mrs Gillander did not lose her calm. She picked up the receiver and demanded, 'Hello, who is it? . . . What? John Golding?' She heaved a sigh of relief. 'Oh, it's you. Thank God.'

The mystery was explained as we helped Helen to the drawing room. John was Jack's younger brother. He was on his way to Glasgow. He had called to say that he would be stopping for a night at Leighton Hall. 'He just said "Golding speaking"', said Helen. 'It gave me such a fright.'

I left them with a polite good night, determined to get away from this haunted place as soon as possible, the very next day or the day after. I tried reading a book in bed, with all the lights on. But it was impossible to concentrate. 'Golding, Golding' resounded from all four walls. I shut the book and stared at the ceiling from where the wretched fellow had hung himself. I could almost visualize his still, lifeless body swaying in the breeze like a bough bro-

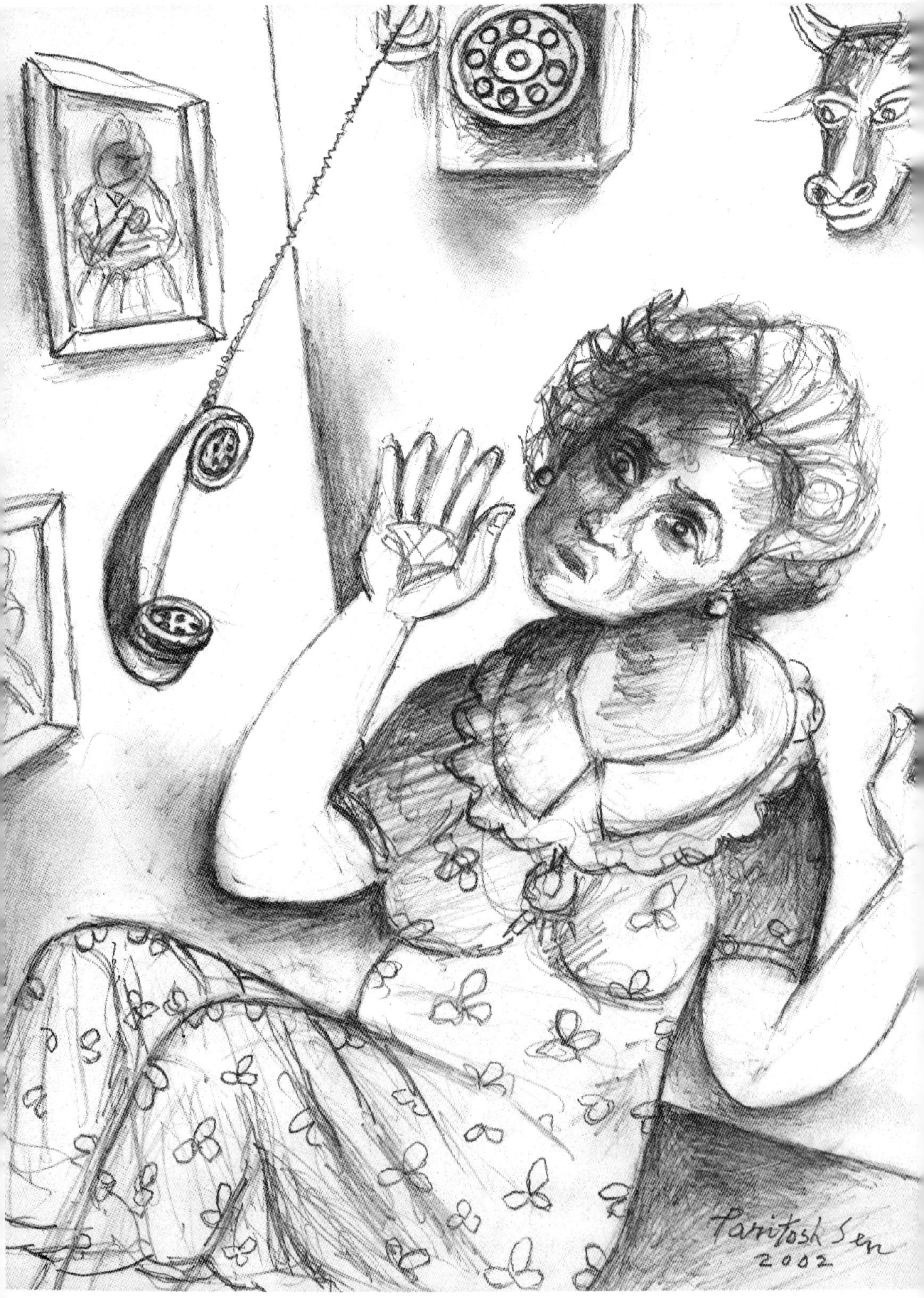
Paritosh Sen
2002

ken loose from a tree. How was I going to spend the night here? To make matters worse, I heard a rustling sound from near the fireplace. It was distinctly odd. I had been sleeping in the room for two weeks without any such distraction. The noise stopped, but started again. 'Let me barge into Helen's room', was the first thought that came to my mind. 'No, no, that would be ridiculous. I must not be unduly scared. Let me try to find out.' Tip-toeing towards the fireplace, I found that the the noise was coming from the waste basket near it. A rat sprang out; my heart almost stopped beating. I raced downstairs and stood in front of Helen's bedroom door. Should I wake her up? She had been through enough already, but I could not go back to my room. It would be much better to spend the rest of the night walking up and down the corridor. However, luck was against me that night. The bulging eyes of the stuffed heads on the walls seemed determined to scare me out of my wits. I ran to the drawing room and settled down on a sofa with a rug. This was certainly the last straw. 'I am not going to stay here for a single day more', I decided.

I cooked up an excuse the next morning and told Helen I wished to leave immediately. She was reluctant to let me go. Stay at least one more day, she persisted. I had no option but to oblige. Dinner that evening was memorable. Garlic soup with poached egge, lobster with fried mushrooms, roast lamb, salad and cheese pudding. The roast was particularly good. Slices of bacon had been inserted into the leg of the lamb before roast. It was then carved and served flambéd with brandy. There was an excellent sauce to go with it – a mix of red wine, tomato pureé, bone marrow, thyme and nutmeg.

It was the first of September, the official beginning of autumn. White and grey clouds flitted across a deep blue sky. The village wore a picturesque look with a play of sunlight and shade. I was ready to leave for London. As I packed my bags and came down, I found the entire family assembled at the front gate to bid me goodbye – Mary, Judith, Gilermina, Melba, Jeuletta, Isabella, Mrs Penelope Gillander. Even the dogs were there, staring at me. I shook hands and exchanged greetings and got into the station-wagon. The dogs began a peculiar, muffled cry. What were they trying to convey? I had no way of knowing. As the train pulled in at the station Helen kissed me warmly on both cheeks and shoved an envelope into my hand.

I opened it in the train. It contained fifty pounds and a short note: 'I hope you will find this useful. Look after yourself. Come back to Carnforth again. Love.'

It has been a long time now. Helen's body has returned to the dust. But our bond is still intact and will remain so even after I am gone. I was her one and only Indian friend. Why did she feel so drawn towards me? That will forever remain a mystery. There are some people who are born only to give, never taking anything in return. She was indeed a lone Catholic, in that sense.

It would be fitting to quote from the most popular poet of this region as my tribute to a wonderful friend:

The good die first
And they whose hearts are dry as summer dust burn to the socket.

Translated from the Bengali by Enakshi Chatterjee

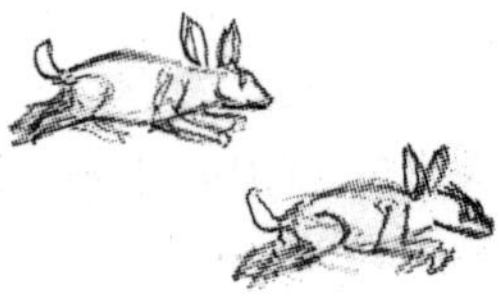

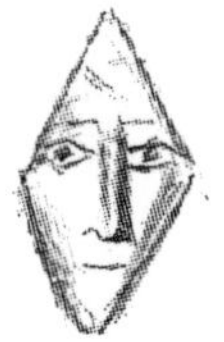

Face to face with Picasso

My first direct encounter with the modern European masters took place through some educated officers of the Allied Forces way back in the early 1940s. During the Second World War there was a sizeable military presence in Calcutta. These British and American officers had brought with them large colour prints of Van Gogh, Cezanne, Gauguin and others. We, members of the Calcutta Group of painters, developed a friendship with the officers and were thrilled to see these prints. In those days foreign books and periodicals on art were available in the city, to cater to the needs of these people. Pretty soon we came to know about the works of other masters like Picasso, Braque, Matisse, Paul Klee, Henry Moore and Brancusi, but the small prints we saw only whetted our appetite for the originals. It was not easy for us to satisfy our desire as most of us were hard-pressed for money. But if the will is strong enough there is bound to be a way. At last, I did set forth for the land of my heart's desire with just the ticket and a few hundred rupees in my pocket. With the gracious assistance of the Indian Embassy at Belgium I was able to hold an exhibition there and earn some money. Thus I arrived in Paris, my actual destination. It was early winter in 1950.

In Paris at that time the art firmament was aglow with all the major stars of the modern age. Painters like Matisse, Braque, Picasso, Roualt and Chagall, and sculptors like Brancusi, Henry Lawrence and Gabo showed at regular exhibitions attended by thousands. Despite the devastation of the World War Paris had once again become the Mecca of the art world. The art market too was picking up, thanks to American patronage. With about 400 art galleries and nearly 40,000 artists from all over the world, the city was a happening place in the true sense of the term. Several Indian artists, like Nirode Majumder, Raza, Akbar Padamsee, Ramkumar, Sankho Choudhury and I, lived there. Souza used to visit from London occasionally. Husain too came for a two-month stay. Among other visitors were some Bengali women artists – Kamala Roychoudhury, Haimanti Sen and Amina Ahmed Kar.

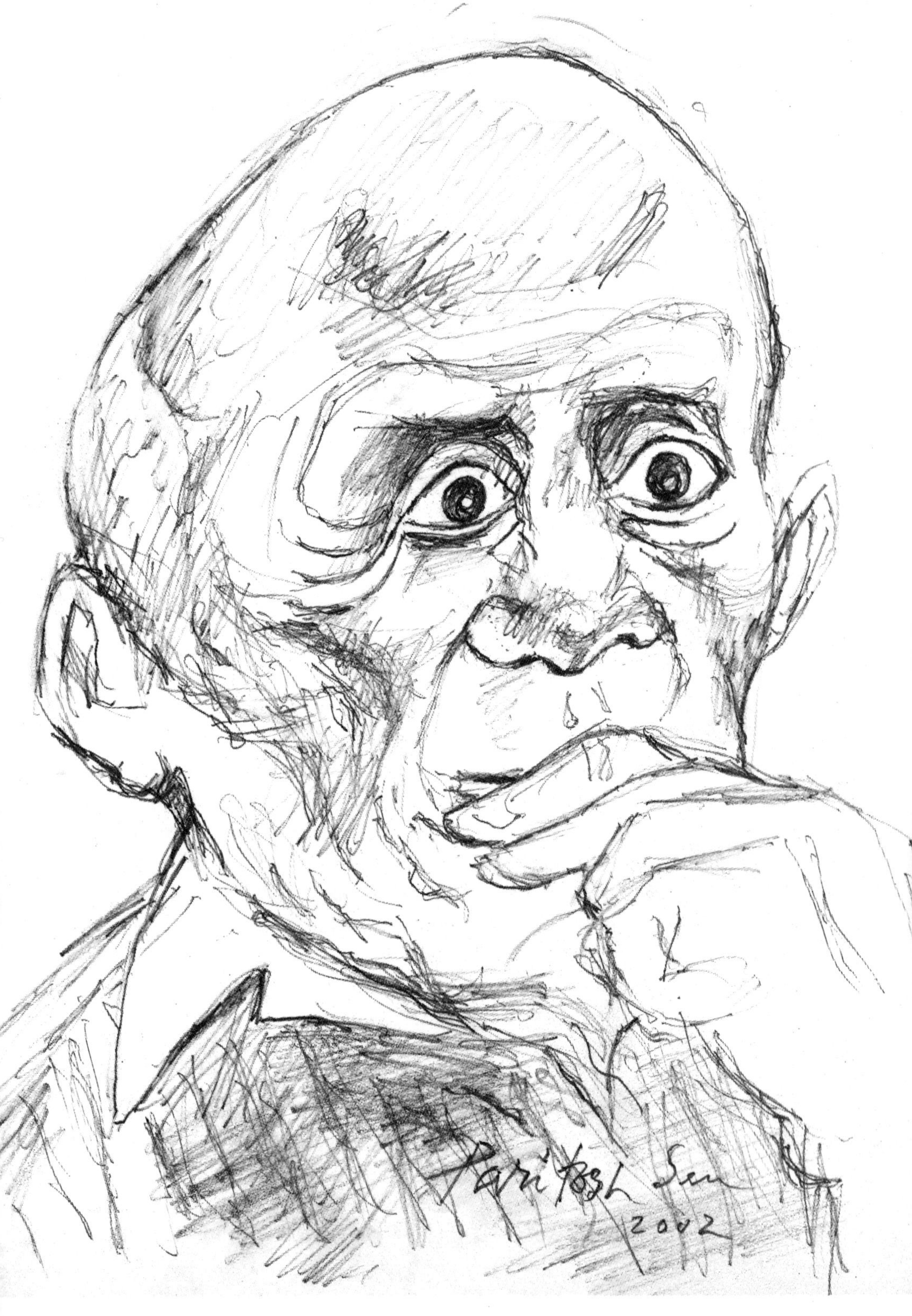
Paritosh Sen
2002

Except for Brancusi all the modern masters lived outside Paris and came to the city only occasionally in connection with their work. Nirode Majumder and his wife were very close to Brancusi. One morning they very kindly took Sankho Choudhury and me to Brancusi's studio at Montparnasse: an altogether unforgettable experience that I shall talk about later.

During the fifties, an annual international art exhibition called the 'Salon de Mai' used to be held in Paris on a very grand scale. I have no idea if it is still held. On 1 May 1953, armed with an invitation card, I arrived at the venue for the inauguration ceremony. As I entered I was captivated by an object of art placed right in front: a magnificent bronze sculpture by Picasso – a full-size figure of a pregnant she-goat standing on her legs. Its monumental quality, the absolute originality in skilfulness of composition, the show of strength, the use of discarded readymade stuff, the masterly control of form – all of these in combination have given it an important place in the history of sculpture. I will come back to this later.

After viewing the figure from all angles I proceeded to the front hall. The first thing to greet my eye was a crowd of people around someone I could not see initially. My curiosity prompted me to move forward, and then I saw him. This was a more stunning experience than the sculpture I have just described. At the centre of the crowd was none other than the great Picasso himself. A thrill of excitement raced through my veins. This was the fulfilment of a long-cherished desire, almost like the fulfilment of a pilgrimage. For me, Picasso is one of the three greatest figures in the world of art and literature, the other two being Rabindranath Tagore and Charlie Chaplin. And here he was, in flesh and blood, right in front of me. Silently, I paid my homage to the great artist.

The crowd consisted of painters and sculptors whose works were on display. They were taking Picasso around, each keen to show him his work. With polite words of compliments Picasso moved from one hall to the other. I joined the throng. As I was debating how to introduce myself, suddenly I found myself face to face with him. I lost no time and extended my right hand, saying I was an Indian painter. I also told him that I would like to show him my paintings. When and where could I meet him? He gave me the address of his studio in a very gentle voice, and asked me to come and meet him the day after the next at ten in the morning. Then he moved on.

In thirty-six hours I would have the good fortune of showing my work to Picasso! A wild surge of excitement ran through my being.

On the appointed day and hour I was in front of his studio at Rue de Grande Augustin. With me was Barin Saha, the film-maker, who was then studying film-making in Paris. We climbed the stairs and towards the studio. Some people were coming out and as we entered, and inside we found quite a few visitors already present. Worse still, we heard Picasso's secretary and childhood friend Sabartes, himself a Spanish poet, announcing to the assembly, 'Picasso will not be coming today. Please leave your name, address and telephone numbers. I will let you know in a couple of days time.' So it had been an empty promise, just a ruse to get rid of undesirable people. But refusing to be put off, I quickly planned a strategy in consultation with Barin. Pretending not to have heard Sabartes, we moved to the far end of the studio and got busy admiring Picasso's collection of grotesque African masks, some animal heads of unknown ritualistic significance, a figure contrived of wicker baskets covered partially with plaster, corrugated paper, board and all sorts of junk, and paintings by himself and other painters.

Picasso had a number of studio apartments in Paris, but this particular one was of special historic significance. This was where he used to work during the German occupation. The agony of those days is clearly reflected in his work of that period. Human and animal skulls, grotesque crabs and fishes, the distorted face of a crying woman, dead people flung in a dark corner – pictures like these bear witness to what he went through. He had scornfully refused the offer of an art-loving German officer to supply coal to this studio. Picasso had preferred the terrible cold to accepting charity from the enemy.

During the pre-war and post-war years, Picasso was deeply involved with many women, of whom two stood out – Marie Therese in the first phase and Francoise Gillot in the second. These two women influenced his art and also played an important part in the days he spent in this studio. The great writer Balzac too had lived in this studio, using it as a refuge to avoid his creditors. The studio has been associated with other famous names as well, like the actor Jean Louis Barraut, who used to rehearse here. Thoughts like these flitted through my mind as we waited.

After everybody else had left Sabartes peered at us over his glasses and was about to repeat what he had told the others, when he suddenly changed his mind. I told him that we were from India, more specifically from that part of India known as Bengal, and he immediately warmed to us. He said that he was the first writer to translate Tagore's poems into Spanish. (He had done this from Andre Gide's French translation.) He then expressed a desire to take a look at my paintings. He studied them intently and appeared to be impressed. 'Let me call Picasso. If he agrees I will take you to him right away', he said, as he picked up the phone.

After a long conversation in Spanish over the phone, Sabartes asked us to pick up the paintings and accompany him, not forgetting to warn me that the visit should not exceed fifteen minutes. After a short walk we climbed up to the master's apartment-cum-studio, on the second floor of 9 Rue Gay

Lussac. Picasso himself opened the door. Sabartes's stern warning to Barin to wait outside became meaningless.

We were introduced to Paloma and Claude, his two children by Francoise Gillot, who, like his other children, have figured in many of his canvases. Sitting on the floor, they were drawing something with coloured chalk.

The interior of the studio was almost bare except for a few old sofas, a couple of chairs and two freshly painted canvases on the wall. Picasso was dressed in gray gabardine trousers, a brown shirt, a blue tie and a light gray cardigan. I had heard and read a great deal about this person who combined many contradictory traits. He was said to be extremely gregarious, yet fond of seclusion. He was reputed to be both shy and arrogant. Known to have a shrewd business sense, he was equally generous with his money. Much has been written about his eyes, describing them in the following terms: 'precious black stones', 'eyes radiating fire', 'the pair of unblinking chestnut orbs that reached out to lasso everything around him'. But during the short time I spent with him that day his eyes exuded nothing but gentleness.

We had known him as the painter of Minotaure – one of the key personages in his work and with which he is often identified, his totem and his double; sometimes guilty, sometimes gratified, and at other times embodying the terror of the beast and the endearing weakness of man, pathetic, lovable and innocent of monstrosities. And we knew about his Odyssey – his voyage to the subterranean world from where he brought up so many symbols, of victims of desire, of cruel dreams. Was I really sitting here, before that master of the tragic? Didn't he also invest his oeuvre with a Rabelasian humour? And last but not the least, wasn't he the modern King Midas, turning everything he touched into gold?

With characteristic humour and perhaps from a desire to make us feel at home, he remarked that Barin Saha and I could easily pass off for Andalusians. Meanwhile I had unpacked my canvases and propped them against the wall. Picasso looked at them intently and remarked that they were well done and had beautiful colours. He was joined by Sabartes who had earlier warned us not to make our visit too long. Now that Picasso himself was showing interest in my work, Sabartes had to retract. He started saying something in Spanish when a young lady entered the studio, obviously in a hurry. She was none other than the artist's companion and mother of the two children, Francoise Gillot.

Her appearance confirmed what I had heard about her, that she was almost half a century younger than Picasso. She was darker than the average European, closer to a wheat complexion by Indian standards. A long, brick-coloured dress clung to her body; she wore a thick leather belt round her waist that accentuated her wonderful curves; and her hair has pulled back in a tight bun. Though she wore no make-up her eyebrows were certainly tampered with. I was familiar with her through many sketches and drawings and photographs. She struck me as a charming blend of beauty and sex appeal. Though a mother of two, she had retained her wonderful figure. By her own admission, she was instructed by Picasso to move around the house in the nude because that was when she looked her best and also because he wanted to study her form before putting it on canvas.

Of the many women in Picasso's life, Fernand Oliver Olga, Marie Therese, Dora Marr, Francoise Gillot and Jaqueline Roque were the most significant. He married only Olga and Jaqueline. His paintings reveal that Picasso showed singularly good taste in the selection of his companions. No wonder his friend and contemporary Braque had observed, 'In matters of women you are a perfect traditionalist.' Interestingly enough, contradictory qualities in women attracted Picasso. Marie Therese was chosen for her gentle nature, well-proportioned body and quality of total surrender. Dora, on the other hand, attracted him with her intelligence, independence, artistic sense and ability to argue knowledgeably about art.

There comes a time in the life of every woman when she resembles a perfectly ripe fruit, to use a common cliché, the peak of womanhood, so to say. Then a decline sets in. Francoise seemed poised at the right side of this dividing line. We were introduced to Picasso's companion of ten years. She whispered something to him and left as hurriedly as she had come, flashing her enchanting curves.

Since our stipulated fifteen minutes were over, I started packing my things. Picasso interrupted me. 'I am still looking at the pictures. Are you in a hurry? I am not.' He said gently. Picasso seemed quite relaxed but since Sabartes had been so tough, I began to wonder. Did he really have the time? Was he impressed by my work, or was he just being polite?

At this point the bell sounded. Sabartes opened the door. A middle-aged woman in black entered. She was greeted by Picasso with a warm embrace and kisses. We were introduced to her. She was Mme Paul Eluard, one of the most well-known poets of France, a leader of the Communist Party and a good friend of Picasso. We knew that Eluard had passed away recently. She was Eluard's second wife. The first wife, Nusch, had been used time and again by Picasso as a model for his drawings and watercolours and oils. She had a fragile beauty and vulnerability that attracted artists and other intellectuals of the city. Though not a voluptuous beauty, she had very strong sex appeal which posed a kind of challenge to men.

Sabartes came up and asked me to pack up. I was about to do so when Picasso interrupted me again to say, 'Please leave them alone. Wait till I ask you to take them away.' He then turned back to Mme Eluard and resumed conversation.

The bell rang again. The visitor this time was a young woman with a crown of golden hair. After the usual French greeting Picasso introduced her as his daughter Maya, one of his favourites. Maya was the daughter of Marie Therese. As I watched her profile I detected a striking similarity with the facial features of her famous father, only the eyes were different. They were bright with youthful fervour rather than the keen and penetrating look of the father. 'You know, you are the first Indians I have met', she said, adding that recently she had seen an Indian movie and been impressed by the beauty and colourful clothes of Indian women. The picture was *Aan*, featuring Dilip Kumar, Nadira and Nimmi, and directed by Mehboob. What kind of impression could she have formed from this *masaala* film of Bombay, we wondered. Incidentally, this was the first Indian film dubbed in French to have a commercial release. I had had something to do with the French rendering of the dialogues. 'I wish I could visit your country', said the young girl, 'a land of such an old civilization.' She was interrupted by her half-brother and sister who dragged her inside.

My attention was drawn towards three small canvases on the wall, all obviously recently done because they still smelt of oils. Though not in the realistic mode, I could make out the features of Francoise. The artist had broken the form; then, keeping the main characteristics intact, redrawn them using his insight. No other artist has this unique ability for formal reconstruction. Picasso has drawn thousands of faces, but no two nostrils or eyes are alike. This kind of inventive power is rare in the history of art. By reconstructing the visual world with the help of original thinking, he brought about a sea-change in the concept of art, influencing other art forms in the process. Although moving towards the abstract, he never believed in total formlessness.

His genius had begun to manifest itself from his early teens. His father, who was a professor of art, was amazed at the talent of his son and admitted that he did not have anything more to teach him. I remember the astonishment I had felt at seeing a work painted by him when he was just seventeen. This was at the Picasso Museum at Barcelona. The eight by six foot painting was rendered in a classical, realistic style, and showed the artist's mother on her death-bed, his father by her side, feeling her pulse with one hand and looking at his wristwatch on the other. A young nurse holding a lovely, angel-like baby stood on the other side of the bed. At very first sight the viewer is impressed by the mastery of the brush strokes, the use of colour, the composition; it has all the imprints of a great master. I do not know if any other European artist, from Leonardo, Raphael and Michaelangelo to El Greco and Rembrandt has shown such mastery at such a young age.

In this connection, let me relate an incident that was narrated by the famous artist Fermand Leger at a reception held to celebrate Picasso's seventieth birthday. The two of them, according to Leger, were visiting a collection of Rembrandt in Holland. The next morning Leger was astonished to find that Picasso had reproduced one of the Rembrandt paintings they had seen the day before. It was an exact copy. Nothing is impossible for a genius, Leger concluded.

My stream of thoughts was interrupted by Mme Eluard, who was leaving. Picasso turned to me again. 'Sabartes was full of praise for you on the phone. I agree with him.' He said. This was beyond my expectations. 'I have come here to listen to your criticism. I would consider myself highly obliged if you could kindly point out the flaws in my work', I mumbled. Picasso smiled. 'I would say you are moving in the right direction', he said. 'I like your excellent use of mixed colours and considerable skill in composition. You must always pay attention to form.' Then he went on to make a suggestion. 'Have you had an exhibition in Paris? If not, I can ask any gallery to hold one.' Without realizing the implications of this offer I said something very foolish for which I have felt sorry ever since.

What I told him was the truth, that I had decided to go home and that the tickets had been bought already. For some time I had been noticing a monotony in my work. There was nothing new to learn here. Perhaps the atmosphere, the colours, the smells and the people of my country would inspire me and lead me to newer paths.

How I wish I had not told him the truth! I could have said instead, 'I cannot think of anything better. It would be my greatest good fortune to have an exhibition sponsored by you.' To think where my luck could have taken me! With Picasso's support my destiny would certainly have been different. The next thing he said was even more unexpected. 'I have seen your pictures. Now let me show you mine.' I was so overwhelmed that for a moment I wondered if I had heard him right. The most celebrated artist of the present time, one of the creators of modern culture, inviting an insignificant Indian painter to take a look at his work! Such modesty is the sign of a truly great man.

There are many stories about Picasso's modesty. Once a well-known abstract artist from England met him outside a café. 'I am Victor Pasmore, a painter', he introduced himself. 'So am I', said Picasso, shaking his hand.

Time was standing still for me. But it was almost twelve noon. Picasso's secretary was anxiously glancing at his wristwatch. Finding Picasso determined to spend more time with us, he finally decided to withdraw from the scene. Picasso led us to his studio downstairs. From the look of it the room seemed like a temporary studio. Actually the artist spent most of his time in his chateau in the south of France and came to Paris very rarely.

A couple of sculptures on pedestals greeted us. They were owls. I had seen photographs of these before. Some of his recent still-life paintings were on the wall. Books on painting stood on shelves and lay scattered on the floor. Apart from the painting paraphernalia there were only some ordinary chairs.

In his long career Picasso had also tried his hand at sculpture, using different mediums like scrap iron, bits of wood, dried tree branches, broken porcelain cups, in fact all sorts of waste material. Nobody was allowed to throw away such junk. They were preserved, waiting to be brought alive by the magic touch of the master.

To illustrate my point, let me give an example: take the full figure of the goat I mentioned earlier. In his residence in southern France Picasso had many pets including a goat. The form of a pregnant goat fascinated him so much that he went about collecting materials to give his idea concrete shape. He began by making a plaster of paris structure and let it stand on four dry branches. This not only created the illusion of a four-footed animal but gave an idea of the mass apart from serving the purpose of carrying the weight. Then a broom with a handle was stuck between the front legs to indicate the neck. The brush was tied with a piece of cloth and then covered with plaster of paris. Next, the dried branch of a date-palm was given appropriate shape and attached to the head so that the semblance to a goat's head was complete. The bulging stomach was created with the help of a basket and drum. Part of the basket was kept exposed to give an impression of ribs. The smooth branch of a date-palm put between the head and the tail served as the spine. Two planks were used for hip bones. Thus, with pieces of wood and dried branches he effectively created the impression of the bone structure. Two porcelain milk jugs were used in the place of tits. The ears were made of cardboard and the horns with a curved grape branch. The enlarged vagina was not forgotten either. He folded the lid of a can to do this. All this was done keeping in mind the principles of modelling and using plaster of paris throughout.

Such bold technical experiments mark Picasso out as a creative explorer of the highest degree. Usually his subjects were determined by the material available. By scanning the trash piled up in the garbage bin he would decide on the forms to be created. A discarded porcelain flower vase would be placed on a pedestal, a few paintbrush handles would be stuck on it, a couple of inverted butter dishes on the top, and the whole thing looked like two flowers in bloom. A clothes-pin placed on the third stem resembled a bud. A few more touches here and there and you had a bouquet of flowers and leaves – a very common subject but an unconventional and bold experiment in sculpture. Many of Picasso's post-cubist sculptures were done in this manner and later cast in bronze or other metals. They can be seen in museums around the world.

Looking at the owl sculptures before me, I felt that they too had been first given shape with various scrap materials before gaining their final shape in bronze. One of the owls had black and white patches. In fact painting sculptures is a distinct feature of Picasso's art. He used different colours on all his sculptures done in the cubist period. In the guitar and violin series done with the help of cardboard, paper, thread, rope, cloth, corrugated board, light iron sheets and so on, he successfully reduced the distance between two-dimensional painting and three-dimensional sculpture. These original creations are regarded as among his best achievements.

In ceramics too he made splendid use of colours such as brown, red, black and saffron. Here too he was unique, though following the classical method. Except for a few like Alexander Calder, no other sculptor had used colour. As Picasso was both a painter and a sculptor, the use of colour in sculptures must have come naturally to him. But he was against using colour unnecessarily.

A middle-aged lady appeared at the door to announce that lunch was ready. Picasso simply nodded and then turned to the paintings on the wall. They were all still-life studies of a bottle on a table with some cherries. In some there was a knife next to the fruit bowl. All his life Picasso had made countless still-life studies of ordinary kitchen paraphernalia – water jug, a loaf of bread, fruits, coffee pot, candle-stand, traditional table lamp, pots and pans, fishes, sea urchins, crabs, bright red lobsters, dressed chicken or duck, even a cat attracted by fish. Nothing, not even the most trivial thing, was overlooked by him. Every time he presented them from a different angle and never repeated his earlier studies. He has presented a guitar in so many different ways. To quote him, 'There is no absolute truth.' One is reminded of the film *Rashomon* by Kurosawa where a single incident is described by four witnesses in four different ways, each claiming his version to be the most faithful.

All the still-life studies on the wall were remarkable for their use of just three colours: white, black and a mixture of the two. Such excellent use of these three colours was indeed rare in European painting, although mention should be made of George Braque who used to combine white, black and grey with brown. Talking of black, it might be relevant here to mention a remark of Matisse: 'We have discovered the use of black as colour only recently. Artists of the Orient had discovered it a thousand years ago.' Clearly, what he had in mind were the black ink scrolls drawn by the Chinese and the Japanese.

Picasso picked up a book and showed it to us. The open page had a photograph of a bull fight. 'Have you ever been to Spain? Ever watched a bull fight?' Without waiting for an answer he went on. 'If you have not, do go and watch the full-length documentary they are showing in one of the cinema halls of the city. You will like it. The dry climate with a clear sky and fresh air has brought about a warmth and passion in the people which has found expression in their bull fight, flamenco dance, in art and literature.' We could not agree more. Cervantes, the author of *Don Quixote*, Goya, the creator of the *Inquisition* series, and last but not the least, Picasso, the creator of *Guernica*, were all children of the Spanish soil. Which other country could have produced such sons? The Spanish creative mind is easily swayed by agony, violence and cruelty. Its response is always emotional, reason is secondary. In Spanish dancing the theme of frustration in love has been taken to the greatest artistic height.

It was almost one o'clock in the afternoon, but Picasso still showed no desire to bring this meeting to an end. Needless to say, we were ecstatic and wanted to make the most of the opportunity.

Another book lying on the table with Matisse's name inscribed on it prompted me to ask if they were in touch. Picasso replied, 'Yes, I and Francoise visit him often. He is confined to his bed but he carries on his work nevertheless. He sketches, paints, and with the help of assistants, cuts coloured paper to make collages. As enthusiastic as ever.' I had noticed among the still-life paintings hanging on he wall, one by Matisse. They used to exchange paintings, so I had heard. I asked Picasso if that was actually the case. 'Oh yes,' he said, 'we have exchanged eight so far. But you know he is stingy. The ones he has given me are smaller in size than the ones I gave him.' He turned the pages of the book to point to some works of Matisse, admiring the originality in the harmonious use of colour. Those pictures were painted between 1910 and 1920. This was considered his best period and the most spectacular for combining the essence of cubism with the two-dimensional quality of the East, for the importance given to lines, calligraphy, ornamentation, abstraction of form, for the remarkable use of pure colours, specially black. Picasso lit a cigarette, his thoughts going back to earlier days. 'You know, we were great rivals in our younger days and never met socially. But all that has changed now. Why, only the other day he said to me that we should meet more often because there are things we cannot discuss with a third person. And pretty soon one of us will be dead.'

To quote Matisse: 'What I dream of is an art of balance, of purity and serenity devoid of troubling or depressing subject matter, an art which might be for every mental worker, be he businessman or writer, like an appeasing influence, like a mental soother, something like a good armchair in which to rest from physical fatigue.' In this he stands in direct contrast to Picasso who, by means of violent distortion, wished to shock, not soothe the viewer. As he has said, 'the possibility of recognizing nature, which is after all a kind of struggle between my interior life and the external world as it exists for most people. As I have often said, I don't want to try to express nature, rather, as the

Chinese put it, to work like nature. And I want that internal surge – my creative dynamism – to propose itself to the viewer in the form of traditional painting violated.'

I then ventured to ask him about his relation with Braque, who had been very close to him in his cubist period. 'He lives in Normandy now and you live in the south of France. Do you meet?' 'Well, no, only when both of us happen to be in Paris at the same time.' I asked him about his impressions of Braque's latest exhibition in Gallery Maeght, the theme of which was 'The Bird and its Nest'. Picasso said he had not seen it but he had formed a good idea from the catalogue. He praised the artist's control over emotion and his judicious use of a few colours – black, white, blue, brown, ochre – and their mixture. I had seen the exhibition. It seemed to me that the bird was a symbol of Braque's own soul. The bird coming back to its nest was the soul finding its destination. When I told Picasso this he admitted the truth of my observation, adding that it was highly successful aesthetically. After a pause he added, 'You know, I have exchanged paintings with him too at one time. I have some of his excellent still-life studies in my collection.' Finding the great master so communicative, I made bold to ask another question that was uppermost in my mind. 'In many of your paintings you have broken the form to take it very close to near-total abstraction. But you have not gone into complete abstraction. May I ask why?' 'There is nothing called abstract art', he said emphatically. 'There can be no art without figure. That is my firm conviction.'

This reminded me of some of his statements in response to critics: 'There is no abstract art. You must always start with something. Afterwards you can remove all traces of reality. . . . One cannot go against nature. . . . We may allow ourselves certain liberties but only in details.' Elsewhere he has said, 'Nor is there any figurative and non-figurative art. Everything appears to us in the guise of a figure. Even in metaphysics ideas are expressed by means of symbolic figures. . . . See how ridiculous it is then to think of painting without figuration.' This is what he sincerely believed to his last day.

About the source of his astounding variety in concept and style, he had this to say: 'One should not mistake my different styles as an evolution or a search for some ideal. Whenever I found something that called for expression I painted it without any consideration for past or future. Different subjects demand different treatment. I accept it wholeheartedly without going for trial or experiment.' Was his art an open book, the various moods indicating his mental states at different times in his life so that, for his fans, his life and art became one? To this his reply was: 'I do my sketches and paintings much in the same way as people write their biography. They are like pages of my diary, complete or incomplete. And meaningful. Only the future can decide which of these are to be preserved, it is not for me to make a selection. . . . Whatever I

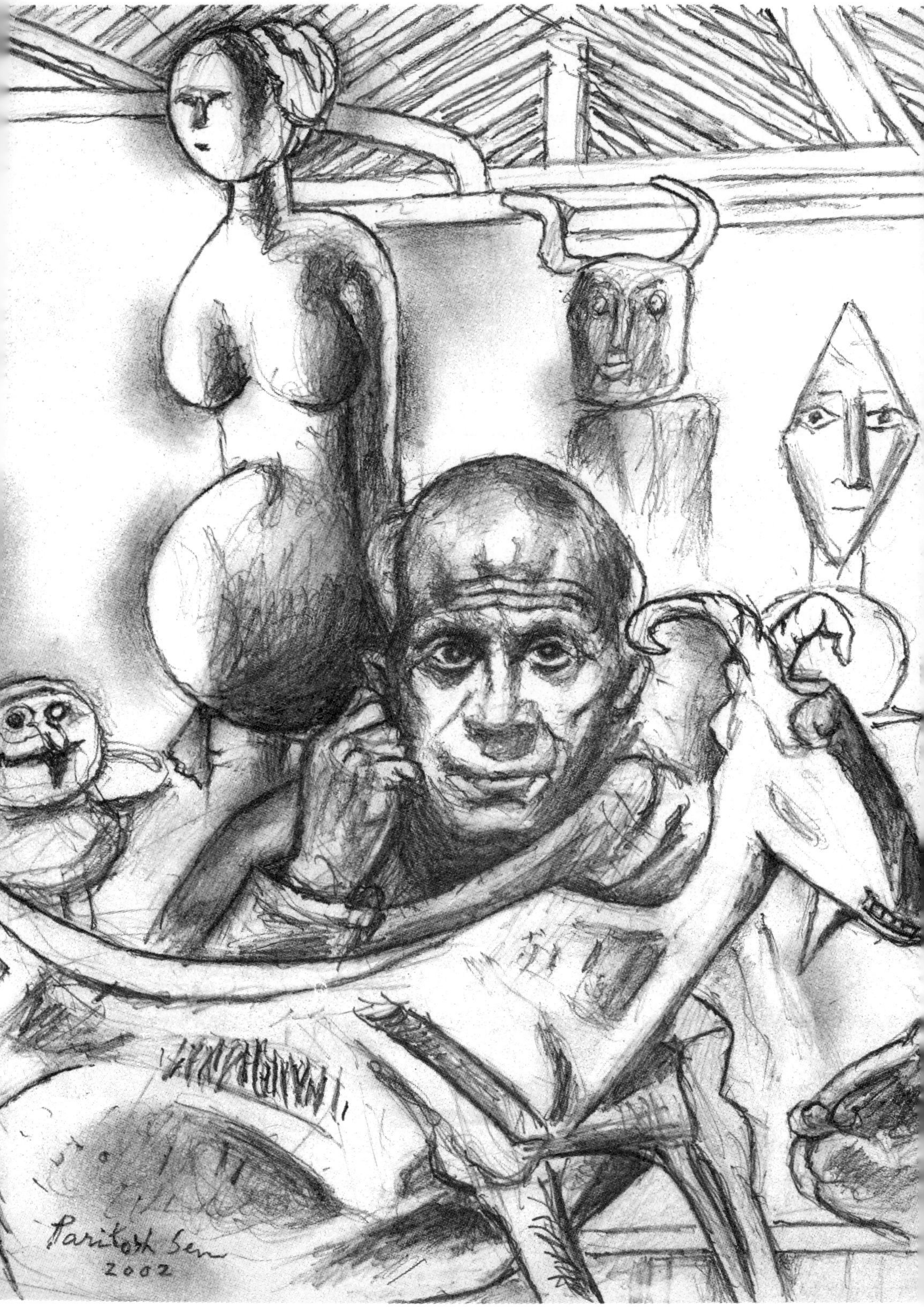
Paritosh Sen
2002

create is an expression of my inner self, yet contact and communication with the outside world is also very important for me. That is why every morning I keep some time separate for meeting people. When it comes to my notice that my secretary has driven away visitors I feel deprived and hurt. Perhaps I have lost something I should have learnt from them. You see I am not like Braque. He loves solitude, he gets his inspiration from within himself. Not that they always have something to give but they satisfy my inquisitiveness and only they can do it.'

Encouraged by his plainspeaking and his indulgence towards me I posed more questions. 'I have heard that you never take respite from work, even in times of great personal conflict. Secondly, you have changed your medium often. You have given respectability to such lowbrow mediums as linocut. What has prompted you to do this?' 'I believe in renewal', he said. 'When I come back to painting after working in a different medium, it gives my work a new lease of life. I look at things in a different way. The most crucial problem in linocut was how to get prints of different colours from the same plate. I encountered such technical problems while doing etchings or lithographs. I told the technicians, it is your problem, not mine. I will tell you what I want and leave the rest to you.' However difficult the task the technicians did it to the satisfaction of the artist. In bronze-casting, particularly in dealing with *The Flower Vase, The Pregnant Goat* or *The Skipping Girl*, an expert caster like Valsuani had initially thrown up his hands in despair, saying he couldn't do it. Valsuani was the best known caster in Europe, much sought after by all sculptors of repute. Our friend, the sculptor Provash Sen, had also been an apprentice to this renowned caster. Somehow Picasso persuaded him to take up the job. This is how, faced with stiff challenges, technicians have been able to devise new ways of printing and casting. In fact, technicians are no less creative than artists.

I reminded Picasso of the reception for Charlie Chaplin when he had come to Paris for the release of *Limelight*. Picasso had been present on the stage. He had embraced Chaplin and kissed him warmly on the cheeks to the thunderous applause of the spectators. 'How did you like *Limelight*?' I asked him. 'A little disappointed', he replied. 'The earlier Chaplin was absent in this film. To me he is a great mime actor and is able to communicate without words. To use language, description or analysis seems totally irrelevant. Besides, I do not see eye to eye with him about the sentiments expressed in the film. A woman I love, however young she may be, will walk away with another lover and I will be a mute spectator – well, I am not ready to take that. Anyway he did what he considered good, why should I complain?' In spite of Picasso's opinion *Limelight* ran to packed houses in Paris.

The middle-aged housekeeper appeared at the door again. Picasso finally stood up. By then I was completely overwhelmed by the attention paid to an insignificant artist like me, especially by someone who valued time. 'Time. That's the thing. When it is gone, it's gone for ever. No argument. Like a taxi metre ticking over.' These were his own words. Only a truly noble person can be capable of such generosity, such magnanimity. It was difficult to believe that this was the same Picasso about whom the most commonly used adjectives are 'arrogant and aloof'. He has been called 'richer than the Bank of France'. Such a man could justifiably act in a boastful manner but surprisingly I found him to be extremely simple and modest. Not for a moment did he make me feel that I was face to face with the creator of the greatest painting of the twentieth century, *Guernica*. He did not show the slightest trace of the stubbornness of the man who had refused to leave German-occupied Paris; who, unlike his colleagues, had refused all help from the Germans; and who had not set foot in his beloved country Spain as long as it was under fascist Franco.

I had heard such contradictory reports about him – that he loved company as well as solitude, that he was proud as well as modest, that he had a shrewd business sense but was very liberal as far as money was concerned, that he was cruel yet affectionate. In her book *Life with Picasso*, Francoise Gillot gives some examples of his cruelty which I find difficult to believe. Apparently Picasso had pressed the lighted end of a cigarette on her cheek just to teach her a lesson. But she also relates instances of his kindness to animals – how he used to feed pigeons and caress the owl living in the attic. He always had time for children, to play with them, to find ways to entertain them. He has said, '*Es una cosa muy rara*', meaning this is a very rare thing. What a wonderful response to the fundamental question of what is the purpose of life. The desire to be at one with birds and beasts, worms and insects, people, in fact with all of creation, is evident in his life and work. The same person who created the paintings and etchings of the Blue and Pink periods, expressing sadness and solitude in the early phase, also presented us with paintings such as *Guernica, War and Peace*, *War in Korea, The Charnel House* and so on. Vengeance, hatred, violence, injustice find expression on his canvases alongside unforgettable documents of the struggles of peace-loving people. Such juxtaposition is indeed rare. He does not have any message, only an aesthetic statement. His *Women Before the Mirror, The Three Musicians*, the sculptures and paintings of the cubist period, all mark him as an artist forging new paths, a path-finder and a guru.

Having packed our canvases we were heading to the door when Picasso did something quite unexpected. There was a full-size convex mirror by the door. He placed his hands on his waist and started making funny faces at it. Bursting into chuckles, he kept at his antics. 'Look, how funny it looks', he said as he doubled up with laughter. Naturally, being convex, the mirror was throwing up distorted reflections. Picasso was almost unrecognizable. He was as delighted as a child with a new toy. I wondered to what extent this mirror was responsible for the distortions of form in Picasso's art. Why was the mirror there? What purpose did it serve? I was left wondering.

One of Picasso's biographers has mentioned that he was in the habit of drawing lines on his face while shaving till he resembled a clown. He even made teardrops under his eyes. His sympathy for clowns and circus people is quite evident in his paintings of the Pink and Blue periods. They point to his intense desire to identify himself with them in some way.

All of a sudden Picasso stopped his antics and pushed poor, unsuspecting Barin in front of the mirror. The mirror showed amusing distortions, to the utter delight of Picasso. He kept urging Barin to adopt different postures and rolled with laughter. This hidden child inside the great master was a revelation. What a complex and mysterious person! The ardent worshipper of art, the solitary genius, the earnest and serious man whom I had cherished for so long, now showed a completely different side to his personality. This Picasso was at the same level as common people like us. But the moment he enters his studio he is possessed by a demonic power and works till midnight.

The volume of work produced by him is staggering. Just to give an idea of his output, he made 347 etchings between 16 March and 5 October 1968, just before entering his ninetieth year. Between January 1969 and January 1970, he made 167 paintings; 194 drawings between December 1968 and January 1971; 156 etchings from January 1970 to March 1972; 172 drawings from November 1971 to October 1972; 201 paintings from September 1970 to June 1972 – altogether 503 etchings, 368 oil paintings and 362 drawings. He kept up this pace of work till his last day. This is not counting the work not shown outside. (These figures have been collected from a catalogue.) If this was the list of his work at the age of ninety, one can only imagine what the list of his younger days would be like. Enough to put many younger artists to shame.

After a round of warm handshakes we bid farewell and came out on to the street. Outside, the bright summer sunshine danced on the branches of the roadside chestnut trees. The busy traffic flowed past us. We were too overwhelmed to speak. Barin, realizing my state of mind, did not make any attempt to start a conversation. Not in my wildest imagination had I ever imagined that a personality like Picasso, so sought after and who happened to be the presiding star in my heart of hearts, would spend so much of his valuable time with a total stranger like me! What had he got in return? Perhaps it was futile to look for an answer.

The experience was all the more memorable because the situation in our country is so very different. Constantly floating in a sea of mediocrity, we hardly ever come across real greatness. Here, conceit is taken to be a sign of greatness, and most people get a sense of false security under a shelter of pride and conceit. Alas, these people do not have the word modesty in their dictionary.

I consider myself singularly fortunate to have come face to face with real greatness. It is an experience that has enriched my life. In the extended university of life, bits and pieces of experience add up to build up one's philosophy of life. Along with this most valuable experience I am left with an equally staggering remorse: why did I refuse Picasso's offer of holding an exhibition for me in Paris? That opportunity is gone for ever.

Translated from the Bengali by Enakshi Chatterjee

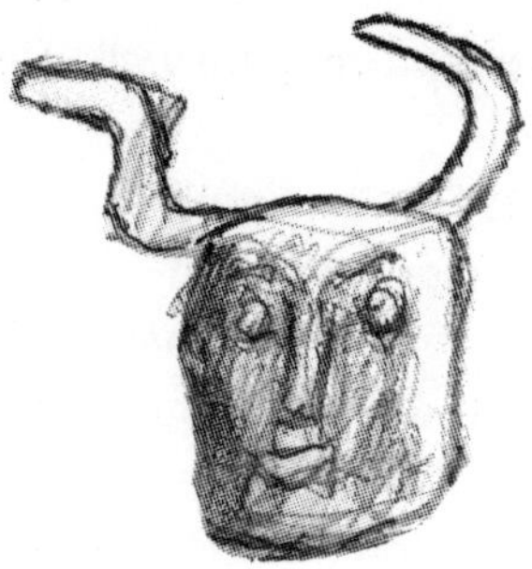

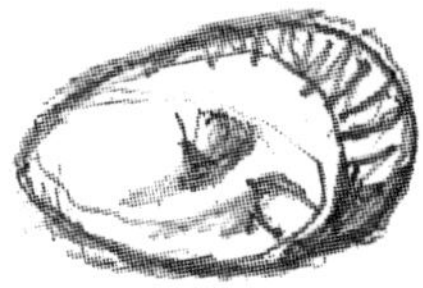

In the studio of Brancusi

It was a Sunday morning. Nirode Majumder called to say that Brancusi had been kind enough to give us some time in his studio. By us, I mean Sankho Choudhury and me. Both Nirode Majumder and his wife-to-be Marguerite knew this master of modern sculpture quite well. We had appealed to them for an appointment with Brancusi.

It was the winter of 1950. On a cold, foggy and windy day in Paris, we arrived at the studio near Impasse Ronsin, at one end of Montparnasse, in our overcoats. The Majumders were already there. Nirode rang the bell as we waited with apprehension for the door to open. Presently, a bearded old man stuck out his head from a slim opening of the door. He greeted the Majumders with *a Bon Jour* but added, 'I am sorry, there is no coal, so the studio could not be heated. Please come tomorrow. By then the coal will arrive and the studio will be warm.' Nirode protested mildly, 'If you can bear the cold inside the studio it will not be a problem for us.' But Brancusi could not be persuaded. 'You are my guests', he said, with a polite smile. 'I cannot treat you in this way. I will be very happy if you come back tomorrow.' He sounded quite firm. We had to admit that his logic was valid. So we turned back, disappointed.

The next day we were received with warm handshakes and a hearty *Bon Jour*. The pressure of his greeting impelled me to have a good look at his hands. I was struck by his large wrists and palms, like those of a farmer. Only such hands could chisel large chunks of marble.

The spacious studio had a glass-covered, high ceiling. Studios like these were specially built for artists and sculptors by the Corporation of Paris and let out at very low rents. Such concern for artists was possible only in France. Sunlight streamed through the glass ceiling to bring ample light to the walls and the objects kept in the studio. The illumination, the sculpted figures and the atmosphere combined to make it an ideal place for work and meditation. A good part of the atmosphere seemed to be due to the simple, unpretentious and quiet inmate of the studio.

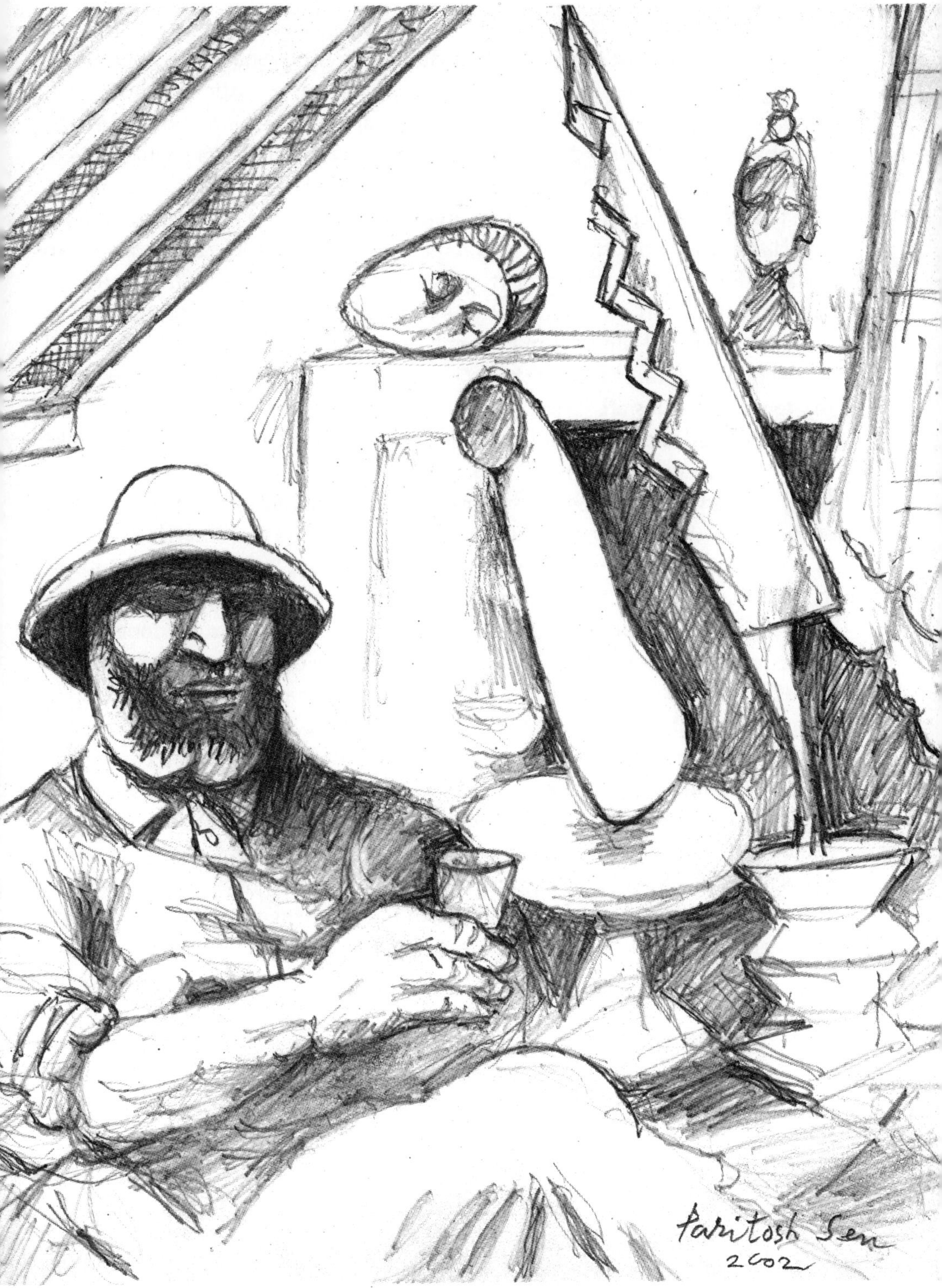
Paritosh Sen
2002

The man we had gone to meet was a celebrity in the art world, although at first sight he was unimpressive with his ordinary dress and unassuming ways. He was not very talkative. There was a rustic air about him. Despite having lived for many years in the capital of fashion and culture, he was absolutely untouched by the artificiality of urban life or its sophistication. It was not that he was unacquainted with the high society of Paris. The impression I had formed of him from photographs was confirmed when I saw him. He was clad in well-worn trousers, a sweater, coat and a worker's cap, and wore an uncared-for growth of beard. His eyes were small and sharp but friendly. A rolled cigarette was snuffed out after a few puffs. The more I watched him the more he reminded me of a man deeply involved in his work, oblivious of all else. All his sculptures around the studio silently declared that for him nothing mattered except his art. These silent figures were his constant companions, he communicated with them all the time. He was withdrawn by nature and spoke to us only when spoken to.

I had seen photographs of many of the sculptures in books. My first encounter with Brancusi originals was in Indore, where I had stayed from 1940 to 1949 as a teacher. I was amazed to find the famous *Bird* series of sculptures in the art collection of the then maharaja, Yashwantrao Holkar. The presence in the Paris studio of some sculptures from the same series, though done differently, prompted me to ask him, 'Where did you meet the maharaja?' He replied, 'I do not remember. I think an American patron introduced us. He bought three of the *Bird* series and asked me to come to Indore to plan a Temple of Deliverance for him.' This struck me as quite incredible. During my long stay in Indore I had formed a different impression of the maharaja. He had seemed to be pleasure-loving, weak-willed and eccentric. That such a person could have planned to build a temple seemed as impossible as an atheist doing so. His art collection did not inspire respect. He had bought many paintings of Nicholas Roerich, paying more than a lakh for each. Then there were portraits of himself drawn by high-society foreign artists who specialize in doing portraits of the rich. What made him buy Brancusi's *Bird* series, I wondered. Had he realized their artistic worth or was he swayed by the artist's name? During my visits to the palace I had never come across any good miniatures or classic bronze or stone figures. Nor was there any good work by contemporary Indian painters. Many wealthy collectors like Raja Ramaswamy Mudaliar of Madras, Narielwala of Bombay, N.C. Mehta of Gujarat, A.C. Laha and the Kanoria family of Calcutta were interested in buying classical and contemporary Indian art in those days.

'I did go to Indore, accepting the invitation of the maharaja', said Brancusi. 'But by that time he had changed his mind. I was disappointed, but that evaporated when I made a trip to the temples of Ellora. That was an unforgettable experience.'

I noticed that he used short sentences which, though unemotional, were loaded with meaning. We went around the studio, examining each and every work from all angles. Some of them were placed on steel or flexiglass motorized pedestals that rotated very slowly. Quite a few shone like glass although made of stone or metal. The metal statues particularly had such mirror-like polish that the reflections were astonishing. The amount of labour and patient handiwork they must have involved made us gape in wonder. We had heard of the dozens of assistants Rodin used to have, to help in chiselling and in other ways. But Brancusi, in spite of his celebrity status, was not in a position to afford assistants. All the hard labour was mostly done by him.

Most of the work was figurative though some of them could have been mistaken as non-figurative. What Brancusi tried to do was to get at the essence of the subject, leaving out the outer form. He did not care for details, as can be seen from the *Birds* series. They were done in different mediums, like bronze, aluminium, brass and stone, with each surface polished to perfection. In each his aim was to present what lies beyond the visual image of a bird. The element inevitably associated with the bird is space. The bird can fly in space with freedom. Its most important features are its wings, which help it to soar. Brancusi's bird creations do not have wings or beaks or eyes or legs. They have, instead, a dynamic sense of mobility, the speed expressed with such economy, using maximum simplification and mathematical precision, that at first sight these sculptures give the impression of being abstract. A strong conviction operates behind this simplification. According to one critic, the 'simplification intensifies the image'. But we have another explanation from the artist himself. 'Simplicity is not a goal in art, but one reaches it despite oneself by getting closer to the real meaning of things. . . . My ambition is to capture the eternal and invisible essence of phenomena, the essential idea rather than the mere appearance.' That is why what we see in his *Bird* series is a presentation of the idea and not the physical form of the bird. There are other sculptures like *The Fish*, *The Rooster*, *Leda*, *Flying Tortoise* and *White Negress* which are similar expressions of an idea.

I think something else needs to be told here: that there exists a twilight zone between figuration and non-figuration. It is only natural that the denizens of this domain will have a semi-abstract appearance. This and many other thoughts crowded my mind as I examined Brancusi's sculptures. It was important to keep these in mind if one wanted to step into the world of his imagination.

At the beginning of his career Brancusi was influenced by various artists. Rodin was the foremost among them. This French master was then a world figure. Brancusi worked for a short period as an apprentice in his studio. He had great respect for Rodin, but other influences were pulling him in different directions, towards the primitive sculpture of many countries, for instance. Truly creative artists are often forced to grope their way through various alleyways before they find their goal. Brancusi, an exceptional genius, was no exception. The same was true for Gauguin, Picasso, Modigliani, the German expressionists and many others. All of them were influenced in one way or the other by Polynesian, Melanesian or Oceanic sculpture. But a true genius has a way of integrating influences and forging an individual style so that the outside elements do not stand out. This kind of give and take has been going on in art for ages.

I believe that Brancusi too was influenced by the art of another country, mention of which is not found in any of the writings on him. I am talking of the sculpture of the Cyclades Islands, part of Myceny. Cyclade art uses the simplification, precision and geometric solution of form found in Brancusi, for which reason it is considered to be very close to modern sculpture. Talking of precision and economy, one is also reminded of Mondrian and the minimalists of a later age. Though their expressions differ, the philosophy is the same.

Brancusi's simplification or semi-abstraction once landed him in a great deal of trouble. The incident may be known to a few, but I think it bears recounting here. Once he sent one of his versions of *The Bird* to an exhibition in New York. The customs authorities there refused to consider it as an art exhibit. They declared it an industrial product as it was made in metal and bore no resemblance to a bird. Brancusi protested against this unfair declaration and sued the customs authorities. The case dragged on for quite some time. Many experts on art came forward to plead in favour of Brancusi and for the right of the artist to self-expression. The judgement went in favour of Brancusi. Needless to say, this judgement is considered a landmark in the history of art.

It is difficult to recognize art from non-art in this age when a virtual free-for-all seems to be the rule. It might be relevant to give two examples here. Picasso created a sculpture of an ox-head with the handlebar of a cycle and seat in reverse. The other is what Duchamp did – he put the wheel of a bicycle on a triangular pedestal and called it a piece of sculpture. What is noteworthy here is the point of view of the artist. Did anyone before Picasso look at the seat and handlebar of a cycle differently? Who knew that an ox-head was contained therein? The same is true about the work of Duchamp. These two artists brought about a sea-change in readymade objects, subjecting them to a thorough dip in their creative imagination. The transformation was truly wonderful. But let me now get back to Brancusi.

Marguerite had meanwhile sneaked away to make coffee for us. She handed us cups of the thick black brew and offered one to Brancusi as well. He was seated on his famous throne chiselled out of a tree-trunk: a perfect seat for the uncrowned king of modern sculpture, a piece of sculpture by itself. It was perfectly in harmony with the other sculptures and wooden pedestals in the studio.

These pedestals deserve special mention as they form an important part of Brancusi's creative output. I do not know if anyone else has treated pedestals as an integral part of sculpture or given them much thought. Most of Brancusi's pedestals are so complicated in design and texture that looking at them is as wonderful an experience as viewing his works. And he is unparalleled in his originality. He used different kinds of wood and stones of different shades, occasionally combining the two mediums so well that they became an integral part of the sculpture. Very often he spent more time and effort on the pedestal than on the actual sculpture. I have a feeling that a particular philosophy was operative behind the shaping of these pedestals. The influence of the wooden furniture and houses of his native Rumania and the wooden sculpture of Africa is noticeable in his work. He never considered the pedestal as a mere support. For him, 'sculpture must start from the ground as it forms a link between the earth and the sky.' This idea is at variance with the modern notion of pedestals. Modern sculpture stands on the ground, with the base below.

An excellent example of the link Brancusi talks about is his creation, *The Rooster*. Made in the form of an arrow, this sculpture has an upward movement. Compared to the verticality of *The Bird, The Rooster* is slanted in orientation. The artist wanted the viewer to look up at it from the ground so that the eye can capture the idea of flight. When the cock crows its entire body stretches upward. To the artist this was the essence of ascension. To emphasize this he made three ridges first on the wood pedestal and then on the stone. These lines were repeated on the body of the rooster in diminishing size till it blended with the tuft. Like his other sculptures, Brancusi made various versions of this work. This idea of ascension in his work may be interpreted in another way. At one time he was profoundly influenced by the mystic philosophy of Madame Blavatsky, as indeed Mondrian, Kandinsky, Kupka, Domela, etc. were. 'As if a spirit [that] has fallen from the divine order into the natural order and is trying to return to his universal state' – this conviction may have pushed Brancusi from descent to ascent. The series called *The Endless Column*, where a number of geometric pillars rise towards space, can be seen as an expression of this spiritual philosophy. The natural course for a soul longing to go back to its universal state is inevitably upwards.

Brancusi had toyed with the idea of a number of elevated editions of *The Endless Column* wherein he had planned a series of columns holding up the sky. He of course knew the practical limitations of such a project. The memorial he built in his native country Rumania in memory of soldiers killed in the war, commissioned by the National League of Women, is truly unique. It stretches along the river Jiu for one kilometre. At the centre stands an endless column 20 metres in height, surrounded by other sculptures. A church dedicated to St Paul and St Peter stands next to it. A round table 2 metres and 15 centimetres in diameter with specially designed twelve chairs around it is another striking installation situated by the river. Named *Table of Silence*, perhaps there is no sculpture equal to this in size anywhere in the world.

The desire to connect heaven and earth has been present in the human mind from time immemorial. Much of it has found expression in religious sculpture, like in the Gothic churches of Europe, in the pyramids of Egypt, and in temples and mosques. Brancusi is probably the only sculptor who gave expression to this mystic idea in wood and stone.

As I went around his studio I was struck by the silence prevailing all around. This was only natural as every one of his works demands concentration. One cannot give them just a cursory glance, one has to contemplate. Each of us was engrossed in his own contemplation, in complete silence. I felt that Brancusi's mature work had evolved around some primary shapes, such as circles, cylinders, crosses, ovals, arcs, diamonds. Of these he seemed particularly fascinated by the oval. Many of his wonderful creations in stone, metal and wood are oval-shaped. Horizontal figures like the head of a child, a newborn infant, a sleeping muse, a blind person, the beginning of the world, and vertical figures like the head of a young girl, the portrait of Eileen Lane, Princess X and the white negress in various versions create a serene mood that moves one. They express themselves by means of minimum statement and are as precise as the parts of a car engine or a plane engine, where not a single piece can be left out. Behind this simplicity, minimality and precision lies the essence of modern art – an affirmation of the autonomy of form. Brancusi was the first sculptor to assert the importance of this autonomy. He emphasized or minimized various elements of form. Coming after Rodin, he was responsible in bringing about important changes in post-impressionist European sculpture – changes that were so revolutionary that Brancusi has been recognized as the father of modern sculpture. Unfortunately this recognition was given by only a few patrons of art and artists like Picasso, Braque, Marcel, Duchamp, Eric Satie, Ezra Pound and James Joyce. He never enjoyed the financial affluence that Rodin did. But his needs were few and he lived a simple life, so the later part of his life in Paris was free from want. The same cannot be said about his early life.

Constantin Brancusi was born on 2 March 1876 in a village in Rumania in southeastern Europe. His father was a real-estate agent. Brancusi learnt the theory and practice of drawing and mathematics and then joined a studio to train in wood sculpture. He learnt the secrets of wood chiselling here. He won a scholarship and several prizes. In 1904 he took the bold step of leaving for Paris, the art capital of Europe. He started out on foot, working his way through the journey by serving as a daily labourer at construction sites in the East and Central European cities of Vienna, Salzburg, Munich, Zurich and Basle. He fell ill with pneumonia before reaching Paris. After a stint in hospital, he finally reached his destination in 1905. There, he worked as an apprentice at sculpture classes during the day and washed dishes in restaurants in the evening. One of his teachers noticed his talent and sent some of his work to the Salon d'Automme. Luckily for Brancusi, Rodin was the president of the jury. He invited the young artist to work in his studio. It was a lucky break for Brancusi. Brancusi has said the following about his guru: 'The situation of sculpture was desperate in the nineteenth century. Rodin arrived and changed everything. Thanks to him, man is once again the measure, the module by which the statue is organized. Thanks to him, sculpture has once again become human in scale and significant in meaning.' I have not come across a better and more precise evaluation of Rodin.

Rodin was then a world figure in art. There was great demand for his work from art galleries and museums. To meet the ever-increasing demand, Rodin was obliged to employ young assistants. Brancusi was one of them. But within a year Brancusi realized that there was no room there for the growth of his own genius. Following the maxim that nothing grows in the shadow of great trees, he left Rodin. The great master's parting advice – 'Don't work too fast or exhibit too much' – proved to be a safeguard in his later career. He followed this advice all his life.

In earlier times sculptors used to make clay models first, then make plaster casts and finally pour the bronze. Nobody worked directly with stone. They even went to the length of using a special technique to get stone carvings made from the plaster, getting it done by somebody else. Rodin's stone figures were created by using this technique, they were not directly chiselled out of stone.

Brancusi was drawn to direct carving right from the start. Two considerations led him in this direction. First, plaster of paris was a rather brittle medium. Second, stone carving was less costly than bronze casting, although it was more laborious. It was an exhibition in Paris that helped Brancusi make up his mind – an exhibition of Gauguin's wood carvings sent from the island of Tahiti. Brancusi was impressed by the brute force contained in these works. Around the same time he was getting acquainted with Asian art in Musée Guimet. The painter Modigliani worked with him for some time, impressed by his sculpture. Henry Rousseau, the painter who became a sudden sensation, had this to say to Brancusi: 'You have transformed the antique into the modern.' A simple yet significant statement.

Influences of African, Egyptian, Khmer and Cyclade art are noticeable in Brancusi's work of this period. However, the way he synthesized these influences show how his genius was forging a new path. He not only concentrated on simplification and precision but also took great care to see that the surface shone like a mirror. I have had occasion to see many examples of metal sculpture but I have yet to find a smoother or more sensual surface. It involves hard labour, respect for the characteristics of the medium, and most of all a focus on its distinct quality. And Brancusi has done such an excellent job with all these that nobody can outdo him. Amixture of sensitivity with hard work: this is a significant quality of his sculpture.

As mentioned earlier, his subjects were limited. Once he discovered their sculptural potential, he spent all his time exploring their various possibilities. In a way he kept himself aloof from art movements like cubism, surrealism, futurism and dadaism, though he was acquainted with them all. His values were contemporary and his concepts were modern. In his own words: 'I am not trying to be fashionable. Whatever is fashionable is soon forgotten like fashion. If you are contested today, it does not matter. Once you have been understood, it will be for eternity.' He had to wait a long time for recognition. His work was initially appreciated by only a handful of patrons and artists. But he had tremendous confidence and he knew that sooner or later the art world would give him his due. And he was proved to be right. The first recognition came not from France but from the United States. Marcel Duchamp held successive exhibitions of his work in New York city. Patrons started collecting his work. Ezra Pound wrote a long, illustrated article on Brancusi. This appreciation had an effect on intellectuals and the general public. Eventually Brancusi's fame reached the shores of Europe.

As I observed the positioning and lighting of his figures in the studio I got the feeling that a lot of thought had gone into these. It was as though they were exhibits in a one-man show. Each sculpture had a very intimate relation with the space around. It could not be moved without affecting the relation. The soft light streaming from the glass ceiling was used most effectively to bring out the three-dimensional, formal and surface qualities to their maximum advantage. Within the limited space of the studio, he had placed the sculptures in such a way as to establish a rapport between the viewer and the exhibit. He was particularly keen to establish this contact. He would get worried about the positioning and light whenever his pieces were taken elsewhere as part of an exhibition or a private collection. He would give precise instructions with the help of photographs. It was his habit to take shots of all his sculptures from different angles and at different hours of the day. When a particular work was taken out of the studio he would show these photographs to the collector to explain how best to place it in its new home. He had very rigid ideas in this regard. Once, a celebrated gallery in Paris wanted to hold an exhibition of his work. He wanted the exhibition to be held in his studio. Needless to say, that was the end of the project. I shall relate an example at the end of this essay which demonstrates the culmination of this attitude.

His photographs were proof of the way his mind worked. He spent a great deal of time taking them. According to many, these photographs are as valuable as his sculptures. To quote one critic, 'Photography provided Brancusi with a means of remaining engaged with his sculptures after they were finished'. The same critic remarks elsewhere: 'One very important function of Brancusi's photographs was an outlet for or expression of the artist's emotional engagement with his work.' Others have taken photographs of his sculptures which are good but lacking in emotional engagement. Moreover, Brancusi's pictures are such that they are not only an expression of his personality but an effort to present the entire studio as a huge installation. This installation was not a static one. He often moved his sculptures from place to place, looking for the perfect position and perfect lighting. After my meeting with Brancusi I came across a long article with reproductions of his photographs that provided me valuable insight into the nature of his art.

After having spent an hour and half in his studio I felt that it was time to take leave of this saintly person. Sankho and the Majumders felt the same way. Most of the time there had been spent in silence and the time had passed very quickly. The studio had a unique atmosphere of its own, made up mostly of silence. Silence seemed to be the key to Brancusi's art. A serene mood blended with a deeply spiritual feeling created an effect whereby the visual became secondary to the inner appeal. That is why it was imperative to view the art in silence. Perhaps in this way a rapport was built with the viewer. Perhaps the artist intended it to be that way.

Brancusi spent his whole life wielding the chisel, hammer, wedge and other tools, working with intelligence and insight with chunks of wood and stone, making apparently simple forms out of bronze, steel and brass, and creating forms that have been hailed as epoch-making. One has to remember that sculptors like Maillol, Rodin, Bourdelle, Despeau and their followers did not ever go in for direct carving; their initial models were always in clay, followed by bronze cast. This is where Brancusi stands apart. For him the first condition of being a sculptor was to carve; he was a sculptor par excellence. To quote him, 'Carving is the true path of sculpture, but also the worst one for those who don't know how to walk.' As mentioned before, he made full use of the special character of each medium, and accorded to the medium he worked with the respect due to it. The love and care he lavished on their surfaces is comparable to the affection we show a child. He lived a very simple life, remaining loyal to art and paying absolutely no heed to name, fame, publicity, sales and other material attractions. In his lifetime of 81 years he never compromised. A proud man, a true artist, Brancusi occupies a foremost place in the history of art.

Throughout our walk around the studio Brancusi sat perched on his throne, his feet up on a log of wood. When it was time to say goodbye, we approached him. We thanked him for being kind to us and giving us his valuable time. He walked with us to the entrance of the studio and said *Au Revoir* with a smile.

A little before his death, Brancusi left all his work, consisting of 230 sculptures, pedestals, furniture, 41 sketches and 1,600 photographs, to his native country. But his will contained one condition. Nothing in the studio was to be disturbed, everything was to be kept as it was. At one point in time the rail authorities were threatening to pull down his studio at Montparnasse in an effort to expand the railway station. Newspapers and journals were flooded with protests, and the rail authorities were forced to defer their decision. Some time after his death on 16 March 1957, work on the expansion of the station began. But the condition set out in his will was honoured and the Musée National d'Art Moderne constructed an exact replica of his studio next to Centre Pompidou. Unfortunately, however, the studio did not attract enough visitors nor was it kept in good shape. Hence it had to be shifted. In May 1995, Centre Pompidou organized a huge retrospective of Brancusi's entire work. It was viewed by thousands of people from all over the world, the present writer being one of them. This was the biggest exhibition of Brancusi's work ever held, and it created a renewed interest in his work – an interest that will only grow with time and spread across the world. As I went through the exhibits I could not help being moved by the greatness of this artist who had fashioned a link between the prehistoric age and the present. The exhibition bore witness to this permanent contribution made by Brancusi.

Translated from the Bengali by Enakshi Chatterjee

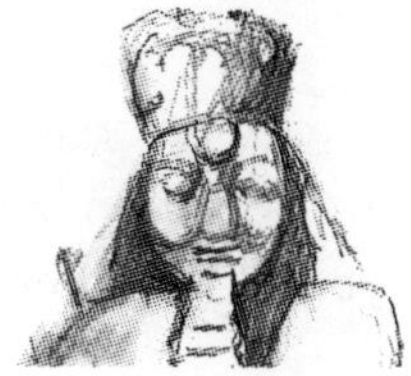

A trip to Abu Simbel

I have crossed the Suez Canal a number of times on my way to Europe. Every time, standing on the deck of a slow-moving ship, I have wondered sadly if I would ever be able to afford a visit to Egypt. So when, about twenty years later, our airplane touched down at Cairo airport, my heart danced with joy – it was the fulfilment of what had seemed an impossible dream.

It was the last lap of a long stint abroad, most of which was spent in France but also included travels in the USA, Mexico, Italy, Spain and England, thanks to the generosity of the French government and John D. Rockefeller the third. What could be a more wonderful finish to my travels, particularly for someone as obsessed with art as I am. Earlier, I had had opportunities to visit South and Central European countries like Greece, Belgium and Holland. This was when I was staying in France. As I traced the sources of European culture – the continuity of the glories of Greece and Rome – I was struck with wonder and admiration.

There must be some secret ingredient in the air, water and light of the Mediterranean, the magic mix of which has fashioned the flesh and blood of the people residing in its surroundings. One can almost call it a magical chemical process. I have bathed in the silvery light and clear blue waters of the beaches of Italy, France, Spain and Greece, trying to fathom the mystery. I have roamed the hills and shores of many countries, but there is something about the Mediterranean air that exhilarates in a way nothing else does. I am still haunted by the memories. Small wonder that so many new cultures have evolved here, in the best climate the world has to offer. All the Mediterranean cultures are indebted to their ancestor – the culture of ancient Egypt.

Our plan was to sail down the Nile observing the antiquities that dot the valley from Cairo to the desert of Nubia. Coming as I do from riverine East Bengal, I am familiar with mighty rivers – the Padma, Meghna, Sitalaksha, Dhaleswari and Brahmaputra. Steamer trips from Dhaka to Barisal, Kolkata and Chittagong are part of my childhood memories. I have always yearned to relive those experiences. Imagine my disappointment, then, when I learnt from my travel agent that the steamer service was suspended because of the Egypt–Israel war. Foreigners were not even allowed to travel by plane. A reminder of India's support to Egypt had no effect. There was no other way but to take the train.

Our destination was Abu Simbel. From Cairo we were to go to Aswan and then to Abu Simbel. On the way back we would visit Luxor, Karnak and Thebes before boarding the train back to Cairo.

My wife and I got into the air-conditioned coupé reserved for us. It was ten at night. Incidentally, we were the only Indian passengers in the entire train. Somehow Egypt has always meant the Pyramid at Gizeh for Indian tourists. They have absolutely no interest in the other wonders of ancient Egypt. The country does not figure even in the itinerary of educated and cultured Indians, whose interests seem to be confined to Western Europe and America. On the rare occasion that it does, it remains limited to Cairo.

Dinner was served in the coupé. We finished our meal and settled down to sleep. The next morning I looked out through the window and found that we were at a small station. It looked like a village station with hardly any of the crowd one associates with railway stations. I spotted some red huts and brick houses under the shade of date palms, gulmohars, eucalyptuses and cypresses. Women in loose dresses and black veils were drawing water from wells in long earthen pitchers. Hauling the pitchers up to their shoulders, they quickly disappeared into the village. A few horses, asses and camels could be seen, tied to the trunks of trees. The soil was yellow, the colour of sand, the like of which can be seen in Rajasthan. Small areas of green which showed up as beautiful little dots were as surprising as they were lovely. Little brown children waved at us from those patches of green, just like the children in our villages do. In fact children all over the world are exactly the same, unspoilt and innocent – they don't recognize the boundaries of space and time.

At around ten in the morning we reached Aswan, a town with no special character. A gentleman from the travel agency, very polite and pleasant, took us to our hotel. We had to fill out some forms meant for foreign tourists. He left us saying he would be back in the afternoon to take us for a boat ride on the Nile.

It was a newly built luxury hotel, set amidst gulmohar and other flowering trees in a secluded spot away from the bustle of the city. It was summer, not the season tourists prefer. The windows of our room on the first floor opened out to wonderful sight. Under the fierce and dazzling sun I could see stone steps leading directly down from the hotel to the river. There, beyond bright red splashes of the gulmohar, lay the Nile – placid and clear, like an ancient reptile basking under the stainless blue canopy of the sky. Jagged sand-coloured hills, untouched by green, fringed the other bank. The bare terrain stretched from north to the south as far as the eye could see, glowing like dull gold.

A couple of fishing boats floated in the middle of the river like a pair of swans that had drifted away from the main flock. From the centre of the river bed rose a small hillock. This island was a fishermen's village. Shouts of joy from the children of the village wafted in the breeze. As I focused my eyes I saw hordes of naked children diving into the water. It filled me with nostalgia. For a moment I felt as if I was back home.

The heat outside was close to 112 degrees and the air was so dry that we could feel it parch the skin. I shut all the windows, turned on the air-conditioner and went in for a shower. My wife came up with a suggestion. How about some cold beer? It was just what I wanted. The beer was ordered. Reclining on the bed, I looked out through the window. The Nile looked refreshing. For the last three months we had been constantly on the move, but all the fatigue now evaporated like the bubbles in the beer. All the strain and nervous tension in us vanished, leaving us with a tranquil state of mind like the wide open sky. As I gazed at the blue expanse I wondered if I had ever seen a river so serene, so unperturbed.

It was hard to believe it was this very river, meandering across 1,500 miles, that floods its banks every year in wild fury. The floods in turn engender life, greening the desert and bringing new hope to the people. It is this river that, from the beginning of time, has kept the heart of this land beating. The river basin of the Nile, for all practical purposes, constitutes the body of Egypt, the blue waters providing its network of veins. Everything else is still, lifeless, dead. It is no wonder that Kipling wrote: 'The weight of the desert is on one, every day and every hour.'

As I sipped at my beer, my mind went back to a dim past when the world's oldest civilization had flourished on the banks of this river, a civilization to which the world is eternally indebted. The first written script, the first organized administrative system, the first calendar, astronomy, agriculture, fibre technology, the census, glass-making, the postal system, music, dance, philosophy, mathematics, poetry, painting, fine arts – the list is never-ending. From about 3500 BC to the first century AD the great civilization flourished uninterrupted, like the continuous flow of the Nile. Those were years that witnessed the birth and death of mighty kings and pharaohs, wars and bloodshed, the making of majestic temples and pyramids, the march of thousands of horse-drawn chariots, barges sailing down the river, gold and precious stones, diamonds and gems, beautiful queens and princesses with their retinue of servants, animals and birds of varied hues, feasts, hunting, music – I let my mind roam this colourful and wonderful fairy-tale land. Except that this was no fantasy – the past had left its mark on the present, in the countless artefacts, the work of Egyptian artists carved in stone, on temples and pyramids, on papyrus scrolls, in sculpture, painting, architecture and poetry.

The effect of the beer combined with strange imaginings of the past had sent me into a dream-world when the doorbell rang. It was our lunch tray, the sight of which brought me back to the present. I suddenly realized how hungry I was. After lunch I lay back on the cool bed and went off to sleep.

At around five in the evening the polite gentleman from the travel agency came to take us to the landing site at the quay below. We climbed on to a small fishing boat. The Arab boatman was pleasantly surprised when I responded to his greeting of '*Salaam alaikum*' with '*Alaikum salaam*'. The sun had sunk beyond the western hills. The shadows of a palm grove created complicated patterns on the surface of the water. A light breeze hit the white sail and set our boat in motion. The man from the travel agency had introduced himself in the morning but I could not remember his name, so I had to ask again. His name was Habib.

The eastern hills slowly took on a mixed colour of gold and copper. Mr Habib pointed to the highest peak and said, 'You see that yellow marble monument – it is the tomb of the great-grandfather of the present Aga Khan. Thirty-five years ago he was the richest man in the world and the spiritual leader of millions of Ismaili Muslims. The mausoleum was built at a cost of fifty crore rupees.'

For a man who had spent most of his life in the south of France, the choice of such a site as his resting place was strange indeed. Why had he chosen such a bare and deserted spot, without a touch of green? I put this question to Mr Habib. 'Well,' said he, 'there is no country in this world which the Aga Khan had not visited. On one of his visits here, he was so struck by the serene environment of this place that he wished to be laid to rest on this mountain peak. This was conveyed to his son Ali Khan. This place would always remain secluded, far away from human habitation. From here he would enjoy the first and last rays of the sun and experience everlasting peace gazing at the quiet waters of the eternal Nile. What better resting place could one imagine for a man who had tasted the ultimate in luxury?'

Mr Habib asked the boatman to turn to the north. After we had sailed for a mile or so he remarked, 'Pretty soon we will see a very famous ancient temple. I am not able to recall the exact name of the temple, but the mighty pharaoh Rameses II built it. I will come to the extraordinary story of Rameses II a little later.'

'In 1972 the dam on the Nile had to be raised for a second time to check inundation and to help irrigation', Mr Habib continued. 'The tower of this temple was submerged. It could not be helped. Built in 1250 BC, the temple still stands unbroken on pillars that are half under water. But very recently the level of the water has started going up again in winter as the height of the Aswan dam has been raised once more. Consequently, the temple may collapse or get completely submerged – this possibility has caused great dismay among Egyptologists. They are considering various measures to save the temple. Fortunately, the topmost floor and the most sacred part of the prayer hall, with six large and magnificent statues of Rameses II, happen to be a part of the hill. This floor is above the water level but it may not remain so for long.' Unfortunately there was no way we could enter the temple. All we could do was to go round the submerged pillars with the sails down. It was an eerie and unreal experience. The temple was infested with bats. This was hardly surprising. What else could one expect in abandoned monuments, where great works of art lie in total neglect? This has been the fate of many archaeological monuments.

'The government of Egypt had appealed to the world for preserving the temple', said Mr Habib. 'The only way this could be done was to take down the entire structure and rebuild it piece by piece somewhere else. This was how the temple of Abu Simbel was saved from the Aswan dam. I will come to that extraordinary effort a little later.'

Mr Habib instructed the boatman to steer the boat towards the hotel. By now the western sky was unusually bright with a tinge of orange and pink. Against the glowing backdrop the trees and the hills appeared almost black. Mr Habib reminded us that it was 21 June, the longest day of the year. Twilight would persist right up to 10 o'clock in the night.

The dense and dark shadows of the trees fell on the river, turning the blue of the Nile into a deeper blue. The masts of boats anchored at the landing of the fishermen's village looked like guards keeping vigil. Our boat reached the hotel landing and Mr Habib left us, asking us to be ready at three the next morning, when we would be picked up for our trip to Abu Simbel. We had our dinner quickly and retired early.

A bell woke us up an hour ahead of the scheduled time. The hotel boy served us tea and breakfast. I was amazed by Egyptian punctuality. Exactly at three, we started for the ferry ghat near Aswan dam from where a hydrofoil or a steam launch would take us to Abu Simbel. I have used various modes of transport in different countries but this was an entirely new experience.

An ass from the village brayed loudly, shattering the silence. Overhead, the stars twinkled like millions of fireflies. The Milky Way seemed close enough to touch. The night sky over deserts is always sparkling and bright. There was no moon; the darkness was as thick as molten tar. There were no sounds, no buzzing of crickets. The river too seemed to be in deep slumber. It was a unique experience – the total silence of a dark night.

The taxi driver greeted us and opened the door of the car. Two young men got into the front seat. For reasons we came to know later, they were not introduced to us. We assumed they were tourists. The headlights of the car were able to pierce only a part of the impenetrable darkness, giving us the feeling of travelling through a long tunnel with no beginning or end. The uneven surface of the road restricted the speed of the car to about 30 or 35 miles. The two young men in front chatted with the driver, exchanged cigarettes, and stole surreptitious glances at us from time to time. It was a bit scary but we tried our best not to show our nervousness.

The headlights lit up huge boulders flanking the way with no trace of green anywhere. It felt as though we were driving through a stone desert. We finally stopped after an hour and a half. The driver lit a torch and asked us to follow him. Where was he taking us in this murky darkness? I felt a flutter of fear. My wife held my hand in a tight grip.

Without a word, the two young men kept behind us like shadows. I was distinctly uncomfortable by now. The silence was ominously broken by the scraping of our shoes on the pebbles. It was a perfect scenario from an American suspense thriller – the two of us could have been smugglers in the hands of ruffians determined to find their way to an illegal store of gold and silver. Any moment they could fish out a pistol or a knife.

There was urgent whispering behind. What will happen next – I wondered. Just then I spotted a dim light in the distance – a pirate perhaps. All of a sudden the driver stopped in his tracks. Highly mysterious. He pointed his finger in the direction of the light and declared, 'Look, there is your hydrofoil.'

What a relief!

A handsome young man with a torch in hand was waiting for us. He led us to the hydrofoil. He was evidently the captain of the ship. The deck had a capacity of a hundred seats. We were asked to occupy two seats in the front row. To our utter surprise the engine roared into life without waiting for any other passengers. The roar of the engine and the splashing waves created the illusion of a large ocean liner. It was still dark outside. The mystery was deepening. Why should there be such a big boat for just the two of us? Looking behind my shoulders I discovered the two strangers huddled in a corner, smoking and whispering. 'What do you make of this?' I asked my wife. She was so frightened that she came closer to me and clasped my hand tightly. I had no intention of pretending to be brave, so I remained silent. At this point the two young men came up to occupy the adjoining seats. We froze. What were they up to? If they decided to throw us overboard we would go straight down into the water that was as dark as chinese ink. There was not a soul around this strange and weird place. Nobody would have an inkling of our watery end.

As such thoughts kept coming to me, one of the men dug his hand into his pocket sending further shivers down my spine. He flashed an identity card at me. Thank god it was not a weapon! He was from the intelligence branch and his friend was from the police. Then he bombarded me with questions. What was my name, my profession, who was this lady, what did she do, how many children do we have, our home, our destination, the foreign currency we were carrying, was it in pounds or in dollars, and most importantly, what had brought us to Egypt, how long would we stay, did we know any one here, and so on. He scribbled in Arabic as I replied to the questionnaire.

I had to guess at most of the questions because his command over English was sketchy. I felt much lighter after the interrogation and lit a cigarette. 'Light one for me too', said my wife. She does not smoke normally, only when she is nervous or tense.

The tinkling sound of cups and saucers came from behind. The two men left. A person we had not seen earlier came to us with a breakfast tray. By this time we had overcome our fear. The simple breakfast of toast, jam and boiled eggs with coffee tasted delicious.

The Serang came up to us. 'Is there anything else you need?' he asked. 'Can I have another cup of coffee, please', I said. He brought the coffee himself. I thanked him and offered him a cigarette. 'Are you expecting more passengers on the way?' I wanted to know. 'We are not stopping anywhere', he said with a smile. 'We are heading straight towards Abu Simbel, a four-and-a-half-hour journey from here.' 'So you are making this trip just for the two of us?' 'Well, we work for the Government Tourist Bureau. During the tourist season we have to take trips to Abu Simbel even if there is only a single passenger. This happens to be the last trip of the season. Then we close for three months. Tourists generally don't come in summer. I must say you are lucky. You would have missed the chance to visit Abu Simbel if you had come a week later. Winter is the busiest season. We are not able to cope with even three trips a day. Excuse me', he said, breaking off the conversation. He marched to his cabin leaving us to the non-stop splash of waves as we proceeded towards an unknown adventure.

The side and front windows which had been covered with tarpaulins were now rolled up one by one, revealing a dim landscape like a beautiful backdrop on a theatre stage. The eastern sky looked like a copper plate fresh from scrubbing. This colour gradually changed to light violet till it merged with the dark blue of the west. The quiet expanse of water glistened like a dull looking-glass. Small hillocks fringed the horizon, looking like the smooth backs of hippos wading in the water. We could see no other boats or water birds. A little later a strange sight greeted us. Some triangular objects, we could not make out what they were, dotted the surface. The Serang came to inform us that the sun would rise within a few minutes. 'Look straight ahead. You will enjoy the sight.'

'Tell me', I asked him, 'what are those black triangular objects? And what is this expanse of water called?' Offering me an Egyptian cigarette, he said: 'This is Aswan lake. It covers an area of 450 square miles, and was formed by the construction of a huge dam on the Nile. It is more than three miles deep. This lake has submerged all the bare hills of the area. What you are seeing are only their tips. Somewhat like a drowning man struggling for his last breath', he added, after a pause.

I was glad to find he had a poetic soul.

He continued, puffing at his cigarette: 'Pretty soon a new steamer service will be operating between Cairo and Khartoum, the capital of Sudan. This is a joint project between the two governments. It will be the longest steamer service in the world – 1,200 miles. I hope you will be able to take the trip some day.' He excused himself again and made for his cabin.

Meanwhile the colour of copper had gone from the eastern sky and was replaced by a layer that was the colour of brass. I breathed in the exhilarating air. I could not remember the last time I had breathed such pure air. Perhaps this was the kind of air that encircled the earth in the early days of creation when the molten mass was turning solid. In the earliest stage of its evolution, air, one of the constituents of living matter, must have been absolutely unadulterated, like this.

I kept gazing in front of me. Sunrise and sunset are dramatic, colourful and mysterious events, equally appealing to artists and common individuals. The more one watches them the more wonderful they become. Every such experience is so unexpected, so strange, that the heart is filled with unspeakable happiness. Each sunrise is a new discovery, as is each sunset. One never knows in what colours the next sunrise or sunset will be painted. Everything changes appearance during the course of the day – beaches, mountain peaks, fields, the colour of the sky. The changing seasons too add to the variation.

As I sat meditating, the centre of the eastern horizon lit up with an unusual brilliance, as though invisible fingers had turned on a million kilowatt spotlight. I had never seen a sky so crystal-clear, so brittle and transparent, with not even a bird dotting the scene. A morning sky without birds was a novel visual experience for me. One usually associates it with the chirping of birds flying about in gay abandon after the forced confinement of the night. Even the monotony of the ocean is sometimes broken by the flight of sea gulls, like white *shaluk* flowers blossoming on the white waves.

The scene that unfolded before us was extraordinary, to say the least. As far as the eye could see, severe and rugged heaps of stone surrounded the water; there was not the slightest touch of green. Elsewhere I have seen how nature can defy the harshest of terrains; green shoots appear through cracks in the barest of rocks. But for some peculiar reason not even a blade of grass could be seen here, despite being so close to a source of water. Nature, it seemed to me, had endowed this place with an expression of anger. The rocks jutting out of the water seemed to underline the fact that this jagged severity was in order here, for it had a beauty of its own. It was a different kind of beauty, distinct and painted in brown – unusual but delightful.

Meanwhile an unearthly phenomenon was about to be revealed to us from beyond the glowing eastern horizon. With dazzling flashes of light, a chorus of millions of cymbals, the blowing of conches and cheering by female voices, it heralded the coming of a divine presence.

My eyes were dazzled by the luminous circle growing larger by the minute, yet I could not take my eyes off it. I was hypnotised. What terrible beauty! What a strange union of opposites! Pharaoh Akhinaten, one of the founding fathers of the great civilization which had drawn me here, had sung its praise in words which sound like a vedic hymn.

> Thy dawning is beautiful in the horizon of the sky,
> O living Aton, Beginning of life.
> When thou risest in the eastern horizon,
> Thou fillest every land with the beauty.
> Thou art beautiful, great, glittering, high above every land,
> Thy rays, they encompass the land, even all that thou hast made.

In Egyptian culture, the sun god occupies the highest place in the divine hierarchy. He is known by various names – Ra, Re, Aton. All ritual worship begins and ends with an invocation to Aton. No coronation of the mighty pharaohs and the associated ceremonies would be complete without these hymns. That is why the sun god, represented by an abstract circular symbol, is present in the crowns of the pharaohs.

Egypt is blessed with bright sunlight all the year round. The sun, a mixture of gold and mercury, reigns supreme in the cloudless clear-blue sky, infusing life into the flora and fauna of the fertile Nile valley. Though predominantly a desert, Aton is not dreaded here because he does not scorch and burn the soil as in similar desert countries. Hence there is no reason to appease him through animal sacrifice. On the other hand, he is worshipped as a preserver of life.

The bright circle of the east had expanded till it filled the entire sky. A heavenly light, glowing like powdered gold, spread across the earth and heaven inducing unearthly happiness. A deep spirituality overwhelmed even someone like me who is close to being an atheist. I have had the rare privilege of watching the sun rise and set from Himalayan peaks and at Kanyakumari, on the edge of the Indian peninsula, washed by the confluence of the Indian Ocean, the Arabian Sea and the Bay of Bengal. I have been to the southernmost region of faraway Mexico, to Ukatan, the seat of the ancient Maya civilization. I have watched the sun set from the peak of Kulkulkan at Chichen itza. But what I was seeing today surpassed all else. All my previous experiences paled into insignificance. It was as though I was undertaking a journey towards light. This was no ordinary trip of a common tourist. The water had been transformed into a lake of light and we were driving in a mythological chariot to an unknown destination – a journey like the eternal quest of mankind that has carried on through the ages.

A beam of light fell on us as if in blessing. Instinctively I took off my shirt, not wishing to keep any part of my body hidden from the pure ray of light. I smeared the holy light all over me. The light filled my interior too, with the purity of a white lotus. Everything around – the sky, air, water, mountain peaks – seemed to be a spiritual expression of sacredness and purity. It must have been this luminous presence that Van Gogh attempted all his life to capture on his canvas, like a man possessed. No wonder every object in his paintings – whether it be sunflowers in a vase, a lantern inside a room, the moon, the stars – takes on the brightness of the sun; he is inevitably drawn in this direction. That is why all his work, be it a landscape or an inanimate object or a human figure, are washed in an extraordinary light. This explains the predominance of yellow and blue in his paintings. Yellow signifies spiritual illumination, blue is a manifestation of tranquillity.

Our hydrofoil skirted the triangular rocks jutting out of the water as we continued to move to our destination. I was in a trance-like state. Excitement filled my veins, elevating me, lifting me into the air.

'Would you like a cup of coffee?' It was the Serang. I came back to this world with a start.

'An excellent idea', I replied, and offered him a cigarette.

'Let me get the coffee first.'

To my right I discerned a tiny blob of green far away, exactly where the water met the mountains. When the Serang returned I asked him, 'That vague green over there, is it real or an illusion?'

'It is real all right', he assured me, and went on to explain. 'An effort is being made to settle the fishermen wherever the situation is favourable. Fishing and agriculture are being tried on the beaches. It will take time, of course, because of the rocky ground under the beach. It will not be easy. But irrigation has already been started in the plains beyond the hills. We hope that in about twenty years the landscape will be transformed. You know how in this desert country of ours water is really scarce. The Nile is all we have. And our population is increasing fast. Unless we develop more agricultural land we cannot cope with the growing demand for foodgrains. So we have to irrigate thousands of acres of the beach area. Unfortunately the Egypt–Israel war is making our task even more difficult. Every year millions of pounds are being diverted for the war effort and national reconstruction is taking a back seat. At the same time the war has to be fought for our national honour.'

He paused. I took this opportunity to ask him, 'How much longer will it take to reach Abu Simbel?'

He consulted his watch. 'Say, an hour and a quarter.'

Only an hour and a quarter! After that I would have the good fortune of viewing one of the great wonders of the world, a noble monument of Egyptian civilization, a glory of the human race – the temple of Abu Simbel! The very idea was thrilling. A dream that I had nurtured for many years was at last going to be a reality! Hard work, intense desire and singleminded devotion can work wonders, bring the impossible to the realm of the possible – I have seen this happen in my life.

Strangely, the dazzling Kohinoor-like source of light that was flooding the atmosphere suddenly turned into scorching rays. They pierced my bare body like a thousand pinpricks – fierce and terrible. Quickly I donned my shirt. I was told by the Serang that the temperature was close to 114°F, and that it might go up by three or four degrees as the day progressed. Even the surrounding water did not help lessen the heat. I felt as though my body was being burned to cinders. The huge expanse of water was as still as a sheet of glass. There was no breeze. The whole world seemed motionless. The only thing that moved was our hydrofoil.

I fixed my gaze on the horizon, in the direction of Abu Simbel. The row of hills stretching from east to west had not left us; but it had faded in a blur of mist, blending with the sky and the water. Gradually it spread. From a line it became a rough and rugged wall, with nothing to distinguish it from the continuous ramparts we had been seeing all along our way.

A little later a light splash of green seemed to appear on the brown of the hills' surface. It was a bend, hiding something from view. 'That bend you see over there,' said the Serang, 'the temple of Abu Simbel stands just beyond. You will have a clear view quite soon.' His words sent waves of expectation down my spine. Impatient as a child, I began to pace up and down, lighting a cigarette to cool my nerves. How I wished I had a pair of binoculars! I felt like urging the Serang to speed up for it seemed as though he was deliberately slowing down, just to test my nerves.

Slowly, beyond the bend, a hill-top came into view, not rugged like the others but rounded, more like a helmet. It resembled a huge sand boulder on which some lines were scribbled. As we approached, the lines became more distinct, they took on concrete shapes. I tried to compare these with the figures I knew were on the rocks and they tallied.

The experience was like viewing a film on a screen, shot with telephoto lens. In an instant the entire temple came to the fore in a close-up; the camera then zoomed to the statues and finally settled on just one. It first focused on the face, next the eyes and then closed in on just one eye. The eye covered the entire screen. Hundreds of violins, drums and other percussion instruments struck up ear-shattering music. My senses were numbed, my consciousness overwhelmed. Never had I seen such an extraordinary film.

The footsteps of the Serang broke into my reverie. 'Here we are', he announced. 'Will you have lunch now or after the visit? We will return in four hours.' 'First things first', I said. 'Let us go to the temple. Lunch can wait.' My wife and I got down.

Let me at this point say a few words about the maker of the temple – Pharaoh Rameses. The life-story of Rameses the Great or Rameses II is excellent material for an epic. Compared to his the life of any other king or emperor pales into insignificance. His superhuman energy, valour, love of women, devotion to god, love of art and the power to build make him a most colourful figure, greater than Alexander or Napoleon, not just in the history of Egypt but in the history of civilization itself.

Rameses excelled in both the art of warfare and administration quite early, even when his father was alive. Soon he conquered Mesopotamia and Libya in the north, extending the frontiers of his land up to Nubia in the south, to become the emperor of a vast kingdom. His treasury was filled with riches as never before. Architecture, sculpture, painting, poetry and various technical arts flourished in his reign. Under his patronage huge and wonderful temples were built on both sides of the Nile, dwarfing the buildings and monuments built by other kings in other parts of the world.

This brave king had more than a hundred wives and fathered at least a couple of children through each. As was the prevailing custom, he married some of the more beautiful daughters himself. He did not want his daughters to give birth to weak children. I do not know if the common people of the country enjoyed such rights. He lived to be 90, ruling over Egypt for 66 years, a world record by all counts.

This lion of a man was singularly fortunate in his choice of wives, of whom one deserves special mention. She was Nefertari, not to be confused with the other famous Egyptian queen, Nefretiti. Extremely beautiful and accomplished, this queen was a particular favourite of Rameses. She was a Hittite princess, offered to the king as a peace gesture by the fierce community when Rameses had engaged them in a bloody war. Of all his queens, only she can be seen next to the statues of Rameses.

As a symbol of his eternal love for Nefertari, Rameses had a special temple built for her in Abu Simbel. We made a tour of this temple too. But before I go on to describe it, let me pause to comment on a particular engineering feat, a marvel of present-day technology.

I have already mentioned the huge dam built on the Nile at Aswan and the 400-diameter lake. When this lake threatened to inundate Abu Simbel, a prospect that worried the entire civilized world, UNESCO, determined to save the great monument, sent urgent appeals to countries across the world for financial help and plans for preservation. Many plans were submitted but most were rejected as being too expensive. One such plan was to cover the two temples with thick polythene sheets and keep them under cover for two centuries, during which time most parts of Egypt would become green and fertile, thanks to the network of canals utilizing the waters of the Aswan lake. As far as I know, this absurd proposal came from an English engineer. Many other schemes were also examined.

Finally, a Swedish model was unanimously accepted and taken up. The proposal was to take down the two temples, number the fragments, haul the heavy pieces, each weighing more than a hundred tons, up a nearby hill, and reassemble them in exactly the original style. Then the surrounding area would be reconstructed. This painstaking reconstruction was undertaken, and after it the reassembled temples look exactly like the old ones, in every detail. Every detail, including the shrubs and the grass, has been retained. All this has been recorded in large format photographs.

A similar though much smaller-scale reconstruction project was undertaken and completed very successfully in our country about fifteen years ago, near Hyderabad. This happened when the huge dam at Nagarjunakonda, giving rise to the enormous Nagarjunasagar lake was threatening to inundate many excavations of the Buddhist age. They were taken down and reassembled in the same way, a feat of which every Indian should be proud.

The temples of Abu Simbel, buried under sand for centuries, were rediscovered in 1813, creating a sensation in the archaeological world. The temples of Rameses are remarkable for various reasons. Let me point to just one. As in our Ajanta caves, the main temple here was scooped out of a sandstone hill, keeping the roof intact. For thousands of years sand accumulated on top of the hill. The thousands of tons of stone lying between the temple and the hill-top were replaced by a hollow concrete dome during the process of shifting, which incidentally became the world's largest hollow dome. Huge quantities of sand were poured over the dome to replicate the original hill. Midway on the surface of the dome is a place to stand, surrounded by railings. From here one can get an idea of the size and ground plan of the temple. The temple of Queen Nefertari was not buried in sand, so no dome was required to reassemble it. The effort of scientific genius and the unimaginable resources

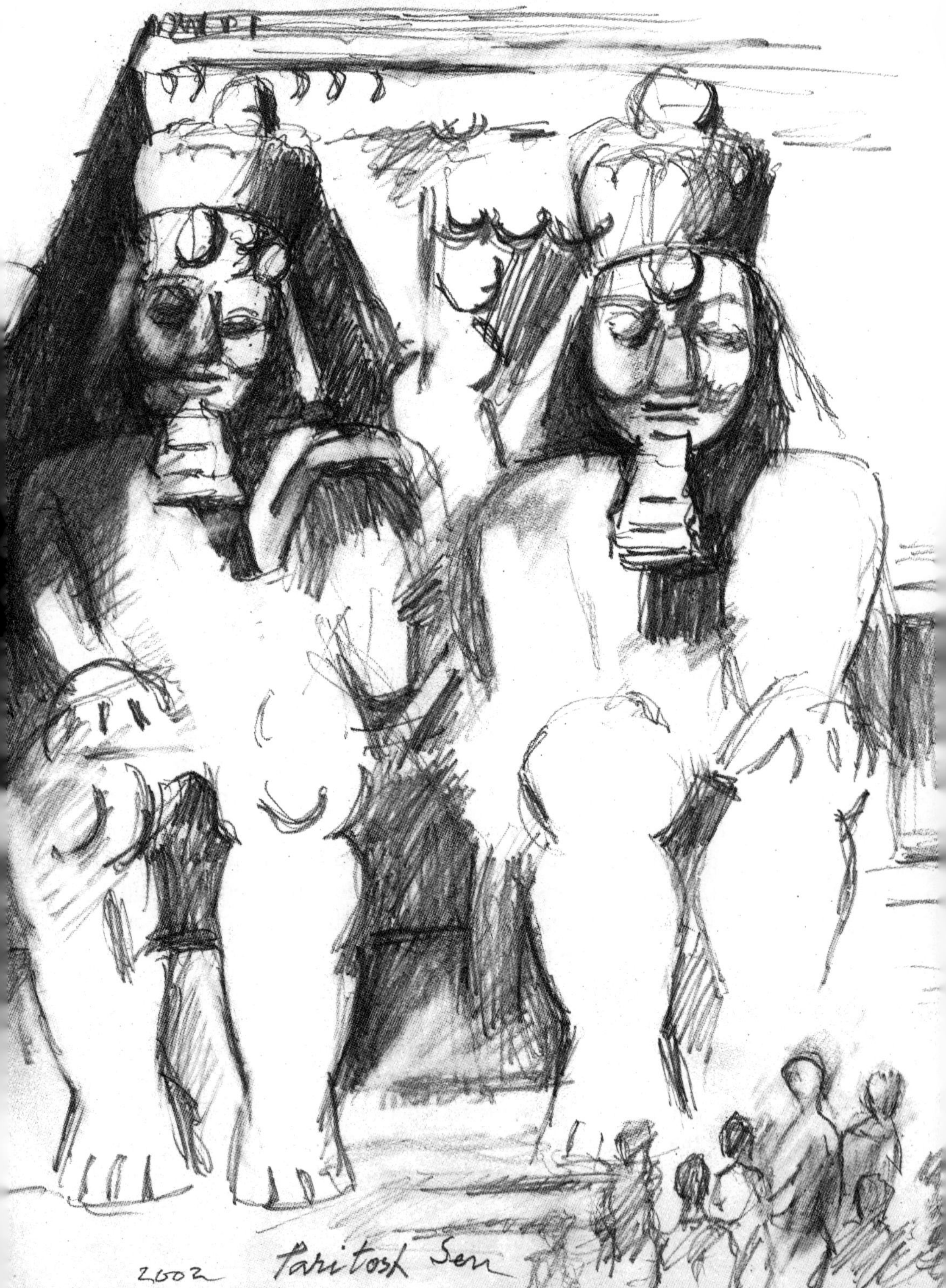
2002
Paritosh Sen

that went into this venture of reconstructing the temples are no less wonderful than the building of the temples themselves. The only difference is that in the ancient days everything had to be done manually, there were no sophisticated stone-cutting and other construction equipment. The reconstruction venture, a marvel of engineering skill, was accomplished at a cost of fifty crore dollars. The credit for its success goes to Swedish planning and Italian technology, proving that there is no limit to what can be achieved through international cooperation.

Abu Simbel was but one of the many temple complexes built during the time of Rameses. There are other, though smaller, temples in Abydos, Memphis, east and west Thebes and Luxor (now known as Karnak). Most of these, however, have not withstood the ravages of time. The temple of Karnak is remarkable for its size, durability and beauty of structure and sculpture. The path leading to it is lined by a hundred lamb-headed sphinxes. The inside of the temple has numerous mammoth pillars, each 70 feet in height and about 12 feet wide, which support the ceiling of a huge hall. The pillars have inscriptions all over them in praise of God Amon-ray or Emperor Rameses II. The top of each pillar is circular and wide enough to accommodate a hundred people. There are also smaller halls and prayer rooms, full of relief sculptures. The distance from the entrance to the centre of the complex is about a quarter of a mile. The structure originally stood on an area covering 62 acres. About three-fourths of the ceiling now lie in ruins.

Equally impressive is the Ramesseum, in Thebes, on the western bank of the Nile. This temple too now is in ruins but whatever remains of the original structure is mind-boggling. Marble pillars and a gigantic statue of Rameses still stand erect, defying the 3,000-year-long onslaught of time.

From this description of the structures, obelisks and sculptures the reader can easily understand why history had few equals of the stature of Rameses as far as construction of monuments was concerned. Rameses thought himself to be the son of the sun god Harekti. Naturally, therefore, all his creations were god-like in size.

Getting down from the hydrofoil, we climbed up the mountain. As we sat on a low wall facing the temple, four figures of Rameses guarding the entrance greeted us. It was the practice to set up huge statues of the king both inside and outside any temple that he built. As mentioned before, these statues as well as the entire temple had been scooped out of a sandstone mountain slope. Such single rock-hewn temples exist in our country as well, in Elephanta, Karla, Kanheri and Ellora. Comparisons are odious, yet in all fairness I must admit that I was more impressed by Abu Simbel for its simplicity of conception and boldness of sculpture and structure.

Stone as a medium has its own character which is different from that of earth, wood or metal. The Egyptian workmen understood this very well and did not try to impose the qualities of one upon the other. Whatever they worked with, be it gold, silver, copper, stone or wood, they applied their imagination to extract the maximum advantage. Stone is a solid and static object, its lack of motion being most evident in portraiture, divine or human. But this principle was not followed by the workmen in depicting mythological or historical events. Their success in imparting to stone a dynamic virtue has given Egyptian sculpture a special place in the history of art.

The gigantic statues of Rameses are a constant reminder of this. The 70-foot figures represent not the pharaoh but the son of the life-giving Ra-Harekti, the immortal god and the representative of god on earth. On the day of his coronation the sun god himself is believed to have crowned him. Little wonder, then, that such a man would possess superhuman energy, might, bravery and kindness.

The temple of Abu Simbel was built in honour of the sun god, and his son presides over the entrance, wearing his divine crown. The colossal statues filled me with wonder. What magnificent conception, what excellent execution! What regal stances, what powerful looks, what superhuman proportions! If the seated images were to stand up wouldn't their heads touch the sky? The only statue comparable in size in India is, as far as my knowledge goes, the standing Digambar Jain statue at Sravanabelagola in Mysore. It is a little shorter, 60 feet in height, but equally astonishing though very different in concept and style.

As I stared at the statues I wondered if one would have sufficed instead of four identical ones. Would it have been possible for only one statue to create the same sense of wonder? I think not. Rameses and his innovative sculptors had indeed been successful in generating a great sense of wonder in the beholder.

Rameses occupies the most prominent place among those kings of Egypt who had invested themselves with divine virtues. Perhaps, according to them, this was the best way of subjugating their people. Let me relate a story in support of my thesis. Princess Hatshepsut, daughter of the first Thutmose of the eighteenth dynasty, married her brother, the second Thutmose, after the death of her father. They had a daughter, who later married an illegitimate son of her father and was declared to be the future pharaoh. Hatshepsut was not ready to accept this son of dubious origin as the future king a took over the reins of government herself. So far the line had passed from king to king, a woman ruler was unheard of. The people, and above all the priests, could not accept this. But despite the prevailing sentiments against her the bold and ambitious Hatshepsut ruled with the might of a male pharaoh. In order to create awe and fear in the minds of the people she went about depicting herself as a daughter of god in paintings and sculpture. As if this was not enough, she went further and invested herself with divine qualities. Also, not to be outdone by her male predecessors, she had a very large monument built for herself even before her death. To what lengths vanity and the craze for power can take humans!

My wife and I rose from the wall on which we were sitting, to enter the temple. The interior, 180 feet deep, was full of surprises. The huge front hall was supported by eight 35-feet-high pillars, with a standing figure of Rameses in full royal grandeur inscribed in front of each. The ceiling was decorated with paintings of flying vultures and a star-studded sky. A wonderful relief of the victory over enemy Nubians marked the eastern wall. The passion of vengeance and the utter helplessness of the enemy are portrayed with such skill on this relief that it stands out as a first-class example of Egyptian relief art. Also inscribed are battles with the Hittites and other war victories. The myth that depicts Rameses fighting 2,000 Hittite horsemen singlehandedly may be a bit exaggerated but there is no doubt about the historic validity of the incident. The overdoing is meant to invoke awe, much in the style of the macho heroes of American westerns or Hindi films. The frescoes had retained much of their original brightness, thanks to being buried in sand for so many years. The dry weather of Egypt had proved to be a boon in the preservation of ancient paintings.

From the front hall we entered another hall, flanked by eight store rooms. This hall was half the size of the earlier one and was supported by only four pillars. The frescoes on walls portrayed scenes of Rameses being blessed by the gods – in some he himself was depicted as a god. Crossing the hall and going past a narrow room, we entered the inner chamber of the temple. Full figures of three gods, Ptah, Amen and Ra, and a fourth figure of Rameses himself promoted to the status of a god, stood on a platform. Every morning the first rays of the sun light up the faces of these figures, so exact are their conception and execution.

By the time we came out of the temple of Rameses the sun had risen to the mid-sky, and was directly overhead. Its rays were scorching. After the darkness of the inner chamber the white light of the liquid mercury dazzled our eyes. Dark glasses were not of much help. The temperature was around 115°. The sun's rays pierced us and we felt absolutely parched, as if we had been lost in the desert for days on end. We asked the temple guard for water and drank up quite a few glasses. There was a hotel close by where cold drinks including beer were available, but since we had only an hour and a half left before sailing back across the Aswan lake, that idea was dropped.

We proceeded instead towards the temple of Nefertari, the queen who usually appears as a much smaller figure by the throne of Rameses or by his side or between his legs. Next to Rameses she is depicted insignificant proportions, somewhat like our Mahadev in the frame over the image of goddess Durga. But in her own temple the queen was in her full glory, as large as Rameses. Six standing figures, 35 feet in height, three on each side, flanked the entrance. They were placed on tall cases, the space between the figures serving as buttress walls. There was a statue of the queen between two Rameses figures, not as mere ornamentation here but as an empress in full regal splendour. As in the other temple, we entered a hall on whose walls were depicted various scenes relating to Nefertari's life, such as the queen by the side of her husband, in the process of defeating the Nubians and the Libyans, being crowned by Isis, the goddess of love, and offering prayer to various gods.

We passed the hall and went through three small doorways to enter the square inner chamber. The wall on one side had an image of God Hathor with the queen by his side carrying incense sticks; on the other side was the king pouring wine for himself and his queen.

Compared to the temple of Rameses, Nefertari's temple was smaller but no less remarkable in conception, architecture, sculpture and masterly execution. The artist had made a beautiful synthesis of earthly and divine qualities in fashioning the image of the stunningly beautiful queen – instilling loveliness, sex appeal and other subtle feminine virtues in her. Small wonder that of his hundred odd wives, Rameses had chosen Nefertari to be his empress. By reverse logic, how could a woman as incomparable as Nefertari have chosen a lesser person than the mighty Rameses II!

The wrist-watch reminded me that we had only forty minutes left. It has always been my practice to study the area surrounding an archaeological site, be it in Mexico, Greece, Mahabalipuram or Taxila. Site selection and the environment are two important elements in the total impact of any building – temple, mosque, church, palace or house. That architects of the ancient age were aware of this is in evidence all over the world. This is true particularly of a religious structure. It needs to be built in a place that can arouse respect, awe, even fear, where the mind can find peace, where man feels humbled before god. The present-day surroundings of the Jama Masjid of Delhi, the Biswanath temple of Kashi and the Kalighat temple at Kolkata defeat this purpose, I am sorry to say. Their original environment must have been different.

I looked beyond the temple of Queen Nefertari. The blue waters of the Aswan lake shone like a huge reflector. Water vapour rising from its surface had turned the distant range of hills misty. Occasional movements in the water sent out sparkles like pieces of diamond. The air was crystal-clear, transparent, with not even a speck of dust anywhere. There was no sign of human habitation. Nobody stayed here except tourists, employees of the archaeological department and the people manning the hotels. The place truly enjoyed the solitude of a monastery. To reach the nearest settlement one had to go across the lake. What better place for prayer could one think of than this, where silence is like an elemental sound, where neither leaf nor air stirred, where no noise of humans or animals disturbed the prevailing peace.

A particular memory came back to me from across the expanse of many years. I was sitting at Sanchi facing the western sky. It was the end of autumn; the time, late afternoon. The open plain stretched up to the horizon, at the fringe of which stood the Vindhya range. The sun had just gone down behind the mountains. A patch of dark cloud over the mountain top had covered its last rays. Then it drifted away, rolling up a stage curtain as it were. And what a spectacular play of colour it revealed! The spiralling columns of smoke rising from the village homes made the scene even more dramatic. The birds were returning to their nests, the cows were going back to their sheds. Dusk fell. Silence reigned everywhere. Indeed a most suitable place to worship the Buddha! I had spent the entire afternoon looking at the wonderful sculpture of the *stupa* gate: the creative power of man at its highest and best. It held me enthralled. For the first time, the realization that man can equal his creator dawned on me. The unknown artists had successfully recreated all the wonders of creation – trees, birds, beasts, insects, human beings – on the solid rock surface. Besides the craftsmanship, what held me in awe was the selection of the site. The surrounding area contributed a lot to my appreciation. That experience of the Sanchi *stupa* suddenly came to my mind here at Abu Simbel.

Though a city man, I am fond of solitude because I seem to rediscover myself when I am alone. That is when I realize the mystery and wonder of creation, feel myself to be one with it, immerse myself in the sun, light and air. In short, I become aware of myself. I must come back to this place, I told myself, and stay here for some time, immersed in the pure light and air that cannot be found anywhere else in the world. The barren terrain which had hurt my eyes earlier began to feel like part of the purity. All these years I had feasted my eyes on the greenery of nature, taking that to be the highest expression of natural beauty. Today another aspect of her beauty had revealed itself to me and I considered myself blessed. Another vista had opened for me as an artist and had made me complete.

Several hootings from the boat reminded us that it was time to return to Aswan: cruel reminders that the best moments in life are shortlived. The pressure of reality cut short the bliss, the melody snapped. The hypnotic attraction of Abu Simbel seemed to bind me to that place. I will come back, I assured myself, and forced myself to walk back to the landing.

Back in the hydrofoil, a sparse lunch awaited us on a tray – sandwiches, boiled potatoes and pudding. The sight of the food made us realize how famished we were; the dry weather had certainly activated the digestive machinery. The food was gone in a few minutes. Do you want more, we were asked. We asked for more sandwiches and pudding. After the meal coffee was served.

On the way back we chose middle seats on the boat and not the front ones. Just as we had watched the gradual unfolding of the mysterious Abu Simbel while coming, we wished to witness its sad fading out. Who knew when we would be able come back here. Both joy and sorrow revolve around our lives, both are important.

The steam-driven boat groaned and splashed forward. I lit a cigarette and stared at the receding Abu Simbel. The reflecting rays of the sun created a film-like mist. Already we seemed to have left the temple far behind. The colossal statues of Rameses II towered over all else. The word 'monumental' rightly describes them, stunning as they are to the eyes of the beholder. Where else can we find such a pleasant blend of architecture and sculpture? And a virile spirit dominates over it all. This was the peak of Egyptian art – unadorned, strong, masculine – the hallmark of Egyptian architecture and sculpture.

Let me add something here, with a little trepidation. The wonderful sculpture and architecture of Southeast Asia, including India, suffers from too much ornamentation. This is true especially of South India. The insides and outside of temples are so crowded with images and ornamentation that the eye gets no relief. I find images in museums or their reproductions in books far more satisfying because then they appear in their total beauty, without getting lost in a host of details. The exceptions are Sanchi and Mahabalipuram, where the reliefs are immensely successful in their detailing.

Any comparative analysis without going into the philosophy of aesthetics is bound to be superficial. The scope of this essay does not permit me to go into it. The classical arts of every country are bound by certain rules relating to technique, balance of the parts, proportion, structural symmetry and so on. These conventions lead to the special character of each art. The most noticeable aspect of Egyptian sculpture is its pose and posture: the stance of standing figures with the left leg thrust forward, the hands fisted and hanging straight down, eyes looking straight ahead, massive shoulders and chests, altogether a picture of firmness and inflexibility; some of those qualities are present even in the seated figures. They contribute to the effect of monumental sculpture.

The finest contribution of the Egyptian civilization is its fine arts. Insularity, years of uninterrupted peace, discovery of the gold mines of Nubia and the expeditions to the north and south under the able leadership of Thutmose III and Rameses II led to the flowering of various forms of art, including its massive architecture and sculpture. The developments of this period are so spectacular that people may wonder if developments in similar fields in the subsequent 3000 to 4000 years mark any progress at all. One rarely finds such glorious examples of art in the service of mankind. Yet civilizations rise and fall following the inevitable laws of nature. Like human life, even the highest monuments of civilization move to their inevitable end.

Thoughts like these crowded my mind as the hills of Abu Simbel receded into the far distance. Between the blue sky overhead and the vast expanse of water below everything appeared through a veil of smoke. The intense sunlight on the noble face of Rameses was dazzling, like the gold pitchers on the top of Hindu temples. What a magnificent scene, what a beautiful conclusion to a memorable trip! It is unforgettable and will remain so as long as I live.

I was ecstatic that my long-cherished dream had come true. All my life I have flitted from land to land, undeterred by hardships, just to have glimpses of beauty. And yet, there is so much more to see. In today's world, where the ugly raises its head even in realms of beauty, fortunately there are specimens like Abu Simbel that continue to provide man with spectacles of beauty; to assure him that he has not completely turned away from beauty and hopefully never will.

As I gazed at the sun-bathed statues of King Rameses, the courageous ruler, patron of art and creator of Abu Simbel, whose great work aspires to touch the heavens, whose contribution has enriched human civilization, my head bowed in instinctive homage.

I bow to you, great Rameses, son of the sun god Ra Harekti.

Translated from the Bengali by Enakshi Chatterjee

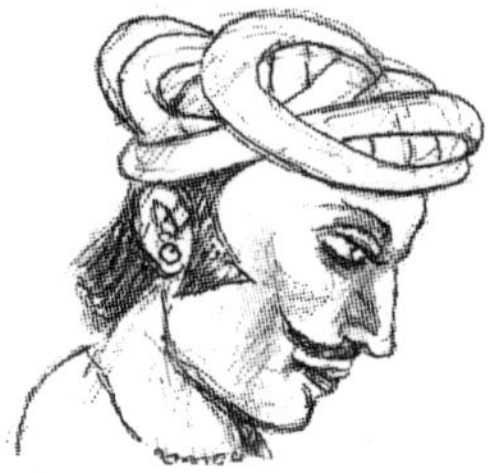

In the role of a prince

It was the month of May in the year 1951. Spring was in the air and the entire city of Paris and its environs – the sky, the foliage, the men and women, the children with their pets – in fact all of creation, was in a mood for celebration. On one such day I was summoned by my Hungarian painter friend, Monsieur Né. 'There is good news for you', he told me on the phone. 'Come as fast as your legs can bring you.'

M. Né was well known in Paris for his semi-abstract paintings, which were cubist in style and nature-based. Older than me, he was affectionate and genial, his French wife more so. M. Né was deeply influenced by the writings of Romain Rolland on Sri Ramakrishna, Vivekananda and Gandhi, and through them had developed a special interest in India. Perhaps that was why he was drawn to me, a struggling young Indian painter in Paris. I had free access to his home. Whenever I visited, whether it was morning or evening, I was never allowed to to leave without being fed liberally.

I took the metro and in no time reached M. Né's third-floor studio flat. What I learnt from him was as follows. One of his old flames, a dancer named Niyotai Iniyoka, had acquired a reputation as an exponent of Indian dance. (There is a mention of her in the autobiography of Amala Shankar, wife of Uday Shankar.) M. Né had just received a phone call from her asking him to send a handsome young Indian man to her if he knew of any. She wanted him to act in her newly composed ballet. It was an urgent request. M. Né patted my back and with a merry twinkle said, 'I think you answer all her requirements.' At a loss, I replied, 'But I have no idea what her requirements are and how on earth I am going to meet them.' 'You'd better go to Iniyoka right away. She will explain everything. It might bring in good money. And a visit to Italy as bonus. Have you been to Italy?' 'No, sir,' I replied, 'though I've been wanting to, ever since I went through a book on World Masterpieces at a neighbour's house in my home-town Dhaka. That was my first acquaintance with Da Vinci, Raphael, Michaelangelo and the other masters.'

The first possibility, however, seemed more attractive to me at that particular moment. My financial state was at its lowest ebb. I was at my wit's end for a way out. Fortunately, I had kind friends, about whom I have written earlier. It was only because of their love and generosity that I did not go hungry even for a single day. I thought over the proposal and finally decided to give it a try. I set out for the home of Niyotai Iniyoka.

She opened the door herself and received me warmly. She lived in a flat in an upper middle-class neighbourhood. 'Né just called', she said. Her next sentence was both mysterious and embarrassing. 'I have been looking for a good-looking man like you. You seem to be the right type for the role. Do come in.' I could not make head or tail of what she was saying.

The furniture of the spacious drawing room had been moved to one side to make room for dance practice. About eight young girls of various skin colour, clad in tights, were rehearsing dance movements in front of mirrors. My entry interrupted their actions and they flopped down on the floor in small groups. Niyotai Iniyoka took me to the next room. Let me take this opportunity to relate to my readers the background of this colourful woman, as gathered from M. Né.

Her family roots were spread over many continents. On her maternal grandmother's side she was a Trinidad Hindu, originally from India. Her grandfather had been brought there from Senegal in North Africa. Her mother was much married: her first husband was a Thai residing in Paris; she left him to marry a man from an aristocratic family in Madagascar; finally she married a Japanese. Niyotai was her second child. The family had a few drops of English blood too along the line, as I came to know later. It is practically impossible to give a full picture of this product of mixed strains. But her oriental features were so pronounced that nobody could possibly mistake her for a westerner, not even for a mulatto.

My first impression of her age was that she was on the wrong side of fifty, but very well preserved. She was short in stature, probably a little over 5 feet, her complexion was a few shades lighter than the 'bright dark' of matrimonial columns. Her skin was taut, her eyebrows pencil-thin. Her dark black hair was done up in a tight knot. The eyes were kohl-lined. The diamond-studded nose had a distinctly Thai look. In the way she looked and carried herself she retained the coquettish ways of her youth. She had adopted the sari as her attire, changing into other costumes only to meet the demands of her various dramatic roles.

'Monsieur Né must have told you what I am looking for.'

'Well, not much. I would be much obliged if you could kindly elaborate.'

'Very well.'

She drew closer to me, our bodies almost touching. Her sari slipped to reveal shapely breasts under the blouse. Artists in general and I in particular have a special inner eye which can penetrate through covers to get to the actual shape of the female breast. I could not help but admire her well-preserved bustline. She certainly did not look her age.

What she told me was, briefly, this. The city of Milan in Italy is the biggest centre of the silk industry in Europe. The silk mill owners' guild spends millions on publicity every year. This year they had thought of a new strategy. Iniyoka had been asked to produce a ballet on the history of the origin of silk. A handsome Indian prince figured as a character in the ballet.

At this point I interrupted her. 'But I am ignorant of the A-B-C of ballet dancing. I am afraid you have chosen the wrong person.'

She was unfazed. 'You don't have to worry. I will tell you what to do. I am an expert in training even rank amateurs.'

I kept saying that what she expected from me was beyond my capability, that I had no training or experience in the field. But she was adamant. 'I won't let you go till you say yes.' Then she mentioned the amount I would be paid and my head whirled. It was more than I could hope to make by selling even ten of my paintings. Given my financial status, I had no alternative but to swallow the bait.

'Will you please explain to me what exactly I have to do?'

'Yes, most certainly. But let me tell you the story first.' She inched closer. 'Your role is so romantic that you will leap up in joy.'

Then she narrated the story. Many years ago, even before the coming of the Buddha, an adventurous Indian prince crossed the Himalayas and reached China. Apparently in those days too there was plenty of bonhomie between India and China. The prince desired an audience with the Chinese emperor, to which the emperor complied readily. With due ceremony the prince was received at the court. After taking his seat the prince looked up, and who did he see before him? An exquisitely beautiful girl in a rich embroidered dress fanning herself with a paper fan. She was introduced to him as the youngest princess. It was love at first sight. A meaningful glance from the princess revealed to the prince that she reciprocated his feelings. Naturally the prince was overwhelmed but thought it prudent not to show his emotion in front of the emperor.

After a few days the two met accidentally one misty morning in the palace garden where the princess had gone to pick flowers. Both were taken aback. On recovering his senses, the prince kneeled before her and spoke of his love. The princess acknowledged it with a smile and disappeared into the mist. They met in the garden every day after that. Gradually the prince began to feel the urge for lasting union with his beloved. But the princess made it very clear

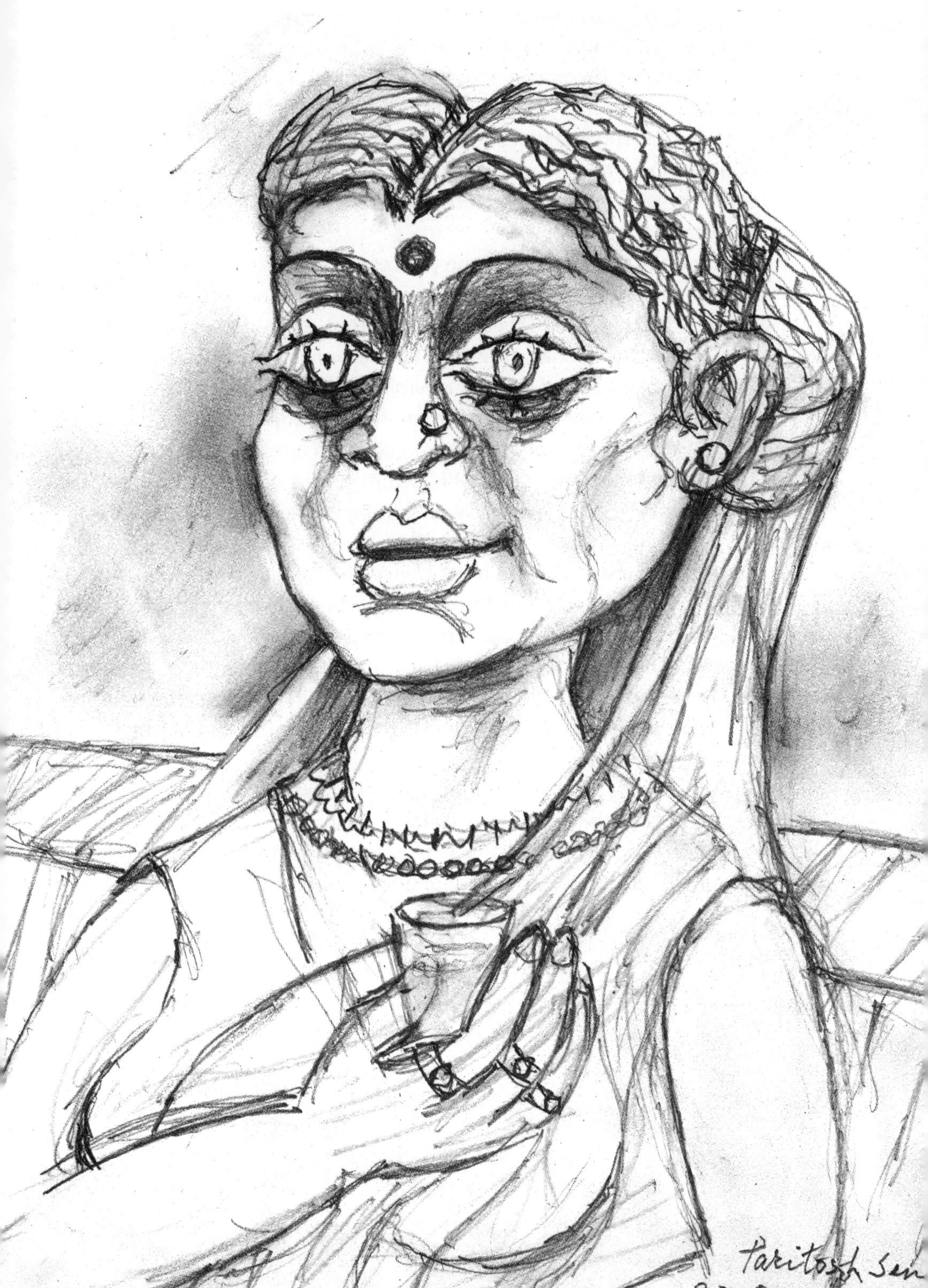
Paritosh Sen
2002

that unless her father agreed they could never be united in marriage.

The next day the prince accosted the emperor on his way to the royal court and knelt before him to express his heart's desire. The emperor was startled at first, but his surprise was soon replaced by anger. 'I can never allow foreign blood to mix with our own, not in my empire!' He frowned darkly. 'You must leave the royal guest house tomorrow. ' He shouted out his orders and marched towards the court.

Meanwhile the prince and the princess fell deeper and deeper in love. They continued to meet secretly outside the palace, behind shrubs and bushes. They exchanged garlands, bouquets, rings and trinkets with inlay work. One of the gifts given by the Chinese princess to the Indian prince was a tiny box. 'Please keep it', she implored. 'This is a symbol of our everlasting love.'

The news of their secret meetings reached the emperor through his spy network. He sent some of his chosen guards to arrest the prince. As soon as they appeared, the prince drew his sword and a pitched battle ensued. Suddenly he was hit from the back by one of the emperor's men hiding behind a bush.

In the final scene we find a sad prince back in his palace in India, staring at the tiny jade and gold-lined box, which was a gift from his beloved. He has no interest in the seductive dancers performing to the tune of lilting music in front of him. The dance rhythm begins with a slow tempo, then goes faster and faster. But the prince is lost in his thoughts. Slowly he opens the lid of the box. There is a silk cocoon inside. A silk cocoon, which is a symbol of eternal love. Thus the story ends.

I had no way of verifying the historical antecedents of this story. Iniyoka believed that the origin of silk was in China from where it was transported to India. But the story was her own invention. Her sponsors, the mill owners of Milan, had given her complete artistic freedom.

I was also beset with doubts about my role in the story and how far I would be able to do justice to my part in this complicated musical ballet. Except for the money, what purpose would it serve me? While I was pondering over these, the shrewd lady winked and held my hand in a tight grip. 'I am sure you find my story fascinating. You will enjoy it immensely. All you have to do is make love to the Chinese princess.' She paused, and then went on with a sly smile. 'Don't you like my story? I have found a suitable princess for you. She must have arrived by now. Let us go to the sitting room. Although the story is about a Chinese princess, this girl is Japanese. I hope it will not make much of a difference on the stage.'

My curiosity about Iniyoka had been mounting as I listened to her story. Finally I threw all politeness to the winds and asked, 'Madam, who trained you in dancing, who is your guru?' Though a little taken aback at first, she soon regained her composure. She gave me a strange answer, which only added to my confusion. 'My guru is the great Nataraj himself', she declared, in a perfectly serious tone. 'I have been attracted to Indian classical dance since my childhood and was determined to learn it at any cost. But no teacher was available. I knew that meditation was part of the philosophy of Indian art, in any form. That no artistic expression is possible without meditation. That is the secret behind the excellent creations at Ajanta and Ellora. So for years I chanted *slokas* in praise of Lord Shiva, sitting in front of a Nataraj idol, praying for his blessings. One morning, imagine my surprise when I found myself dancing in front of the Nataraj! Oh, the ecstasy of it! Heavenly bliss coursed through my entire body. I can still feel that happiness in my veins. So you see, I do not have a guru in the strict physical sense.'

I could hardly believe my ears! I was completely confused by now. On proceeding to the drawing room I found that more girls had joined the dance practice. A woman of mixed blood, probably an assistant of Niyotai Iniyoka, was giving them lessons. A girl sitting at a distance from the group came up to us. 'This is your princess', Niyotai said, introducing her to me. 'Yoko Tani.' (She subsequently acted in a film, *Reap the Wild Wind*, which was shot in India.) I in turn was introduced to her. 'This is our prince.' I was also introduced to the rest of the company. While one couple seemed to be French, all the others looked like cross-breeds. One was from Indonesia. But all of them had been brought up in France. 'Another Indian dancer is going to join us in a few days', announced Iniyoka. She looked at the princess and me and said, 'You two must come thrice every week for a two-hour rehearsal. The other girls will carry on their practice every day. We will rehearse in Paris for a month, then move to Venice, the floating city of palaces, to rehearse on a palace stage for two weeks. A gala opening will follow this. We will perform before the elite of Italy's art world. It will be a spectacular affair. I already have quite a few dinner invitations. Media people are making inquiries too.' Turning to me, she added, 'How does that sound? Fabulous, isn't it? So start your rehearsals from tomorrow. You two don't have to sing or dance. All you have to do is make overtures of love.' She then turned to the princess. 'You certainly are lucky. I am already feeling jealous of you. You have to do some mime. Don't worry, I will show you.'

Like the rest of the group, I too started addressing Iniyoka as Madam. On leaving her house I began to have doubts again. This would be a really weird experience. The story of the origin of silk was absurd enough, even more absurd was the story of her initiation into dancing by Nataraj. I took the metro and reached M. Né's place. I told him everything including my apprehensions about Madam's authenticity. He did not seem the least bothered. 'Don't you worry', he assured me. 'You will get good money, good company, good food

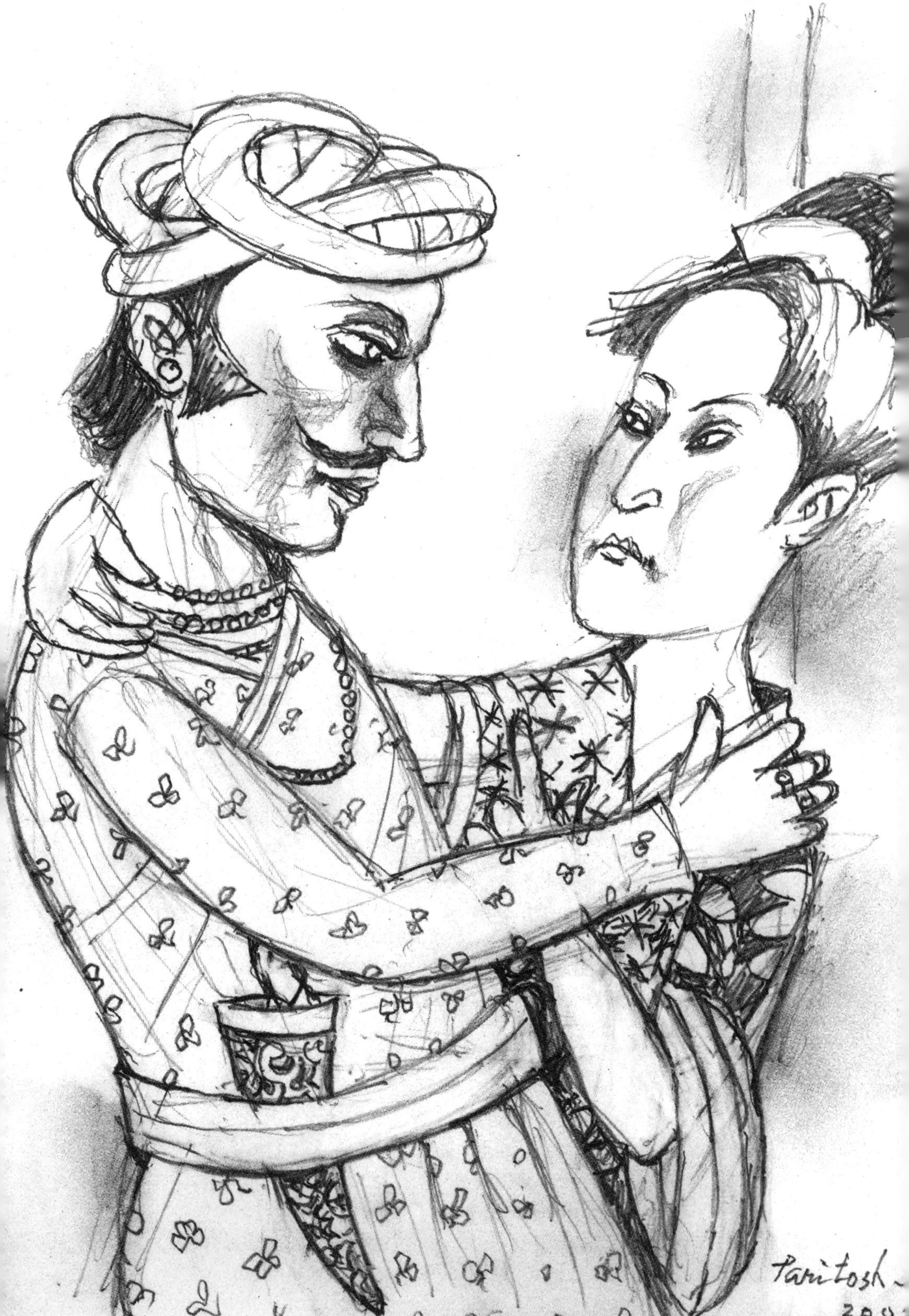
Paritosh

and a chance to travel in Italy. What more do you want? So go, grab it, man.'

The rehearsals started the next day. Let me now move straight to the stage rehearsals in Venice. In the first half of the play my role was confined to meeting the princess secretly behind the bushes. Then comes the order of the emperor and I am banished from the royal palace. Faced with the dire prospect of losing my beloved for ever, I, the Indian prince, begin praying to the god of love, Madanmohan, the son of Nanda. Madam herself played the role of Madanmohan or Krishna. It was an unforgettable scene. Madanmohan is busy frolicking with Radha and her companions under a *kadam* tree overlooked by a full moon. Krishna wore dark blue leotards (the tights worn by ballet dancers which cling to the skin, making every curve visible to the onlooker). Imagine! A Krishna in underwear instead of a *dhoti*, with a crown on his head on which the plume of a peacock had been stuck, plenty of ornaments on his body and a flute in his hand! Madam had tied her breasts so tightly that her chest looked absolutely flat. The tune they played was, most incongruously, a folk-tune-based Tagore song – *Gram chara oi ranga matir path* (The red soil track which goes beyond the village).

Try to visualize the scene! Madam as Krishna frolicking to this music, swinging her hip and throwing her arms about. A group of girls in equally strange costumes prancing about to the rhythm of the band. I have had the opportunity of watching dance performances by masters like Uday Shankar, Bala Saraswati, Rukmini Arundale, Ram Gopal, Gopinath and others, but this was an altogether unique experience. I felt ashamed as an Indian to think that this was being passed off as classical Indian dance by a person who claimed to have been blessed by the god of dance Nataraj himself. Classical Indian dance had created quite a sensation in Paris in the thirties, when Uday Shankar made his debut. (Let me remind the readers that Uday Shankar began his career in Paris and acquired quite a reputation in Europe and America. He was given a royal reception at home when he returned to India in the mid-thirties.)

But from what I could gather from Madam's style of dancing, she had a natural flair for rhythm. Added to this was the still lingering charm of her younger days. Though she had no formal training in Indian classical dance, she had obviously studied the figures at Angkor Vat, Ellora and Borobudur. After making some random movements, she would adopt a classical pose and stay in that position for a while, allowing enough time to create an impression on the spectators. This, in short, was her secret. It was only after the independence of our country that Indian dance troupes had started visiting the west. Before that, Europe had no idea about classical Indian dance. Madam's claim to have learnt her art from Nataraj and her absurd style was funny as well as disconcerting. What am I doing here, I kept asking myself. Why am I a part of this deception? But then I recalled the sound advice of M. Né: you will have good food, the company of women, money and travel. What more could one want?

Meanwhile, a Bengali kathak dancer joined our group: Sukhendu Dutt, originally from Coomilla, who had trained under a disciple of the famous kathak master, Achhan Maharaj of Delhi. This was a very good move. If anyone were to question the authenticity of the dance, Sukhendu was the answer. There was a solo piece by Sukhendu after all the group dances. Sukhendu had brought his own taped music and immediately won a great deal of applause. Even the raw recruits in our group could recognize what was genuine from what was fake.

Let me come back to what was happening on the stage. The fire of love raging in my heart (I mean in the heart of the prince) shows no signs of abating. Lord Madanmohan is powerless to do anything. He advises me to pray to the god of fire to help me out. Since he was the one responsible for starting the fire, nobody else can put it out but him.

As each scene unfolded, a sweet female voice from behind provided the connecting link of the narrative. The scene changes. The illusion of a wild blaze is created by trick lighting in various colours – yellow, orange, dark red. Niyotai Iniyoka herself in fiery orange tights, a huge crown and flame-like ornaments appears in the role of the god of fire. She and her girls dance to the fast tempo of an orchestra playing the tune of a popular Bombay film song broken from time to time by a *dhak* beat. After a good deal of twists and leaps, Madam assumes the Bhairava pose of Ellora, in order to create a mood of fury. The prince, on his knees, prays to the god. 'Get up, my son', says the god of fire. 'It is true that I cause fire to burn but putting it out is not my job. For that you have to pray to the god of air.'

The scene changes promptly. A storm blows on the stage with the help of huge electric fans. Trees sway this way and that. Into this storm-tossed scene the god of wind makes his appearance, his locks streaming in the strong breeze. Madam once again. After giving the prince a patient hearing, the god says, 'I can put out fire all right, but not the fire of love. You have to seek out the god of love. Only he can help you.'

Change of scene once again. The god of love appears with his bow and arrow, riding a cloud, in seductive poses. Fortunately, it is Sukhendu in this role, not Madam. The background music is provided by a female voice singing in the Rajasthani Mand *raga*. The god of love dances in true kathak style to the accompaniment of taped music. He shoots out arrows every now and then, hitting the young lovers and making them more lovesick than ever. A rainbow-coloured light playing across the stage renders the scene as clumsy as the concept. The prince and princess are seen at one side of the stage in a gesture of prayer. Their role is passive – in between the appearances of the various gods they are seen hugging and kissing – that is all. The primary idea was to bring in colourful dance sequences, however incongruous or unnecessary they may be in the context of the story.

I have forgotten to mention that an Italian assistant was engaged to coordinate our acting with the commentary in Italian. Italians are an emotional race. Exaggeration of everything, including the expression of emotion, is second nature to them; they are not happy otherwise. What I am going to narrate now has a lot to do with this national trait. During rehearsals the princess cooperated with me fully on the love scenes, making them seem as natural as possible. But one night, on the stage, she seemed keen to keep me away from her. What was the matter? I was confused. Meanwhile the Italian assistant shouted from the auditorium, '*Malto amora, Malto amora*', which meant love in a more intimate style. We had to come closer. This propelled me to be more aggressive. But as I pulled the princess towards me she whispered, 'Don't, please. My boyfriend is here. He is very jealous, he does not like this. It might lead to a misunderstanding or worse. I am sorry.'

Meanwhile, cries of *Malto amora, Malto amora* filled the auditorium like a slogan. With consideration for the plight of my princess I merely made a show of pulling her towards me. Fortunately the scene changed and we were relieved for the time being. But it was embarrassing for us both while it lasted. How was I to know that her boyfriend had taken a seat in the dark auditorium? I had no idea what he looked like, either. Little did I know of the absurd consequences that would follow when I joined Madam Iniyoka's troupe. This was one among many professional hazards but at that awkward moment I was hardly in any state to rationalize.

The god of love informs the lovers that he is not equipped with the means to extinguish the fire of their blazing passion. The only god who can do this is Indra, god of the heavens. Indra is invoked and he appears in his splendour, riding his elephant, Airavata. He makes the heavens burst forth in rain and thunder, but the fire of love refuses to be put out. Many other gods come and dance away. At last come Shiva and Shakti, but please don't ask me how and in what connection. I have no answer. How can there be any explanation where all logic had been thrown to the winds. To cut a complicated story short, Shiva and Shakti take pity on the lovers and quench their fire of passion though they are not able to fulfil their wishes. So the Indian prince, banished from China, is obliged to return to his home country. What happens later has already been told.

In our troupe there were twenty young girls and just two men – me and Sukhendu. For some strange reason, Sukhendu was not interested in girls. In no time the girls became aware of this and focused on me. They devised various tricks to get my attention, my princess being no exception. It was quite a problem for me dealing with all the girls, a single man in a large harem. But it was also a most desirable situation for any man, needless to say.

The troupe staying in a hotel in central Venice, the Piazza San Marco. Madam was staying in a different place. After an early dinner we used to go for rehearsal. We spent the whole day together, playing ping pong, bathing at the beautiful Lido beach, roaming around looking at the marvels of Italian art, walking down the alleyways of Venice, window-shopping and chatting over cups of coffee on the spacious terrace of Piazza San Marco, watching tourists from different countries. On the whole we were having a good time.

One day as I was about to go in for my bath, Yoko Tani, my princess, knocked on the door and entered, clad in the briefest *choli* and panties and carrying a towel and a bottle of oil. She saw the towel in my hand and asked, 'So you are going for your bath too?' Then she came closer and placed her hands on my shoulder. 'You know something? I believe you Indians are as good at massaging as you are at yoga and meditation. Will you give me a massage with this French oil?' Before I could say anything, she promptly spread the towel on my bed and stretched herself out on her stomach. The more I tried to convince her that she was mistaken, the more vehemently insistent she became. She kept urging me, 'Try it. Try it. Don't disappoint me!'

The only way to get rid of her quickly was to comply. But how and where was I to begin? I was completely at a loss. Yoko Tani had velvet-like skin, soft to the touch. Perhaps all Japanese women have such skin. The bare portions of her body gave the impression of tight muscles underneath. An irresistible urge to tickle her took possession of me. I controlled myself with great effort. I began massaging her from the toes up. Never before in my life had I massaged anyone, male or female. And she was a foreigner to boot. After a few moments of silence the princess murmured, 'Your touch is like a feather. Do it like a man, can't you?'

I was in a fix. I applied more pressure and kept on. 'You are a liar', said the princess. 'You are doing it almost like a professional. How long have you been doing this? Carry on, I am enjoying it.'

By then my fingers had reached her knees. Undecided which way to go now, I kept pressing the region around her knees. 'Why are you sticking to one spot?' complained the princess. 'Go further up. I am enjoying this very much.'

My hands made a leap to her back, resisting the temptation of exploring the area between the knees and the back, fascinating as it was in its rhythmic ups and downs. We Indians are used to suppressing our natural instincts right from childhood. As a result we suffer from peculiar manifestations of inhibition. People in the west are comparatively free and open.

Suddenly, to my great embarrassment, the princess unbuttoned her blouse to give freer access to my hands. What was I do? My fingers acted mechanically while the princess moaned with her eyes shut and kept pleading with me to carry on. When would this ordeal be over! The princess now turned over and lay on her back. I was quite flabbergasted at this dramatic change of scene. My heart beat faster as the scene unfolding before me was becoming impossible to resist. I closed my eyes but that was of no use. Emotion was about to give way before reason. A wave of heat went over my body and the pores of my skin grew tense. What was the best way to deal with this crisis? Should I take the plunge and resolve the dilemma?

At this critical point there was a knock on the door. It was Sukhendu. I had a huge impulse to punch him hard. A glance inside the room made him realize his mistake and he fumbled. 'I am sorry, I am indeed sorry.' The princess had turned over and was lying on her stomach now. I controlled my anger and disappointment and invited Sukhendu in. 'Do come in.' To the princess I said, 'Now I am going to hand you over to the right person.' Turning to Sukhendu I spoke in Bengali, 'Massage this girl good and proper, will you? I am sure you can do it better than me. This is part of your profession. Besides, your muscles are stronger than mine. The princess will enjoy it.'

Visibly irritated, the princess sat up, buttoned up her *choli* and climbed out of the bed. She put on her slippers and made her exit, muttering, 'You are hopeless! You are less than a man!' I took a vow to show her that she was being unfair, that I did not deserve that humiliating comment.

Meanwhile, the date for our gala opening was drawing near, with only three more days to go. Excitement ran high. I think I was the only person who did not share the general enthusiasm. Somehow I was reluctant to be associated with Iniyoka's absurd hotch-potch of a story of the origin of silk and the presentation of that fantastic tale with generous doses of Indian classical dance, 90 per cent of which was bogus. I was looking forward to the time when the silly ballet would be over and I could set out to see Italy: the country which had brought about a change in European art from the thirteenth to the early seventeenth century; a new age which had begun with Cimabue and Giotto and included Fra Angellico, Masaccio, Uccello, Tintoretto, Titian, Verocchio, Pierro Della Francesca Mantegna, Bellini, Boticelli, Da Vinci, Raphael, Michaelangelo and other such towering artists.

Finally the big night arrived. Our ballet, 'Love in a Cocoon', was to open to its first show. The auditorium was packed to capacity. Eminent citizens from as far as Rome and Milan were invited to the opening. It was a gathering of the elite. A glimpse through the curtains revealed well-dressed and beautiful ladies in the front rows. Italian women are famous for their good looks. I discovered that this was no exaggeration.

Just before the show started, a sweet female voice gave the viewers a summary of the story and of how Niyotai Iniyoka had transformed it into a ballet by her extraordinary choreography. We often claim that Bengali is a very musical language but I think Italian is sweeter. Perhaps it is for this reason that this language gave birth to the opera and that most operas are composed in Italian.

Since I have already described the story line of the ballet in some detail, there is no need to go over it again. Right from the first scene the thundering applause was proof of the audience's appreciation. The lavish sets and excellent lighting contributed a lot to the total effect. The sponsors had not spared any expense. The two best people in the field were employed to take care of these. Whatever may have been the shortcomings in the musical part, the light effects and sets were simply dazzling.

The scenes followed one after the other. I was waiting for the episode where I had to have a sword fight with the spies. I was made to sport a Rana Pratap-type moustache and was clad in the glittering attire of a Rajput warrior, complete with appropriate turban, strings of pearls and a sword hanging from the belt.

Outside the palace walls, half-hidden in a bush, I sat with the princess in my arms, kissing her passionately. It was night. The sky above the wall was studded with stars. The princess was holding me tightly. 'What is the matter? Is your boyfriend out there?' I whispered. She shook her head. So he was not in the audience. This meant she was being serious in the expression of her love. It must have seemed very natural to the viewers. We were lost in a world of our own when our dream was rudely broken by the sudden appearance of a group of armed men who sprang before us. I leapt up to deal with the intruders, brandishing my sword. The strategy was that only one of them would pretend to fight with me, while the others would jump about as though in a hurry to kill me. One of them would stab me from behind. I have always hated the sword. What an irony of fate that I had to wield that very weapon, that too on a stage! My co-fighter too was a novice in the art, like me. So we had come to a gentleman's agreement. We would act out a few hitting motions and then lock our swords in the figure of an X. After some time we would disengage our swords, only to return soon to the X position. Madam's attempts to train us under an expert in the art of sword-fighting had not worked at all. So she instructed us to keep the sword fight as brief as possible. My intention was to keep our swords locked for the most part and keep the brandishing to a minimum.

But on the stage, even as I kept desperately whispering to my opponent to keep the swords locked, he insisted on disengaging and hitting out at random. 'Keep to our agreement', I kept telling him, but it did not seem to have any effect. I was in mortal danger. Why wasn't he paying any heed? Scared stiff, I whispered to the man who was supposed to stab me to hurry up. 'Quick, quick', I said. 'It is time. Act now.' Fortunately he followed my cue and I fell to the ground. The curtains came down.

Later I came to know from one of my co-actors, that the man who was supposed to have a duel with me had appeared on the stage dead drunk, having consumed half a bottle of brandy just before the show. I was lucky that a major mishap had been averted. To come back to the performance, I rushed to change for the next scene. I hurried to the make-up room where the Italian assistant was waiting for me with a new set of costumes. As I took off my robe, he exclaimed, 'What is this? Your vest is soaked in blood!' I took it off and turned to the mirror. True enough, there was a wound on my back, though not a very serious one. But I was in no condition to pay attention to my wound, for I had to be back on the stage soon in the new costume. The make-up man dabbed the wound with dettol and cotton. Donning my Rajasthani prince's costume, I walked on to the stage. Later the mystery of the wound was revealed.

In dramatic performances and films a special kind of knife is used for fight scenes. It is different from a real knife in that the blade slips into the sheath as soon as the tip touches the body. But as ill luck would have it, it failed to work in my case because the knife was being used after a long time and both the cover and the blade had rusted. Instead of slipping in the blade had stayed as it was and pierced my back. Fortunately, the cut was not very deep.

In the last scene we find the exiled prince in his palace, looking depressed. He is holding the ornamental box containing the silk cocoon, a symbol of eternal love. Dejected and heartbroken, he stares at the box. No amount of distraction can revive his spirits, neither the slim beauties fanning him nor the sparkle of the chandeliers or the dancing fountains spraying coloured water. A group of youthful maids appear with wine in silver glasses, followed by dancers clad in the scantiest of clothes. The band plays lilting Hindi film melodies to which the girls dance. It is a queer combination of sexy movements which cannot, by any stretch of imagination, be accepted as dance: a random throwing about of arms and legs and coming to a rest in the posture of a dancing figure from some ancient Indian temple sculpture. I found the entire exercise to be hypocritical. My acquaintance with Indian classical dance goes back to my student days in Madras when I had had the opportunity of watching Bala Saraswati and Rukmini Devi from close quarters, an experience matched later only by the performances of the young Yamini Krishnamurti. And here I was, witnessing an absurd concoction being passed off as Indian dance. When one is not in a position to change an adverse situation there is no way but to accept it, I suppose, however unpleasant.

The open-air theatre resounded with the strains of the dance music. The band was playing an appealing mixture of North Indian folk and film tunes. The sky over Venice echoed with the sounds of the clarinet, flute, saxophone and other wind instruments accompanied by percussion, as well as the violin, cello and other string instruments. What made the last scene unforgettable was the spectacular play of light. And Niyotai Iniyoka leaving the stage to the veteran kathak dancer Sukhendu, who had already captured the hearts of the spectators with his wonderful footwork, exquisite movements and perfect control over rhythm. The audience loved the scene. Gradually, things were moving to the finale, the tempo was stepping up. Anticipating the climax, the audience started to clap. The applause merged with the tinkle of anklets and the beats of the drums as the heavy velvet curtains descended. A great burst of applause followed. The curtains were drawn. Niyotai Iniyoka walked on to the stage and bowed in Indian style. The applause went on. At her signal I and the princess joined Iniyoka and bowed in front of the spectators. Sukhendu was next. The clapping intensified. Then came the dancers, followed by the musicians, the art director and his assistants. The applause continued for ten whole minutes, after which the lights went out one by one, and the clapping too died down. Darkness descended on the seventeenth-century palace by the Grand Canal for the night.

Often we are obliged to take up jobs that are not to our liking. One has to make a living after all, and it is sometimes difficult to draw a line between the good and the bad. Compromises are inevitable where self-interest is involved, or just for the sake of earning a livelihood. But ultimately a time comes when one has to face one's conscience. This may lead to a correction of ways, and enable one to shake off hypocrisy and material attractions and feel proud just to be oneself. But again some people get so immersed in material comforts that they sink lower and lower. Needless to say, their footprints leave no trace on the sands of time.

I could not help pondering over the strange ways of Niyotai Iniyoka from whatever I could gather from the bits of information I knew about her. I did not know what to make of a person who claimed to have learnt dancing from the god Nataraj himself, and who earned name and fame by parading ridiculous dance sequences as classical Indian art. Probably she believed what she was presenting was the genuine thing. At a personal level, we all had reason to be charmed by her warmth of heart. She kept a constant watch on all the members of her troupe. There was no doubting her liberal attitude. All the same, I found it difficult to integrate these two aspects of her character – the generous employer and the daredevil presenter of adulterated art. People do have contradictory traits. But how could I, an artist myself, accept her attempt to deliberately distort art and pass it off as genuine stuff?

That night was our fourth and last performance in Venice. We were taken out to dinner and dance after the show every night by one or the other of the silk magnates of the city. For a poor and starving artist like me, the fabulous food and the company of beautiful, well-dressed Italian women seemed like a dream. The ladies would drag me on to the dance floor, not heeding my refusals. After the food and wine I would be in no condition to dance; besides, I was no dancer at all. But their perfume, soft touches, bare shoulders and the lilting waltz would prove irresistible and ultimately I would give in.

Since all the others except me were leaving for Paris the next day, we had no dinner engagement on that last night. We were left to our own devices, we could roam the dream-city to our hearts' content. It was sheer folly not to take advantage of the attractions provided by Venice – gondolas sailing in the waterways to romantic melodies of the guitar or the accordion, the warm sands of the Lido beach (the setting for the Venice International Film Festival and the Venice Biennale) where men and women of all ages make love. Why let go of these and later regret it for the rest of one's life?

During lunch Sukhendu had a suggestion. Let us take a trip on a gondola tonight, he said. Good idea, I replied. But it was very costly. We needed to be at least three or four to share the expenses. Besides, sailing in a gondola just by ourselves would be kind of unromantic. We must have proper companions. I approached two of our co-artistes, Madeline and Lena, at the next table, and persuaded them to join us. Madeline was married, Lena was still in school.

After dinner we set out on a gondola from the terminus at the Grand Canal. It was a windless summer night but the moving gondola provided plenty of breeze. Once in a while other tourist-laden gondolas crossed us. Accordion music wafted in the breeze. Madeline scoffed at it, saying they were all hackneyed love songs, but I liked them. The Italian language has a charm of its own. The moon shining in the sky, the water murmuring below and the sound of the music, all combined to create a drowsy effect. Perhaps the generous helpings of Italian wine during dinner also contributed. 'I feel sleepy', I told Madeline. She promptly offered her lap. 'Put your head down here. Let me stroke you.' Oh, what heavenly bliss! This just what a night in Venice should be like.

Well past midnight we returned to the hotel, with me holding on to Madeline. She invited me in. 'Please come in. I will put you to sleep.'

Every day I spent in Venice offered wonderful experiences of endless variety. What I have related here is but a sampling of them. I am grateful to Niyotai Iniyoka for giving me that opportunity. The Venice chapter of my life will remain vivid in my memory forever, a kaleidoscope of strange and wonderful happenings.

Translated from the Bengali by Enakshi Chatterjee

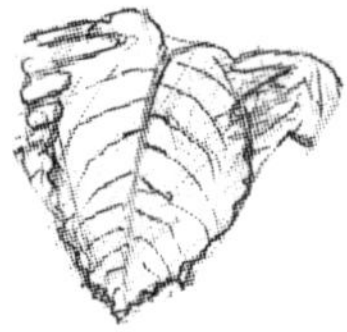

In search of Arcadia

Madeline and I lived in adjoining rooms in an insignificant Paris hotel. During the last four years we had developed a natural and friendly relationship. Madeline worked in the trunk-calls department of the telephone company. She came from a middle-class home in central France but lived in Paris because of her job.

Every summer, during the tourist season in the Mediterranean region, she was posted to a coastal area in the south of France, known as Côte d'Azure, or the Blue Coast. Thousands of tourists flocked to the coast at that time of the year, swam for hours in the cool blue waters of the ocean, basked in the sun, inhaled the invigorating air and recuperated after the long winter. A couple of thousands of government employees like Madeline were transferred there during the summer months, to be of service to these tourists.

One day in early June she told me, 'I have a posting for ten weeks in Le Lavandou. I'll go there first and settle down. Then I will inform you. You must join me as soon as you can. It is a small tourist spot by the sea. You will like it. You may feel like painting as well.'

I had heard and read of Cannes, Nice, St Tropez, Monaco and other such places in France. Famous writers and artists throng these spots. Rich people from all over the world are also known to frequent these places. But this was the first time I was hearing of Le Lavandou. I opened my atlas to find its location. It was about 200 kilometres to the east of Marseilles with a beach in front and hills forming the backdrop.

I had a call from Madeline within a week. 'I have a wonderful two-room flat. You can get a view of the sea from inside the rooms. Even from the toilet. Besides, there is the pure and dry air, life-giving sunlight and delicious seafood. What more do you want? Don't dilly-dally. I am looking forward to your visit.'

In a few days' time I was on my way to Lavandou. I reached Marseilles after a whole day's train journey. I called Madeline to tell her when and by which bus I would be arriving at Lavandou. She was waiting at the bus stop with a bouquet of roses. The sight of her filled me with delight. I clasped her in a warm embrace.

Madeline was a kind, well-mannered and softspoken woman of thirty plus. She had lovely eyes. Though not really beautiful, she had a charm of her own. She was taller than the average Frenchwoman and had a poise that made her quite attractive. Unfortunately, she suffered from an unnecessary inferiority complex because she had not been to the university. This made her shy and withdrawn in front of men. In fact it took me quite some time to break the ice between us. Our friendship was based on the understanding that we had no expectations of each other. We led completely independent lives, yet there was no dearth of affection between us. My heart fills with gratitude even now as I write of her: she was like a guardian angel who saved me from starvation, provided monetary help from time to time and rescued me from the terrible curse of loneliness.

We were sipping Pernod, an aperitif, in her balcony. It is a fairly strong drink if taken quickly, but creates a warm feeling of well-being if sipped slowly. Soon I began to feel as light as a feather, helped along by the Mediterranean breeze. It was a wonderful feeling of unalloyed idleness, of being on a perfect holiday after a long time.

'I have cooked Bouillabaisse for you, a fish dish typical of this area. Made with saffron, garlic, cardamom, cinnamon and herbs.' I had heard about this delicacy and could not wait to have a taste. Instead I said, 'I'm feeling so good that all thoughts of dinner have faded from my mind. Let us stay here a little longer. Moments like this when all material thoughts slip away and the mind is free to soar towards outer space do not come very often.' I was becoming philosophical.

Madeline suggested a stroll along the beach. We did so after our meal. I pointed to a cluster of lights on the sea, quite a distance away, and commented, 'Look, a ship at anchor.' She burst into laughter. 'I am afraid that is not a ship but a hilly island: L'ile du le Vent, or Windy Island. It is quite famous for a special reason. I'll take you there tomorrow. It's a holiday, so we can spend the whole day there.' I wanted to know what was so special about the island but she refused to elaborate. 'I am not going to tell you now. You will find out for yourself. That will be better.'

The barefoot walk on the wet sand coupled with the sea breeze had made me drowsy. We turned back to the flat.

The next morning at our breakfast of coffee and croissants, Madeline asked me, 'Have you brought your swimming trunks? You should get into them once we reach the island. There is a lovely beach on the other side where you can bathe.'

'No, I don't have my trunks with me', I told her.

'In that case, your underwear will do. Actually, it would hardly matter even if you wore nothing at all.'

'What do you mean?' I was puzzled.

She had a mischievous smile. 'That is all for now. Let's proceed towards the ferry.'

It was a small single-deck steamer. About fifty people were already aboard, most of them armed with binoculars, focusing them towards the island. I was the only coloured person. All the passengers were scantily clad like Madeline.

The sky was a transparent blue, a colour not to be found in Paris or in the north of France. Even the paintings of the impressionists do not have this kind of blue. That is because they painted landscapes of northern France. Only when Van Gogh came to Arles in the south of France was this shade of thick enamel blue caught on his canvas.

There was a bracing breeze. The air was free from dust, allowing the sun's rays to penetrate the body. I felt as though I was riding the crest of waves of joy. I had heard how the sun and the air of the Mediterranean act like a tonic. No wonder thousands of people flock here from faraway places to soak in the sun and to prepare themselves to face the bitter winter ahead.

The steamer was drawing close to the island. It was now clearly visible. The binocular-owners were getting alert as though they were expecting something. The French girl next to me, without taking her eyes off the binoculars, exclaimed, 'Ah, what a reception!' All the other watchers laughed, Madeline included. I borrowed the binoculars from the girl and focused them. This is what I saw. On the boulders on the beach two large women in their forties were standing with their back to us, completely naked, drying themselves after a dip in the water.

No wonder the passengers were amused. I returned the binoculars to their owner and asked Madeline, 'What's going on?' 'I want to give you a surprise,' said Madeline. 'In a little while. You will enjoy it.' This increased my curiosity many-fold.

By now we were so close to the island that no binoculars were needed to see what was going on. My suspicions were confirmed. I saw men and women, all without clothes, either sunbathing or enjoying the spray of the waves dashing against the boulders. It reminded me of the wealth of women figures in art, starting from the fertility goddess to the fleshy women of Rubens and the straight lines of the bathing beauties of Cezanne.

'Now you can see where we are and the reason why I kept you in the dark', said Madeline. 'This is France's only nudist colony. It is a wild and lovely place. Thanks to the efforts of our tourism department, it is quite unspoilt too. Huge boulders, undulating walks, an overgrowth of shrubs, rows of pines, an open sky, the ocean around, pure air, a quiet and peaceful environment, and good food to top it all – can you think of a better way to spend a holiday?' We walked up the hilly track and encountered quite a few of the residents of the island on the way, men and women of all ages. The dry heat and the excitement had left me feeling parched. 'Let's go somewhere and have a cold drink', I suggested. 'Let us climb up a little. There is a well-stocked restaurant there. You will get hard and soft drinks, whatever you want.'

The path up was steep and hilly; the beach lay on the other side, away from the public gaze. But even here we met nude men and women, with just some of the men clad in the briefest of underwear. Perhaps these were worn as a precaution. For men in a nudist colony walking about without any underwear could pose a problem. Sexual excitement in the male is clearly visible, unlike with the female. Under the circumstances I was beginning to feel much too overdressed. I had already taken off my shirt. Now I rolled up my trousers, that was the best I could do. But I still felt uncomfortable.

We reached the restaurant. It was on a wide terrace on the top of the hill. A winding grapevine covered part of the structure. The wide expanse of the sea stretched out in front and there were plenty of flowering shrubs. We ordered beer. Surprisingly, the waiters were all fully dressed, in black trousers, white shirts, black bow-ties and white coats.

Except for a few of us all the customers in the restaurant too were in the nude. Some were families: husband, wife and two to three children. The sight of them sitting at the tables without any clothes on but with napkins spread on their knees was odd and amusing. The desire to go back to nature, to get back to primitive instincts, certainly cannot be fulfilled by discarding clothes. It is not so easy to break out of the crippling rules of urban civilization. Besides, we are all such slaves of habit. Would it be sacrilege if a few crumbs of food dropped on one's naked body?

'Since we are here, we may as well have our lunch', I said to Madeline. 'I am sure this place will be quite crowded at lunch-time.'

'You get only seafood here', Madeline informed me.

The cheapest item on the menu card was grilled pomfret and boiled vegetables. But the price was high enough to give me a jolt. 'Forget it', I said. 'Let's order sandwiches.'

'No way', protested Madeline. 'We are not likely to come here every day. We will have the grilled pomfret. I don't mind spending a little money.'

By now I had seen about forty nude people, but most of them were between the ages of forty and sixty. I started looking for younger women. Where had all the girls gone? My disappointment gave way to surprise when a young girl in her early twenties walked in just then. She was about five foot seven, pencil-slim, with a shock of long hair and in her birthday suit.

Nonchalantly she went over to a corner seat, ordered something and turned her attention to the book she was carrying. There was something distinctly carefree in her manner. The other nude women I had seen so far were not as successful in shedding their veneer of civilization. They were out of place in the untamed environs. The only exception so far was this young girl.

'Strange', I exclaimed. 'She is without a companion.'

'I am sure she has one', Madeline hazarded a guess. 'Nobody comes here alone. Must be around somewhere.'

The girl had a beautiful tan, a mixture of the colours of gold and light sand, a product of the sun and sea water. Her hair was a polished gold. Her breasts and the portion below the navel were a lighter shade, showing the effects of bra and panty. Her uncombed hair kept falling over her eyes and she shook it off with a quick and wild gesture that reminded one of wild animals. I found her fascinating. The more I looked at her the more she reminded me of a leopard – the same quick movement, curves, a sense of power held in check. Her body was wonderfully smooth. 'Thank you, Madeline,' I said, 'for bringing me here and giving me the chance to observe such an exquisite female form, comparable only to the Chola sculptures or the wall figures of Egyptian dancers.' That a form in flesh and blood could equal the artist's imagination was something to be seen to be believed.

'Well, if you are lucky you may come across other beauties. Let us hurry and go to the beach. That is the happening place', said Madeline.

(A few months later I was leafing through a popular magazine in a barber's shop in Paris, when the photograph of a girl in a bikini made me catch my breath. It was the same girl. Her name was Brigitte Bardot. She had created a sensation with her first appearance in a movie. I rushed to the nearest kiosk to buy a copy of the magazine. Then I hurried to our flat and showed the photo to Madeline. 'Do you remember seeing this girl before?' I asked her. After giving the picture a good look she suddenly exclaimed, 'Why, this is the girl you fell for, the one you compared to Chola sculptures and Egyptian dancers. Now I remember.')

We went down the slope of the hill past a lot of overgrowth till we came to a clearing from where we had a view of the sea. As we proceeded further the crowded beach and the equally crowded sea could be seen. Needless to say, everyone there was in the nude.

There is a thin line of distinction between nakedness and nudity. The famous art historian Sir Kenneth Clerk has defined it as follows in his book *The Nude*: 'To be naked is to be deprived of our clothes and the word implies some of the embarrassment which most of us feel in that condition. The word nude on the other hand carries, in educated usage, no uncomfortable overtone. The vague image it projects into the mind is not of a huddled and defenceless body, but of a balanced, prosperous and confident body: the body re-formed.'

It was not as if the experience was a unique one. During the course of my training as an art student and then as a teacher I have, on more than one occasion, come across nude men and women. It was imperative to have nude models in art class, at least for some time. But the spectacle of an assembly of nude men and women, of all ages and sizes, was certainly new. Surprisingly, I felt no sexual excitement at all. Curiosity, mystery and sexuality, these are the three things associated in my mind with the female body. But all these sentiments are aroused only when the body is partly clad.

One particular model comes to my mind, one of the most perfect models I have encountered. I met her in the United States in 1981 when I was teaching at a well-known art college. She was a student but from a different department. Modelling for her was a way to pay the tuition fees. This was a common practice in the art schools and colleges there. She had a very ordinary name, Marie, but her figure was anything but ordinary. The perfect symmetry of her body was indeed rare, perhaps one in a million. The very first day, as she took off her clothes one by one, I had felt a pleasurable excitement. The feeling of anticipation, of mystery, persisted as long as the process of disrobing was underway. But the moment she was completely nude and ready to pose for our sketches, all the excitement vanished. She reminded me of Rockeby Venus, the masterpiece by the Spanish artist Velasquez. Naturally, she was in high demand as a model.

Perhaps I should also mention here that very few women are worth viewing in the nude. That is why it is better for them to be robed than disrobed. Nevertheless, the nude female form has a special place in all art, eastern and western. In most art forms it is the youth of a woman that is celebrated, and youth is inseparable from sexuality. The female body is a symbol of nature's bounty and the spirit of creation. The French artists Ingres and Renoir have glorified the female form in flesh and blood, each in his own style. Gauguin has done the same. The vivacious dark beauties of Tahiti found in his paintings are youthful and physical. Turning to our country, the Yakshi of the Gupta era and the Vrikshaka figures, all are portrayed with heavy breasts and ample hips. Everywhere there is glorification of youth and sexuality. The only exceptions to this are the goddesses of the fertility cult, in whom the emphasis is more on the eternal plentiful aspect and less on transitory youth. This exuberance has been equated with the exuberance of nature.

Let me return to the nudist colony. The sea here was not rough but the waves were quite high, rising to about double the height of the swimmers. When the dark blue waves swelled before breaking, the sunlight streamed through, making their blue as transparent as glass. Swimming in the placid waters of a river or lake and tackling these huge waves of the sea seemed to

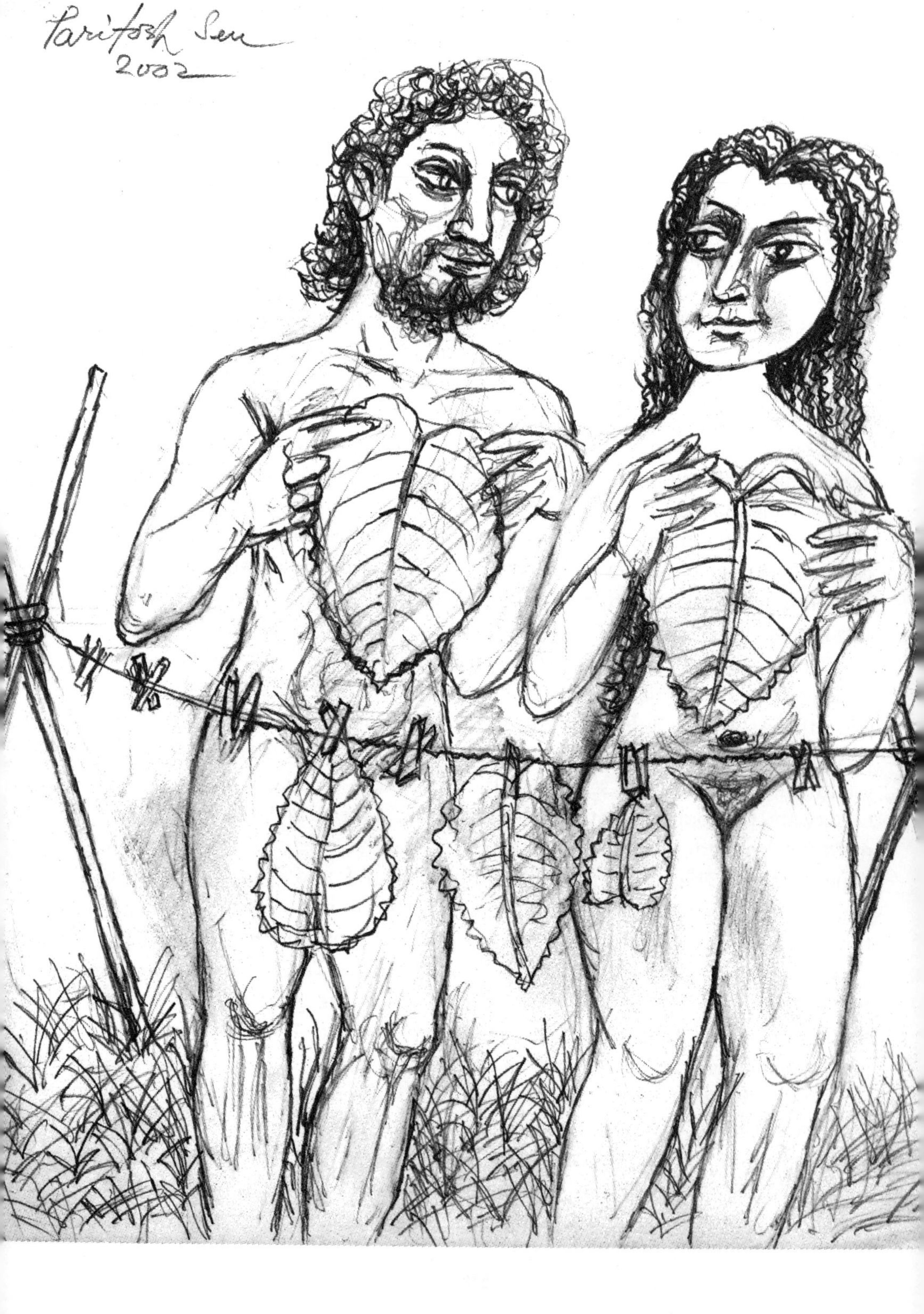
Paritosh Sen
2002

me to be two entirely different propositions. To ride the crest of the waves effortlessly requires a perfect sense of timing. It must be a different kind of thrill altogether. This was corroborated by what I saw before me. The women swimmers were all young with taut bodies. The effortlessness with which they are swimming belonged to creatures of the sea. They seemed very at ease in water. The blithe abandon of the waves matched their equally joyous abandon.

Indeed, if one thinks of the strange and varied ways of entertainment human beings have devised for themselves, one is bound to be amazed. But grappling with sea waves in the nude must be one of the most enjoyable of all sports. I am sure all swimmers would agree with me. The difference between swimming in the nude and with a swimsuit on is like the difference between a complete and a partly done figure in art. In my opinion two other forms of sport, skiing and figure skating, can also lay claim to this distinction because these too combine pleasure with aesthetic beauty. But swimming in the nude has no equal, I had this feeling while watching the young women in the water. Despite the fact that I do not know how to swim I could not help feeling this way. The regret of not being able to swim hit me badly that day, standing on the beach of the nudist colony. I felt sorry for myself, for being deprived of one of the purest pleasures of life. I blamed my guardians for not letting me learn to swim. It was a gross neglect on their part, I found it unpardonable.

I was so engrossed in watching the young swimmers that I did not at first notice that many people were giving me curious looks. I asked Madeline about this. She advised me to take off my trousers and walk about in my underwear. I realized that in a place where to be free of clothes was a precondition, even underwear would be superfluous. Another reason why I was being stared at was the colour of my skin: I was the only dark person in an assembly of whites.

'Let us go now to the most interesting spot, the area where they live, the actual colony', said Madeline.

We climbed up a narrow track lined by boulders and shrubs. Presently we reached a crossing where there was a notice board across two posts. I peered at it to find a cartoon, amateurishly drawn but funny nevertheless. It was called Adam and Eve's First Washing Day. The drawing showed Adam and Eve hanging up fig leaves to dry. It reminded me of another famous cartoon: four famous men under a tropical tree dressed in grass skirts like South Sea islanders – they were Levi Strauss, Roland Barthes, Michel Foucault and Jaquemont Lacanne. The dandiest among them sported a bow tie. The cartoon, which made fun of the four great intellectuals, appearing under the title *Le dejeuner des structuralists*, had created quite a sensation a few decades ago. One of the reasons why they were shown in island garb was perhaps because of the research done by Levi Strauss on the mental processes of primitive peoples. In a way the nudist colony too could be called a caricature of primitive life.

The notice board made it clear that it was mandatory to follow the rules of the colony. These applied to tourists as well. It also said that within the jurisdiction of the colony nobody was allowed to wear clothes except at night. I was quite startled by this.

'Does this apply to us too?' I asked Madeline with some apprehension.

'I have no idea. Let us get there first. Then we will see', replied Madeline.

It was an open space surrounded by trees, providing perfect privacy, in which a number of colourful tents had been set up. An idyllic setting that brought to my mind a famous mural by Picasso titled *Peace*. It was one of two large murals done in 1952, called *War and Peace*. I had had a chance to see them in a place called Vallauris in the south of France. Picasso says, through these paintings, that the greatest good is happiness. One condition for achieving this is culture, for which social organizations are a must. The *Peace* painting shows people engaged in all sorts of activities in order to obtain happiness. The same was true of this colony.

These are some of the scenes I witnessed: a girl lying half-inclined, reading a book; a man sitting cross-legged, jotting down something in a note book; a mother breastfeeding her baby; a girl cooking something on a stove; a man strumming his guitar; a couple playing chess lying propped up on their elbows; another couple playing with their two children and a ball. The Picasso painting has, among other things, a ploughing scene, birds in a fish bowl and fishes in a bird cage. Above all these is a multi-coloured sun, the giver of all life. By the absurd presentation of the fish bowl and the bird cage the artist wishe to convey the message that even the impossible would be possible if there is uninterrupted peace on earth.

Pictures of Arcadia can be seen in classical European paintings. Titian's *The Shepherd and the Nymph* is one example: in a beautiful natural setting of trees, flowing water and soft light, a shepherd plays his flute while his companion, a voluptuous half-clad woman, sends inviting signals. That painting has just two characters while in this nudist colony an entire society had come together in search of Arcadia. There was a feeling of communal harmony here and an atmosphere of contentment. The colony, I was told, lasted for four months a year, from May to August. You sunned yourself, swam, relaxed, breathed the bracing sea breeze to your heart's content, drove away all tension, excitement and worries, and let the mind roam, ate healthy food, danced and sang, spread the message of universal brotherhood, and made friends with everyone. Could there be a happier life?

Let me digress a little here to tell my readers about Arcadia. Arcadia

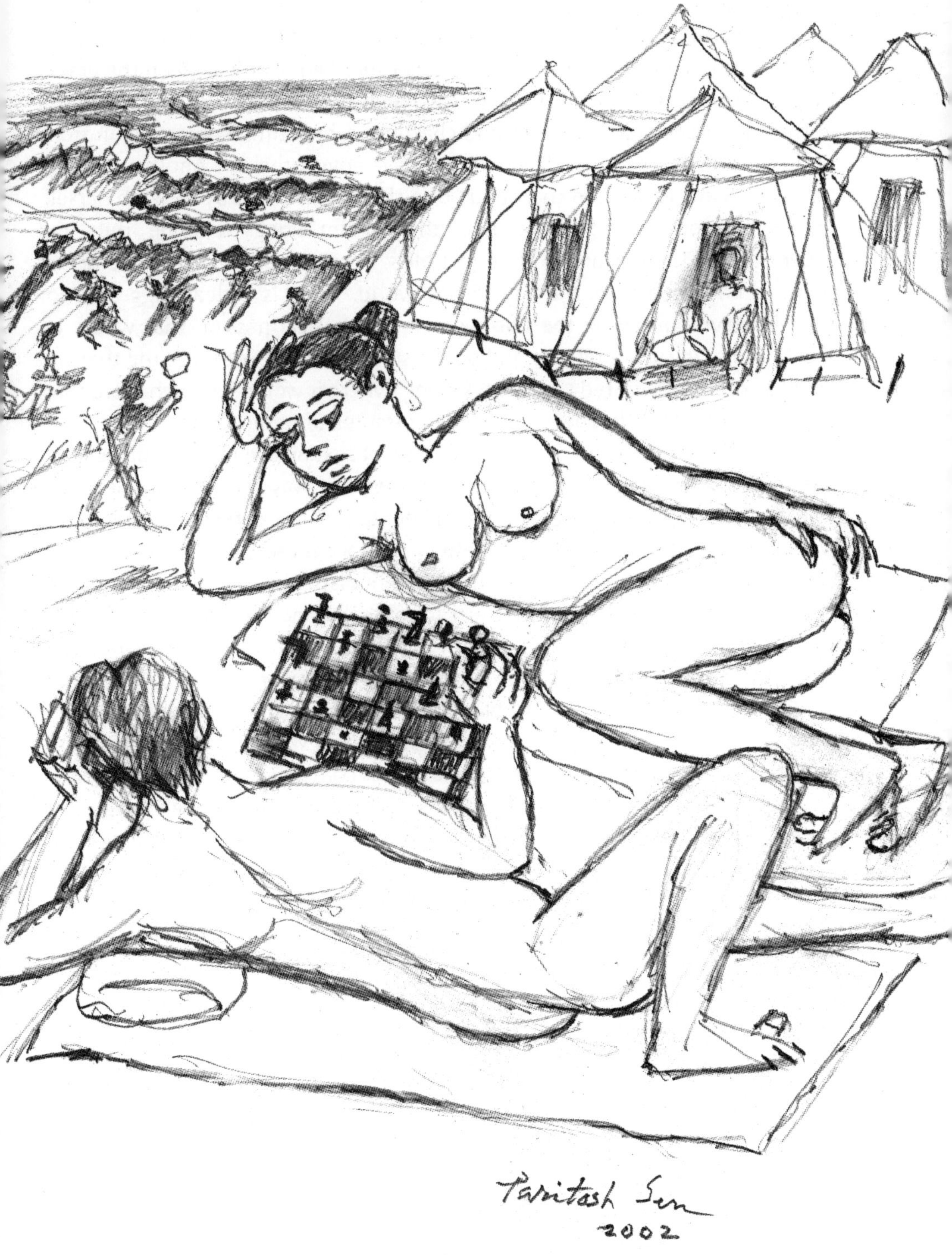
Paritosh Sen
2002

was a small province in the south of Greece whose inhabitants were mostly shepherds. It was the favourite dwelling place of the god of the shepherds, the fun-loving Pan. Poets eloquently sang praises of the simple way of life of the people who lived in this inaccessible place. So the name Arcadia came to be associated with simplicity and innocence. The description of Arcadia brings to mind another famous painting – *Le dejeuner sur l'herbe*, or 'Lunch on the grass', by the French artist Manet. It shows two well-dressed men reclining on grass in the cool green shade of trees and chatting. A beautiful woman sits in front of them in an inviting pose. She does not have any clothes on. Another woman, half-clad, leans forward in the waters of a shallow lake nearby to wash herself. In the foreground are the clothes of the women alongside some fruits and other edibles. There is an air of perfect bliss, in search of which the characters seem to have fled from the day-to-day world. There is a clear suggestion of sexuality, symbolized by the two women, of physical passion that would be most natural in such a remote and poetic surrounding. It seems to me that the act of sex is ideally suited to such a setting, where it would be much more than a matter of habit as happens under the pressures of urban living.

I did not come across any exhibition of sexual love in the nudist colony barring a few embracing couples behind trees. Yet was certainly an ideal setting for arousing physical passion, and the act, in the darkness of the night, would be natural and unfettered. Later, I had occasion to discuss the subject with friends who had spent some time in a nudist colony. They felt that nudism is a necessary experience not just for physical and mental health but also for community living. The kind of harmony found in such a colony is not visible in city life. All inhibitions drop away one by one as one joins this life; many hidden qualities get a chance to blossom forth and a true feeling of happiness is experienced. Though temporary, the experience is valuable. At the same time one should not forget that nudism is meant for cold countries. It is natural only for people who, for a good eight months of the year, have to wear layers and layers of clothing, and therefore crave for the feel of fresh air and the sun against their skin.

I was nagged by doubts. Would these people revert to their old sentiments of anger, envy, meanness, once they got back to their original settings? Were they now merely putting on a mask? Or would the memory of the idyllic days spent here in amity and brotherhood and in harmony with nature bring to them glimpses of a simpler lifestyle? No easy answers were available because the human mind is entangled in complexities like in a spider's web. The intricacies of city life do not easily enable one to get out of it. But even anti-nudists must admit that exposure to nature along with relaxation is certainly good for the body.

These were the thoughts going through my mind as we approached the colony. My attitude towards nudism was changing from negative to positive when we found ourselves face to face with a bearded man in his late thirties, smoking a pipe. Needless to say, he did not have any clothes on. We saw him emerging from a nearby tent. Fishing out an identity card from a pouch attached to his waist he addressed us firmly: 'Don't you know that the first condition of this colony is that any kind of dress is forbidden? Haven't you seen the notice board?'

'Oh yes, we did see the board but did not read the instructions. We should have. We are sorry and beg your pardon', replied Madeline.

The man, who happened to be the secretary of the colony, was not satisfied. Determined to teach us a lesson for breaking the rules, he called out, obviously in an attempt to embarrass us, 'Come out and welcome the bride and the groom!' The bride, meaning Madeline, was wearing a bikini, and I, the so-called groom, had on my underwear. At once the colony-dwellers were out clapping and shouting. 'The bride is here, the groom is here, three cheers for them!'

The nude crowd closed in on us. 'Run, run', I whispered to Madeline. 'Pretty soon they will be tugging at our clothes.'

'Wait a second', whispered Madeline. 'Do as I am doing.'

She too started clapping and joined the forty-strong crowd in their chorus. I followed her, amazed at her presence of mind. The next moment she did something quite unexpected. My eyes almost popped out. Without batting an eyelid and keeping a smiling face, she threw away her bra and then her panty. I had no option but to undress too. This action pleased the crowd. 'Bravo, bravo', they shouted, still dancing and clapping. We found ourselves joining in their wild jubilation.

Translated from the Bengali by Enakshi Chatterjee

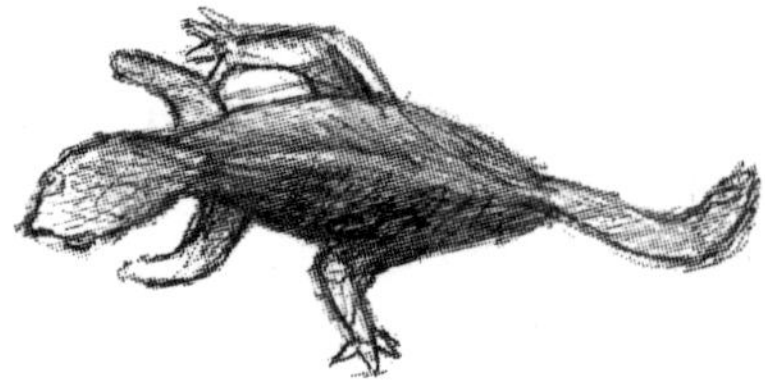

Union and separation

ONE

The backyard of our house in Dhaka was a veritable paradise to us. Stacks of unused bricks, household junk, medicinal plants, fruit trees and shrubs made it a happy hunting ground for worms, insects, snakes, lizards and various other creatures. It was here that we were introduced to the mysteries of the living world for the first time. It was a constant source of endless wonder and thrill, a site for strange new discoveries. I still remember the excitement I felt when I discovered *pathar chunar* leaves that had dropped from the plant striking roots in the ground, and the growth of another plant in that place.

One morning my elder brother and I were exploring the area under the *shiuli* tree when something soft and golden brown inside an earthen pot caught our attention. They were two tiny mongoose cubs, looking for all the world like balls of wool. We were very excited. Carefully we lifted them out of the pot and procured a bird cage to shelter them. We put some gram and water in the cage for the baby mongooses and decided that the wire mesh stretching over the courtyard would keep them safe. The parents of the cubs or a cat would not dare enter through the mesh. Thus assured of no interference, we – my brother and I – went into the house. It was time for school and we had to rush through our bath and meal. As we were about to begin our early lunch, a faint screeching sound, somewhat like a wail, alerted us. This was certainly not the sound of pigeons, of which we had quite a horde in the house. Leaving our meal unfinished, we rushed upstairs. We were most unprepared for the scene we witnessed from the verandah. By some incredible means the mother mongoose had climbed up the wire mesh and was trying desperately to open the cage door. Despite all the differences between humans and lower animals, the maternal instinct is the same in both species. God has bestowed this quality in the same measure in all his creations, high or low. How the mongoose had managed to climb up the wire mesh still remains a mystery.

We tried to shoo it away. The mother mongoose snarled at us exactly like a man-eating tiger. We were so scared that we ran to the safety of a room

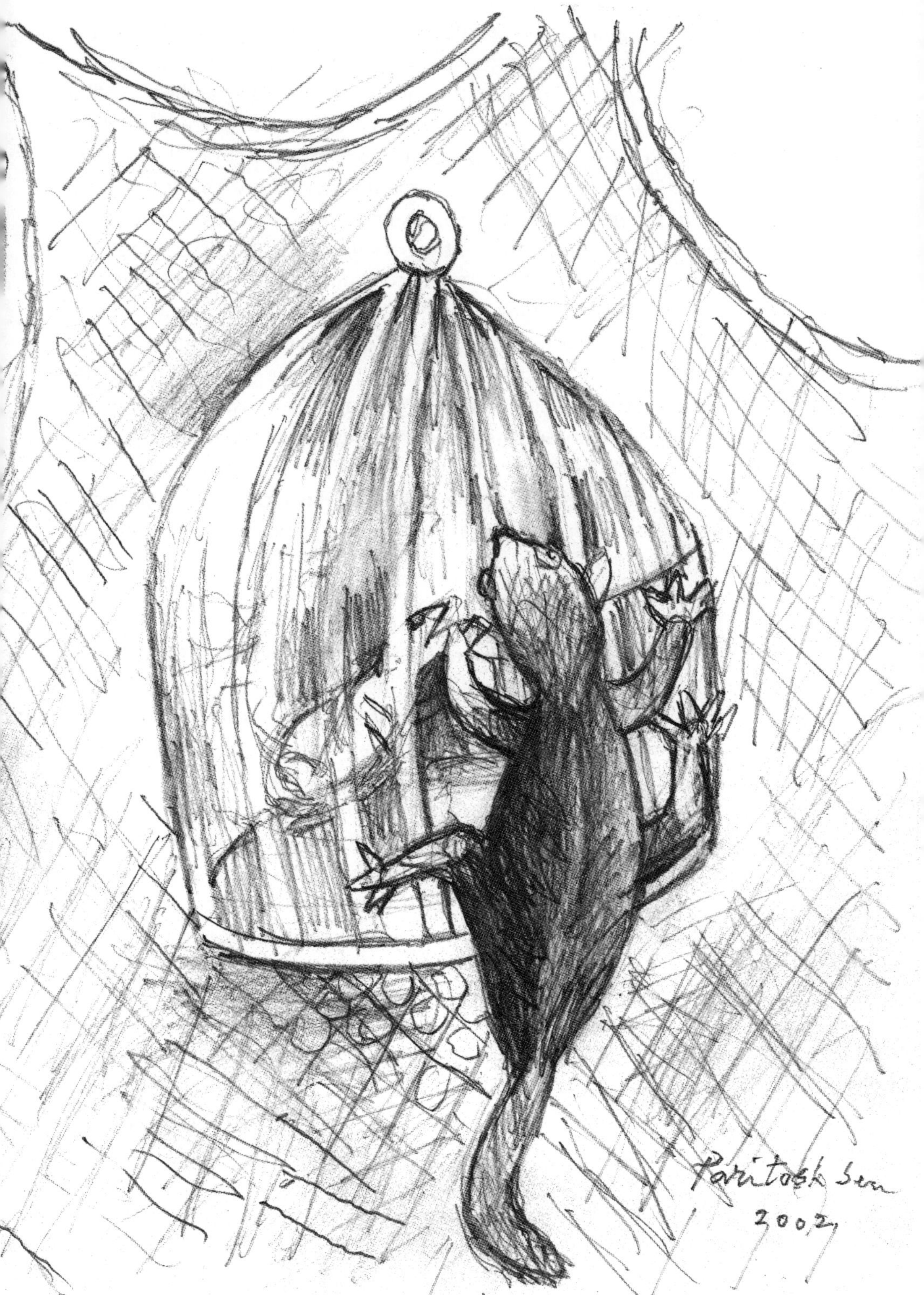
Paritosh Sen
2002

indoors, bolted the door and peered out through the window. We could hardly trust our eyes. That a mongoose could so passionately want to be reunited with its offspring was unimaginable. It was behaving exactly like a human mother would have, under similar circumstances. We were in a dilemma. Should we keep the cubs for our pleasure or accept the right of the mother over her children? We did not argue, for some instinct told us to set the cubs free. The agony of the mother mongoose was unbearable to watch. Armed with two sticks, we first drove the mother to the back garden. As we descended the stairs carrying the cage, there she was again, confronting us. The red tip of her nose and her shining bead-like eyes glowed in the dark. It took us quite an effort to make her retreat to the far end of the garden. Then, opening the door of the cage we put it on the ground and ran back to a safe distance. Like a flash of lightning the mother mongoose was at the cage in an instant. The siblings and the mother were reunited in a perfect expression of love, an uncontrollable urge that could not be denied. It was as though all of nature, all the trees and shrubs in the garden, rejoiced at the spectacle. This incident left such an indelible impression on my mind that later in life I could never bring myself to keeping pets of any kind.

TWO

It was the year 1948. I was teaching in a college at Indore, the one-time capital of the Holkars in the Malwa valley, in the northwestern part of central India. It was an early winter day, in the month of November; there was cheerfulness in the air. From my window the view of trees in the distance and the red tiled roofs of the teachers' bunglows looked exactly like a scene from Cezanne. Zinnias were in bloom in my garden, attracting butterflies; they flitted about looking for pollen. I was alone in my six-room bungalow, down with malaria. My head hurt terribly. At this point the servant Tolaram brought me a postcard. Written in faded blue ink, it was from my brother, written at my mother's instruction. I knew that *Ma* had not been keeping well for quite some time. She was completely bedridden now, her body shrunken like hay. The letter conveyed her request that I should come immediately; she had a feeling that her days were numbered.

It is relevant to mention here that Mother had lost her youngest child, my youngest brother whom I was very fond of, at the tender age of nineteen. He had died of snake bite in a remote village in the district of Sylhet, away from the family. My mother did not ever get over the loss, in spite of the fact that she had eleven other children. She was often seen on the terrace of the house, staring unblinkingly at the sky. 'What are you staring at, *Ma*?' would be answered by a mysterious 'Don't you see, he is beckoning, I have to go to him.' And she would point to the sky. From then on I and my elder brother became her special favourites. She had her reasons for this. I have dwelt on this subject at length elsewhere.

In my childhood, deprived as I was of her proximity, I never knew what it was to be loved by my mother. My heart longed for her tender touch just as *parijat* flowers wait all night long for the sun. No other person can invoke the same sense of attachment and devotion. However beautiful, the moon can hardly make flowers bloom or fill them with honey. Yet, circumstances have stopped so many mothers from bestowing affection on their children. Family duties prevent them from being close to their offspring and they are hardly ever able to attend to them unless they fall sick. But the latent store of affection always remains deep down in a mother's heart. By some peculiar magic the child can always understand the frustration of the poor mother who is thwarted by circumstances from reaching out to her child. Nobody else can gauge how this communication takes place. It is like unseen waves coming from faraway heavenly bodies.

My mind goes back to the mid-twenties. It must have been the height of summer in Dhaka, for I remember the copper-coloured leaves that the fig tree in our back garden had just sprouted had turned a dead brown. But in spite of the terrible heat there was great excitement in the air. Thousands of people, Hindus, Muslims, young and old, rich and poor, were infected by it. In the afternoon, when people usually rest indoors, they were out in the streets instead, filling up lanes, house-tops, branches of trees. Dhaka had never witnessed such scenes before. The people were waiting with bated breath, thrilled, proud, hopeful, happy, expectant. Even the famous *Janmashtami* procession did not draw such a jostling crowd. It was Gandhiji's first visit to the city.

I had to hurry through lunch to ensure my place in the crowd. Suddenly I felt a terrible shooting pain in my chest, no doubt brought about by the excitement and the rush. This was accompanied by palpitation. It was a bad time to be sick since all the menfolk were already out of the house, lining the streets, and the women were up on the terrace. My mother came to my rescue. She went down to my father's dispensary and brought some old ghee. She heated it up and massaged my chest. Wild roars of '*Mahatma Gandhiji ki jai, Mahatma Gandhiji ki jai*' rent the air. But I was not there to see him. The shouts came to me from a distance while I basked in the warmth of my mother's care. How soothing her tender touch was. Even having a glimpse of Gandhi, a very rare opportunity, seemed of no consequence to me at that precious moment. Gradually my pain subsided but from the depths of my subconscious the frustrated longing of a young boy, unfamiliar with such demonstrations of motherly love, burst out in sobs.

All my life I hungered for that love, as I did not have the good fortune of receiving it in childhood. Very often this hunger bordered on the ridiculous.

That is why when I fell in love, I wanted my loved one to be a mother figure as well.

As soon as I read the news about my mother's illness my headache and fever seemed to evaporate. I must leave for Calcutta right away – that was all I could think. It was an uncontrollable desire. Not a moment's delay would do. I must see my mother, I must reach her bedside somehow, for I might never see her again. But it was the end of the month and I was without money. What could be done? Ask for a loan, but from whom? I was worried sick. As various possibilities flitted through my mind, there was a knock on the door. I wished it would be some kind friend, an angel of mercy. I staggered to the door. Almost as an answer to my prayers, the caller was the driver of a lady I knew very well. He had an envelope for me. I tore it open and what I found inside took my breath away. I felt as though I was confronted with the eighth wonder of the world. It was a letter with a cheque for four hundred rupees pinned on to it. The short letter said that I had to accept this cheque, otherwise she would never see me again. This was a strange coincidence indeed. For a non-believer like me who scoffed at miracles, there was no explanation for this sequence of events. Wonders never cease. What mysterious power had come forward to solve all my worries at one go? Had my mother guessed, lying in her bed in distant Kalighat eleven hundred miles away, that I was in dire financial straits and that some solution must immediately come my way if she was to have a last meeting with me? The more I thought the more puzzled I grew.

Not a moment was to be lost, though. I wrote a hurried note to the English principal explaining the situation and asking him to send me cash in lieu of the cheque. Let me unravel the mystery of the cheque now. The writer of the letter had liked some of my paintings so much that she had a couple of them on the walls in her room. For the last four years she had been asking me how much she owed me. Each time I had avoided a direct answer because she had been very kind to me and I was grateful to her. I had not wanted her to pay for the paintings.

The same evening I set out for Calcutta, armed with ample doses of quinine and a month's leave. The train chugged along the metre-gauge track through the densely forested and hilly terrain of Malwa. It was a journey of thirty-six hours. Would my mother wait for my arrival? What if she left before I reached? My last wish to see her, would it remain unfulfilled? While these questions persisted in my mind like fixed centres of an ultimate disaster, a faint ray of hope kept peeping through the dark clouds of despair.

I reached home and rushed upstairs to the room where *Ma* was. As I stood at the door I felt an air of foreboding. There was my mother, pale and thin as a sheet, lying on her side, her eyes shut. I crept up to her and tried to touch her feet. She opened her eyes, looked at me and gestured. She showed no surprise to seeme at all, as though she had known I would come. She spoke a little later. 'So you are here. Now I can take my leave in peace.'

She did not touch me but I could feel her blessings. Her words left me in wonder and gratification at the same time. I was indeed fortunate. By what supernatural power does a human being postpone the inevitable arrival of death? Is such a rare power reserved only for such occasions as the reunion of a mother and her son? Was this manifestation of miraculous power caused by the fire of longing, did that provide the spark? I wondered. I still wonder. I stood bewildered and confused. It was not in my power to unravel the mystery.

Then my mother spoke again. 'You know, the doctor has given up all hope. Actually I should have gone two days ago. They had all started weeping. But I told them, how can this be. I can't leave without seeing you. Now that you have come, I am ready to go. Please call the others.'

She talked to each one of her children as if she was going away on a long journey, in very clear tones, giving specific instructions, wishing them well. To me she said, 'I had so wanted to see you settled. But it was not in my fate.' I controlled the surge of emotion that was welling up within me with great effort. I was overwhelmed by the unfathomable mystery of life and death. She looked totally at peace, there was no touch of regret. It was as though some invisible hand was giving her solace, asking her to be happy. How could this frail body which had refused food and water for the last few days have retained so much mental strength? From what supernatural source did she derive such power? Who could be the giver of this power, from which part of the universe did it come?

She seemed to be floating in a sea of bliss. Her eyes were closed. My doctor brother felt her pulse. It has stopped, he murmured. Suddenly her eyes flew open. She called my youngest brother by his name and said softly, 'He is asking me to join him. Let me go.' And she was gone, beyond the limits of all earthly pain, away to the heavens beyond. She had shown us a glimpse of the immortal beyond earthly life, revealed to us the essence of beauty. She had accepted death willingly. Fire would soon devour her earthly remains, but she had not seemed the least bit afraid.

Did my youngest brother ever know that his mother had nurtured in her so much love for him? Perhaps children are acquainted only with the perceptible form of the mother, and her other self, that is beyond sense perception, forever lies beyond their grasp. Our physical eyes are limited. They do not see the greater, the more pervasive form of the mother. She had never told me of her feelings for me in this transient world. Now through her death she had laid open her vast store of love in silence. In my childhood the demands of the family had always created a distance between her and me. She had made up for all that now, at this final moment of departure. It was as though the curtains had been drawn and the ultimate truth stood before me in all its beauty, compensating for all the neglect accumulated through my childhood days. By bringing me into this earth, she had been a part of the creativity of nature, the great mother. All earthly bonds severed, she had parted the curtain separating life from death and revealed her real self: the eternal mother in her true manifestation. For four long years she had suffered the loss of her youngest son in silent agony, which was like a smouldering fire. This fire now assumed the cool beauty of an emerald lake, scattering a shower of white flowers. Blessed is the son who has a glimpse of the eternal mother, the icon of motherhood.

THREE

It was afternoon. Sitting on the steps outside the living room, I was idly watching the busy world go by. Suddenly a taxi pulled up and I saw my eldest brother emerge carrying his wife, looking distraught. *Boudi* looked seriously ill, pale and emaciated. Her eyes were half shut. Promptly I helped my brother stretch her on the cot. Meanwhile my mother and other members of the family rushed down from the upper floor. *Dada* broke down. From what we could gather, *Boudi* was seven months pregnant and was suffering from tuberculosis. Her condition was critical. As *Dada* wept like a child, my mother too was deeply moved. *Boudi* seemed to lack the energy to even look at us.

Her family, who lived in the same neighbourhood, was informed. *Boudi* had only a widowed mother and a younger brother called Noshu. They hurried to our house. A gynaecologist was called. After careful examination he prescribed some medicines but he took my brother aside and confided to him that it was a touch-and-go situation. He would have to watch for at least a couple of days before he could say anything definite.

After three days *Boudi* gave birth to an undersized infant. My mother, with the experience of bringing up twelve children of her own, took every care to ensure the child survived. But *Boudi* grew from bad to worse. She had all of us worried. Noshu was the most affected. He visited the Kalighat temple every day, offered flowers and sweets to the deity and prayed for the recovery of his dear sister. He sat by her bedside all night. Ever since they had lost their father, this *Didi* had supported the family, working in a primary school. In fact it was she who had brought up her younger brother and put him through school. *Didi* was dearer to Noshu than his mother. He would confide in *Didi*, tell her whatever was on his mind. She was the most important person in his world. He was very upset when, after her marriage, *Didi* left home. And now his *Didi* was lying in a critical state. Naturally, Noshu was miserable. His concern for *Didi* was so overpowering that he went without food or sleep, and ran from the temple to the small *puja* shelf in their one-room flat, trying to please the gods and goddesses. Before her marriage it was *Didi* who used to do the daily *puja* after her bath, placing the traditional sweets, flowers and water in front of the images of the gods. Now Noshu took over. He would touch the offered flowers to *Didi*'s forehead and put them under her pillow. He would buy bananas, eggs, *sandesh* and other nourishing food for his ailing sister. But in spite of all his efforts *Didi* showed no signs of recovering. Her condition slowly deteriorated after the birth of the child. She grew paler, even opening her mouth and eyes were an effort. A few drops of liquid were all she could ingest.

At midnight her pulse began to race, and her breathing became unusual. My brother and everybody else waiting by her bedside were sick with anxiety. Poor Noshu, at the point of tears, kept stroking her forehead. Hoping for a miracle, he placed a hibiscus flower from the Kalighat temple on her head. The next moment he joined his hands and murmured some prayer. *Boudi*'s mother too was at her bedside, she was busy chanting the name of Srihari. This went on for some time. Suddenly *Boudi*'s breathing slowed. *Dada*'s fingers were on her pulse. She was almost gone, he told us. In a few moments she was truly gone. *Dada* broke down as he announced that *Boudi* was dead. In the general mourning that followed, there was a sudden loud howl. It was from Noshu. He rushed out of the room into the street, as though driven by some terrible fury. I went after him as he raced through the street in a wild run. The front door of their house was shut. He kicked at it angrily till some of the other tenants appeared to see what was happening. Pushing them away Noshu ran into the house and turned on the light in his room.

Unable to comprehend this wild frenzy, the neighbours tried to hold him back. But Noshu was like a man possessed. He rushed at the images of Kali, Radha Krishna, Mahadev and Durga on the *puja* shelf. Picking up the eggs and bananas he had kept for his *Didi*, he flung them at the images, showering obscene abuses. In seconds, the picture of the goddess Kali was covered in egg yolk and white. Not satisfied, Noshu threw the framed pictures on the floor. Soon the red cemented floor was covered with broken glass. Glasses, tumblers, whatever he could lay his hands on, he dashed to the ground, shouting dirty abuses all the while. Everybody knew Noshu to be a very well-behaved boy, polite and soft-spoken. This seemed to be another person altogether. From where had he got the strength of a hundred elephants? The sudden outburst of violence over, Noshu began to dash his head against the wall. All of us tried desperately to stop him. At some point in the struggle, he flung himself on the cot. Exhausted and tired, he fell into a deep sleep.

How people will react to death is something nobody can anticipate. Certainly Noshu was not at all prepared for the sudden loss of his very dear *Didi*. The shock had generated anger. It was so overpowering that poor Noshu had no way of controlling it. All that was of value to him had collapsed in an

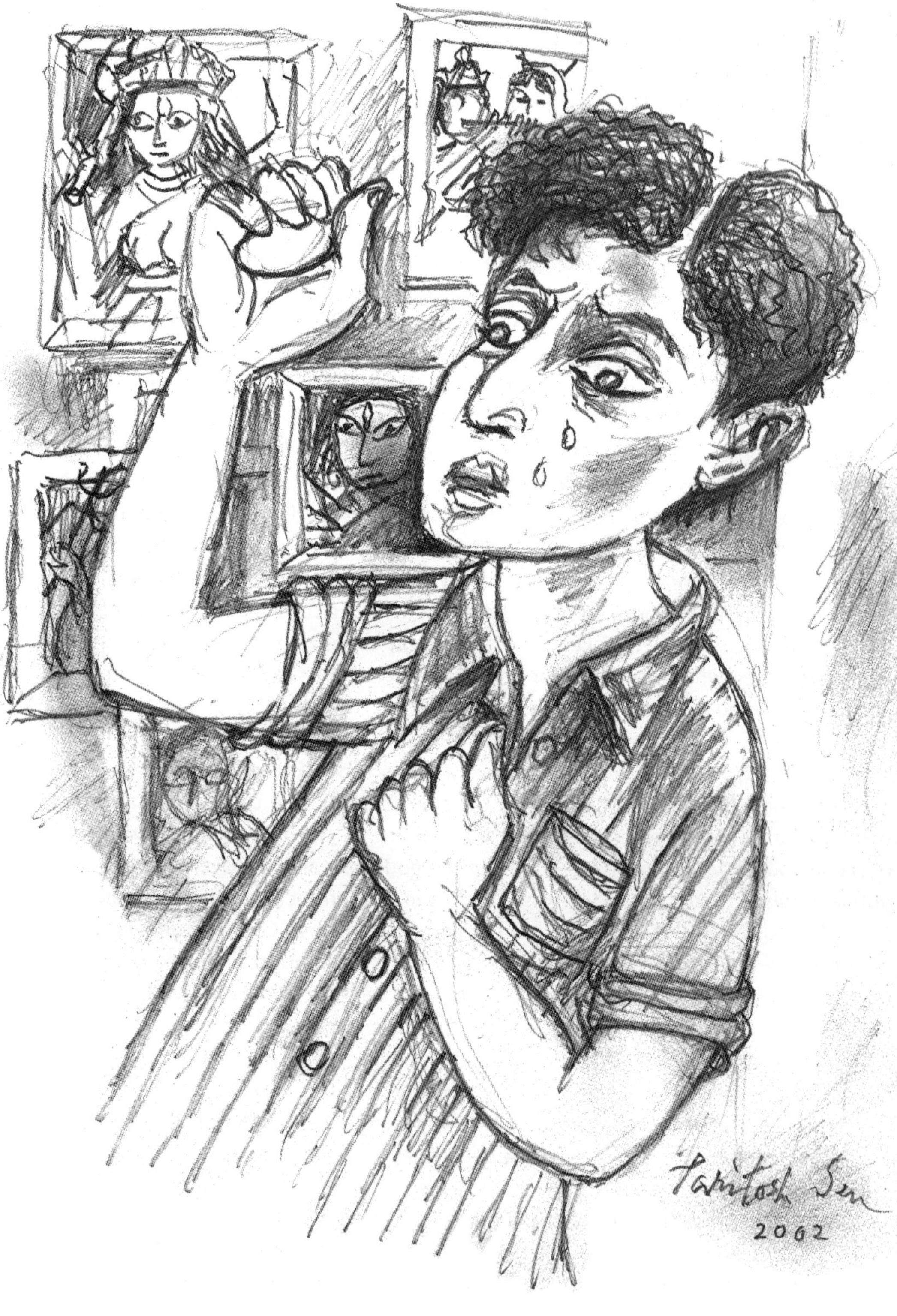
Paritosh Sen
2002

instant, and he was driven to an abyss. He did not know what he was doing, he lost all control and resorted to violence. The inevitable truth that his *Didi* would not come back drove him to madness. It was an admission of defeat he was not ready to accept. Death was his adversary, but who was he to fight against this mighty enemy? The frustration of this realization turned Noshu into a vindictive animal, like a wounded tiger. Noshu's violent outburst was an example of the fact that the expression of grief can assume odd manifestations.

His outburst of grief, though ugly, could not be termed fake or false. It was genuine. The unfortunate brother just did not have the mental make-up to accept the death of his sister. His odd behaviour only established this fact. I was much too young at that time to understand all this but now, looking back, I can sympathize with him. A very simple soul, Noshu had the conviction that the gods had the power to protect devotees against all crises. His belief had received a jolt. His gods could do nothing when the person who was dearer to him than his own life lay dying. This was more than he could take. The nearest analogy I can think of is from Tagore's play, *Biswarjan*, in which Raghupati, in a fit of anger, flings away the image of the presiding deity Tripureswari. Noshu's grief was more genuine. What Raghupati had done was to spread false propaganda in the name of the goddess, with the purpose of serving his own ends. Noshu was not like him. His explosion of grief was firmly based in his own conviction. It may not have claimed respect but one could certainly understand it.

Translated from the Bengali by Enakshi Chatterjee

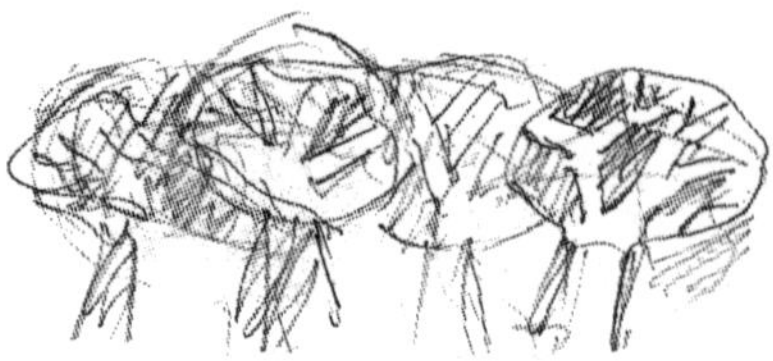

The bull and the devotee

It was winter in Calcutta. The skyrocketing prices notwithstanding, I got tremendous pleasure out of wandering in the market among huge piles of fruit and vegetables, greens and tubers. The cauliflowers were arranged in rows of white bouquets. Next to them were fleshy purple brinjals from Baruipur; the touch of their smooth, soft and rounded surface was nothing short of a sensual experience. Succulent, fiery-red tomatoes against tender green cabbages made for a classic ensemble of colours. Yellow pumpkin flowers arranged on banana leaves seemed to be waiting for a painter. Red chillies placed near fresh coriander leaves flashed brightly like parrots' beaks. A little ahead I could see heaps of spinach and carrots, reminiscent of a dark green Kanjeevaram sari with wide saffron border. At the fruit stalls a pyramid of sun-ripened Darjeeling oranges towered next to blushing rosy rows of Kashmiri apples. The combination reminded me of the bright colours of Tibetan rugs. And what about the maiden from South 24 Parganas sitting on the pavement with a fully grown gourd! It would be too prosaic to describe the scene in words. Only a drawing can do full justice to it. Amidst this riot of colours my mind was temporarily freed from the pressures of urban life.

I walked up to a vegetable shop and just as I was asking the prices the lights went off. Nothing unusual for Calcutta. The shopkeepers quickly lit candles and kerosene lamps and the normal business of buying and selling resumed. 'Run, run fast!' Suddenly a huge cry from the other side of the market Pandemonium ensued. People began to jostle and scramble. Before I realized what was happening, a powerful shove from a matronly Bengali *ginni* sent me reeling on to a heap of cabbages.

Getting up quickly, I saw a couple of young men at a little distance, beating something with long sticks. In the dim light of the candles and lanterns nothing was clearly visible. When I asked the shopkeeper what the matter was, he said: 'Move away quickly, the bull is coming.' Saying this, he too picked up a stick like the other shopkeepers. A jet-black, huge, mountain-like mass could be seen coming towards us, swinging his great head. He was not the least bit

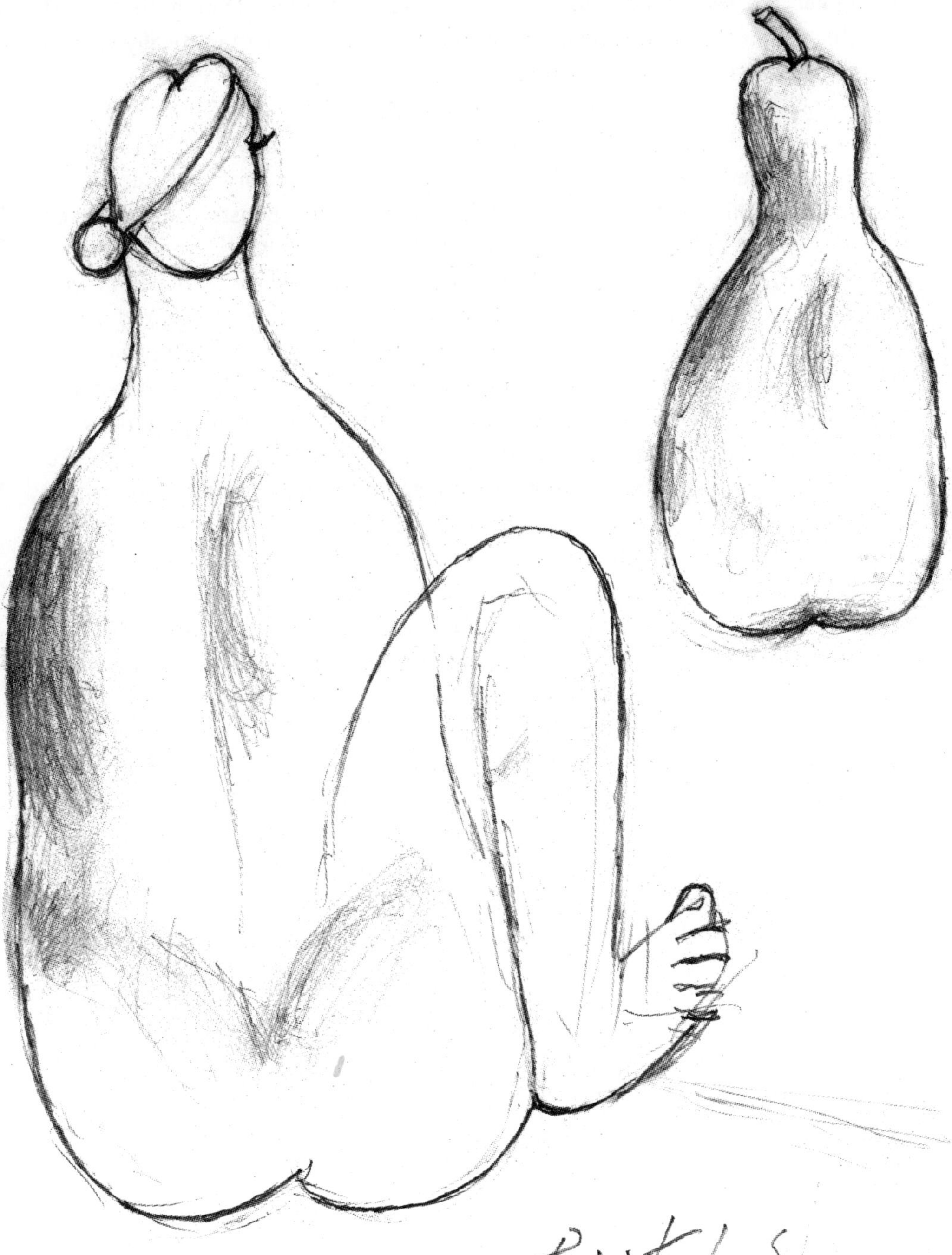
Paritosh Sen
2002

perturbed by the beatings being showered on him. The moment he turned his triangular massive head and roared, his assailants fled. During that short respite, he selected two cabbages and munching on them, majestically walked out of the eastern entrance of the market.

Just then, a man wearing a nondescript shirt, a *lungi* and a caste mark on his forehead, came and stood beside me, wanting to buy peas. He seemed a trifle agitated. He addressed me in English sprinkled with Bengali words. 'There is no difference these days between men and beasts. Did you see? Needlessly the bull was . . .'. He was not allowed to finish his sentence. The shopkeeper, who was weighing the peas, butted in rudely: 'Why don't you invite the bull for both meals to your home? Those cabbages he picked up . . . will you compensate me for them?' Hearing the sharpness in the shopkeeper's tone, the man walked away muttering and gesturing: '*Aiyo! Aiyo! Mahapapam, mahapapam*! What sin, what blasphemy!' He left without buying the peas.

I started for home after finishing my shopping. Having walked some 20 yards, I saw the huge black animal strolling down the pavement. I stood facing him and observed a serene, satisfied air about him. Who could have said that he had created such a tremendous commotion in the market just a little while ago?

Stray cattle are a common enough sight on Calcutta streets. But one seldom comes across such a powerful, handsome creature. The rise of his curving hump from his sturdy shoulders was like the surging wave of a storm-tossed ocean, dramatically breaking over the beach of his broad back and sweeping down. From there the line dropped like a waterfall down the tail to the ankles. Similarly, a supple line travelled down his powerful jaw, slithering down the dewlap to lose itself in his vast chest. From there another long curve flowed to his loins. These dynamic lines contained the powerful body as though in a tightly clenched fist.

Looking at the animal I realized why, down the ages, in all mythologies, the bull has held pride of place in the animal kingdom. Why artists, beginning with Egypt, Phoenicia, Assyria and Mohenjodaro right down to our age, to Picasso and Nikhil Biswas, have portrayed this animal as a symbol of beauty and virility on the one hand, and of majesty, gigantic strength and destruction on the other.

Apart from that incident at Lake Market, I began to encounter the bull, unexpectedly, in the twists and turns of the lanes of our neighbourhood, on the main street, on the soft grass of Southern Avenue, in the afternoons and evenings and sometimes even at night. And whenever I came across him, I watched him enchanted.

One night, after dinner, I had lit a cigarette and was strolling up and down the front balcony as is my habit. It was about 11 pm. Most of the houses

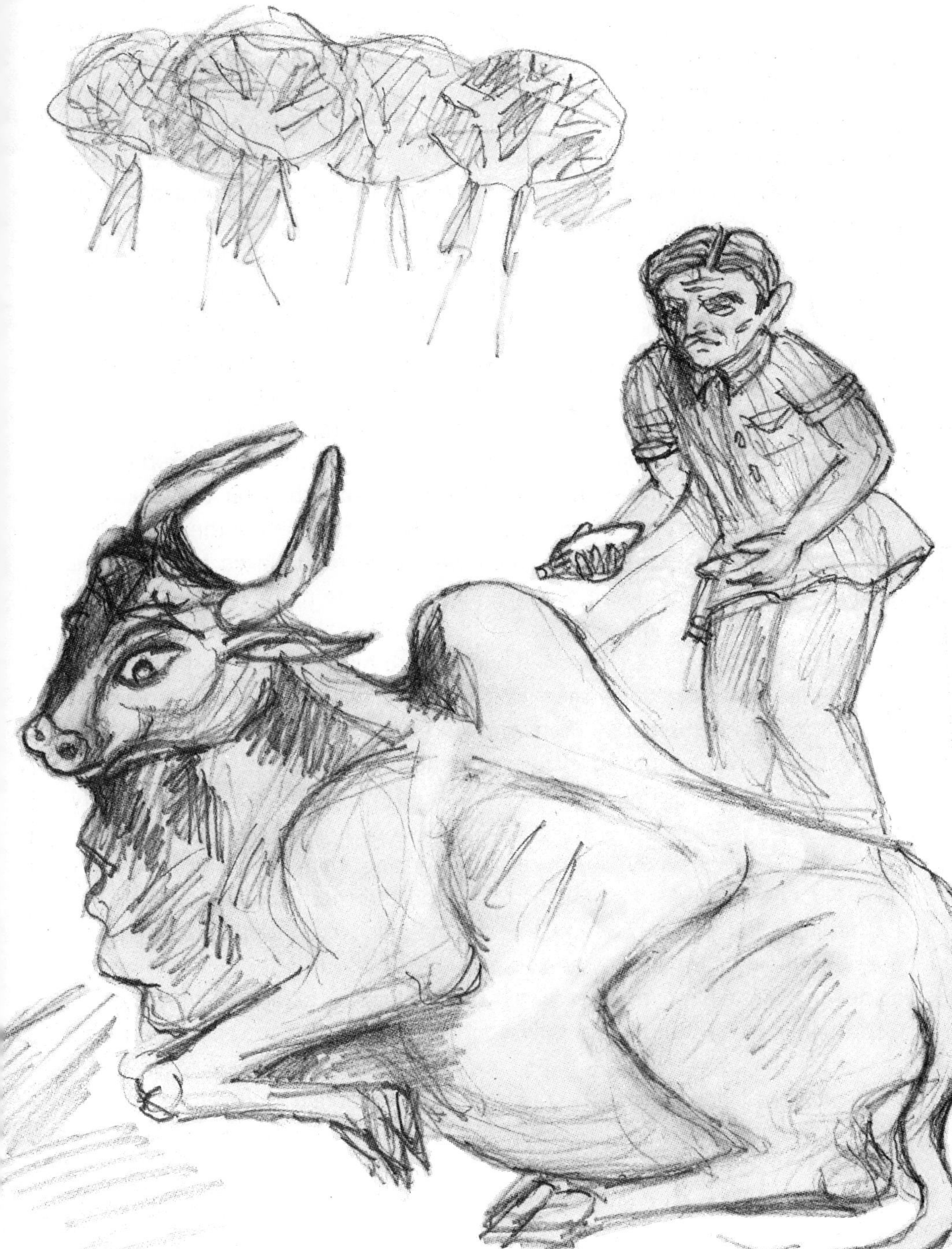
Paritosh Sen
2003

in the neighbourhood had put out their lights. There were hardly any people on the street. In the faint glimmer of a waxing moon, the houses in front made an intricate geometric pattern with the interplay of bluish-green light and shade. My eyes travelled to the road below and suddenly I saw the shining black beast sitting quietly under a street lamp. The light from the lamp was focused on him in such a way that the dark shadows blending with the colour of his skin accentuated his mass. He looked much larger than his actual size. One could have easily mistaken him for the famous Nandi at Mysore carved in stone, enormous, immobile. Entranced, I examined in great detail the grace reflected in every part of his body. I was making quick sketches of him in my mind when all of a sudden I noticed a man approaching with a small bag in his hand. I recognized him instantly. He was the man I had met in the market.

He took out a plantain flower from his bag and held it before the bull, who, with one swift movement, pulled it into his mouth. After that the man brought out a couple of fresh cabbages and placed them before the animal. He then took out some white flowers and *bael* leaves and placed these on the head of the bull. He took out some more flowers and mumbling quietly with half-closed eyes, he touched them to the horns of the animal a number of times, brought them to his forehead and then to his bulging underbelly where his genitals were hidden. He then wrapped the flowers carefully in a plantain leaf before placing them in his bag. After this he stroked the bull's soft dewlap as gently as caressing a child to sleep. The display of this extraordinary devotion to the living vehicle of Shiva both startled me and made me immensely curious.

Three weeks after this event, one evening, there was a knock on my door. I opened it and, to my surprise, I found the man standing outside. His clothes hung loosely on his thin frame. His nostrils were curled up a little, as if they were being permanently assaulted by a bad odour. After ascertaining my name, he handed me a letter with the insignia of a foreign consulate in Calcutta. He was waiting for a reply, so I asked him in. He introduced himself, saying that he was employed in the consulate and lived nearby. His name was Chidambaram Narasimhamurti Kotilingam Padmanabhan Murugan Iyer. It was too long a name to remember easily, so I got up to fetch my address book in order to note it down. Meanwhile, he started explaining the complexity of his name. He had been born in Chidambaram, a great pilgrimage centre dedicated to Shiva in Tamil Nadu; Narasimhamurti, an incarnation of Vishnu, was his great-grandfather's name; Kotilingam was his grandfather's name; Padmanabhan and Murugan were the names of his maternal great-grandfather and grandfather. Confused, I asked him which of these was his own name. He shook his head from left to right and answered: 'All combined – ah – is my name – ah.'

As I was noting down his name and address he started examining my modest collection of assorted books. He picked up one and asked me whether he could borrow it for a day or two. The book's title was *Secrets of Male Sexuality*.

I met him again on Shivaratri. It was almost 10 pm. I was returning home after spending a convivial evening with friends. I suddenly came face to face Mr Iyer near the Triangular Park. He was carrying the small bag I had noticed in his hands on the earlier occasion. In the dim light of the street lamp I observed lines of anxiety on his forehead. I asked: 'How are you, Mr Iyer?' He answered briefly: 'Okay! Okay!' He appeared to be distracted and searching for something. Walking alongside him, I asked: 'How is your Mrs?' He answered, barely glancing at me: 'Okay! Okay!' To keep the conversation going, I enquired after the health of his parents: 'Okay! Absolutely okay'. 'How is everything in the office?' 'Okay! All okay!'

Suddenly he came close to me and asked: 'Have you . . .?' He hesitated a little over the question. I reassured him, assuming a tone of familiarity: 'Go on, unburden yourself. Why should you feel shy with me?'

Heartened, he continued: 'Have you seen that black bull anywhere today?'

'Oh yes, as usual he was taking a stroll at the vegetable stalls in the market and the shopkeepers were trying to ward him off by beating him.' On hearing this, he said: '*Aiyo! Aiyo! Mahapapam*! To hit Nandi on Mahashivaratri is the height of sacrilege. Shame on them! Shame!'

I consoled him: 'No. no. The beating was not too severe. On my way back from the market I saw him calmly wandering about. I am sure you will find him somewhere nearby.'

Impelled by my curiosity about his mysterious devotion to the bull, I could not resist asking him: 'What's up?' Mr Iyer dragged me behind a tree and whispered urgently: 'I must find that bull somehow. He is no ordinary animal, you know!'

'How do you know?' I asked. His eyes bulged. He spoke in an agitated voice: 'Last night I saw him in my dreams. What infinite grace granted to me by Shivashankar! I saw Pashupatinath himself seated on his back! I threw myself on the ground and made my obeisance. The Lord asked, "What do you want my child?" I prayed, "Oh Lord, you are the Master of this world, you are omniscient. You are not unaware of my sole wish!" Do you know, Mr Sen, what Pashupati said?' Impatiently I said: 'Tell me, tell me.'

Mr Iyer continued: 'Pashupati affectionately stroked the black bull and said: "From the auspicious moment of Mahashivaratri you will feed my beloved animal for a fortnight with rice, banana, *sandesh*, coconut and milk and perform *puja*. You will collect a bowlful of the bull's urine. And after mixing it with two-and-a-half litres of Ganga water and generously sprinkling *tej-patta* and *garam masala* in it, you will boil it for a whole hour. You will then bathe your whole body in it before going to bed at night." I feel shy to tell you the rest of what Pashupati said. Receiving this blessing from the Lord himself, assuring fulfilment of my longstanding wish, I felt such surging joy that I woke up from my sleep with a jolt. That is why I must find him tonight, somehow.' Saying this, he walked away in search of the bull towards Jatin Das Road.

A month passed after this episode. It was spring time. The trees were in full bloom. As was my normal routine I set out on my morning constitutional towards the lake. The darkness of night had hardly lifted. The Calcutta sky, usually filled with smoke and dust, glittered like a transparent grey crystal at this hour. The drab urban life of the crowded, noisy, concrete jungle was transformed for a while with the song of magpies, bulbuls, mynas, doves and other birds.

The seasonal extravagance was also apparent on the flowering trees: on the *gulmohurs*, silk cottons, cassias, bauhinias, *amaltas* and jacarandas. They paraded their gorgeous displays like Banarasi brocades. The ripe red fruits of the *bakul* tree were strung along its branches like illumination for a wedding celebration. Some bulbuls were making a grand feast of them.

I walked eastward down Southern Avenue. A *chaiwalla* was making preparations to light his coal stove under a *peepul* tree. The *rickshaw-wallas* sleeping on the pavement were not yet awake. A milkrnan was driving his tiny herd of sooty buffaloes westward. An old man wearing canvas shoes and carrying his walking stick was strolling towards the lake. I overtook him and within a few minutes reached Vivekananda Park.

In the park a tree heavy with pink bauhinias of unsurpassable beauty greeted me. Glancing towards it, my eyes fell upon a sight that brought me to a halt. The black bull was standing on a carpet of turquoise green grass. Its appearance recalled a miniature of the Jehangir period – a huge black elephant against the luminous green. The bull stood rooted, like a statue carved in black marble. And between the black and the green, the flaming red of his exposed genitals made a glorious combination.

A little distance away stood a rain tree. To its trunk was tied a Multani cow, as white as rain-washed jasmine flowers – an eminently suitable mate for this marvellous dark creature. Her horns curved upward like tongues of flame. They were capped with brass that shone like the ornaments of a new bride. Her ears were smoothly folded like fresh canna leaves. Her dark eyes, with an expression of anticipation, were so large and enticing that the name 'Vishalakshi' would have suited her well. The eyes also wore a tinge of anxiety, like those of the black doe in the painting of *Todi Ragini* of the *Basholi Kalam*. Her body was replete with feminine grace and curves. Her supple beauty and the balanced harmony of her form were no less memorable than that of the famous stone carving of the lactating cow at Mahabalipuram.

A few men, probably employed by the owner of a nearby cattle shed, were throwing stones at the bull, trying to drive him away. But used as he was to daily beatings, he ignored these missiles as trifling intrusions. From time to time, the white cow turned her head and fondly looked at him.

The eastern sky was flooded with pink. There was an *aubade* of birds in the trees. The air was redolent with the scent of many flowers. Suddenly the bull rushed forward like lightning towards 'Vishalakshi'. A magnificent chiaroscuro of black and white, a meeting of Purusha and Prakriti, hailed the eternal laws of creation under the blushing sky.

Remembering that I had to do some shopping at Gariahat Market, I was about to leave when I was startled to see Mr Iyer approaching from behind the cattle shed with the ubiquitous bag slung over his shoulder. In one hand he held a fresh cabbage and in the other, some *datura* blossoms. As he walked towards the bull, the men from the cattle shed shouted loudly and warned him against advancing. Mr Iyer walked on resolutely without batting an eyelid.

The bull was standing next to 'Vishalakshi' with his head hanging down. Making soft cooing noises, Mr Iyer went forward and held the cabbage out to him. Again a warning shout was heard. I too thought that Mr Iyer had lost his senses and was about to cry out, when the bull turned towards him. Very gently, the animal accepted the cabbage into his mouth. Meanwhile the man stroked the entire body of the bull including his genitals with the *datura* flowers and then held them against his own forehead and muttered something to himself with closed eyes.

A couple of months after this incredible event, I happened to be walking past Mr Iyer's house on the way to the market. I saw that his house was blazing with lights both inside and outside. There was quite a gathering in the sitting room. An attractive girl was singing *bhajans* in the Carnatic style. Curious to know what was happening, I peered inside and Mr Iyer spotted me.

He came out immediately and dragged me inside. 'Come in, come in', he said with a warm welcome. South Indian snacks were being served to the guests. He pushed a plate in my hand. I enquired: 'What's happening Mr Iyer?' Mr Iyer could barely suppress his joy as he said: 'Oh, nothing! Nothing! Just a simple get-together of a few friends!' He then rushed into an inner room. A guest sitting next to me, sipping coffee, was unable to keep the news to himself any longer. He whispered in my ear: 'Mr Iyer will soon be a father.'

Translated from the Bengali by Ela Dutta